FOCUS ON

GODARD

edited by
ROYAL S. BROWN

A SPECTRUM BOOK
Prentice-Hall, Inc.
Englewood Cliffs, N.J.

FILM FOCUS

Ronald Gottesman and Harry M. Geduld
General Editors

ROYAL S. BROWN, *editor of this volume in the Film Focus series, is Lecturer in French at Queens College, C.U.N.Y. He is the translator of Georges Sadoul's* Histoire du cinéma mondial *and is on the reviewing staff of* High Fidelity *magazine.*

for
Sandy, Cary, and Jason

A SPECTRUM BOOK

0–13–357764–3
0–13–357756–2 (pbk.)
Library of Congress Catalog Card Number 72–4879

Printed in the United States of America

10   9   8   7   6   5   4   3   2   1

PRENTICE-HALL INTERNATIONAL, INC. (*London*)
PRENTICE-HALL OF AUSTRALIA, PTY. LTD. (*Sydney*)
PRENTICE-HALL OF CANADA, LTD. (*Toronto*)
PRENTICE-HALL OF INDIA PRIVATE LIMITED (*New Delhi*)
PRENTICE-HALL OF JAPAN, INC. (*Tokyo*)

CONTENTS

ESSAYS

COMMENTARIES

ACKNOWLEDGMENTS

I would like first and foremost to thank General Editor Harry M. Geduld, not only for his confidence in me, but also for his constant advice and friendship. Pioneer Godard critic Jean Collet spent much time and provided me with a great deal of valuable material, for which I am extremely grateful. Paul Snook of New York provided not only a good deal of the bibliographical information but also many hours of stimulating conversation on one of his favorite directors. My mother-in-law, Mrs. Marcella C. Linsin, was also extremely helpful with the bibliography. I would also like to express my gratitude to the following people, authors or otherwise, who made the obtaining of some pieces a much more pleasant job than it might have been: Kent Carroll (who provided much useful information besides his interviews); Carla Rotolo of Grove Press; G. Coratte, A. Choffrut, F. Boularan, and Mary Kling of l'*Express;* L. LeRoux (for her help in a lost cause) of *Réalités;* Jacques Aumont of *Cahiers du cinéma;* Jean Binet of *Le Monde;* Ruth Valentini of *Le Nouvel observateur;* Claude Mauriac; a lady whose name I never found out of *Le Figaro;* Roger Greenspun (who also provided much useful information); Penelope Houston and Sylvia Loeb of the British Film Institute; Ruth C. Rogin of *The New Yorker;* Mme D. Cusson-Morgat of Minard; P. F. of Éditions du Chiron; Father Alain Tirot (who also provided some useful documentation) of Éditions du Cerf; René Bourdier of *Les Lettres françaises;* Marcel Martin and Henry Mortet of *Cinéma (70 & 71);* Gilles Jacob; Mme George Sadoul; Georges Pierre; M. Humbert of the Office Régional d'Enseignement Cinématographique at Nancy; the staff of the Bibliothèque Municipale at Nancy; the Librairie des arts in Nancy. Thanks are also due to Claude Doubinsky of Tours, for his help with the linguistic problems, and to James Price of London and Roger Viry Babel of the Nancy University for their help on documentation. I would also like to especially thank M. and Mme Antoine Duhamel for their extreme cooperation, for the documentation they furnished me, for their hospitality, and for the insights they gave me not only into M. Duhamel's superb film scores, but into Jean-Luc Godard's whole way of working.

Finally, I can only offer my gratitude and a bit of penitence to my parents, Mr. and Mrs. Joseph Lee Brown, who suffered the consequences of my procrastination on this book, and to my wife, Sandy, and my children, Cary and Jason, for putting up with me while I was working on it. A special thanks as well to my father for his knowledge of the English language and his help with the proofs. And to Sandy, for her gluing, typing and extremely helpful comments throughout. And for doing that thankless bit of busy-work, the index.

I would also like to offer my best wishes to Jean-Luc Godard for a complete recovery from the injuries he suffered in his recent accident.

Introduction
One Plus One Equals
by ROYAL S. BROWN

> Prokosh: *Yes, it's in the script; but it's*
> *not what you have on that screen.*
> Fritz Lang: *Naturally. Because in the*
> *script it is written. On the screen it's*
> *pictures. Motion pictures it's called.*
>
> (LE MÉPRIS)

The recent history of the various revolutionary movements that have taken place within the arts, particularly in France, can perhaps best be summed up by the word "debourgeoisification." As Gilles Jacob has pointed out in his article on Jean-Luc Godard's *Made in U.S.A.*, the word "bourgeois" has come to represent, both philosophically and aesthetically, a much broader concept than that of a simple social class. Today the word implies an entire mentality, a middle-of-the-road way of life involving a halfway materialism justified by a religious confidence in the inexorable operation of a cause-and-effect absolute, and a halfway absolutism whose whole raison d'être is bound up in totally materialistic goals. One of the prime results of the revolts that have taken place against this life-style— and against its manifestations in all the domains of the arts—has been the divorce of materialism and any idealism exterior to it, concentrating, positively or negatively, on either one or the other of these two elements, or, as in the case of Jean-Luc Godard, on both.

Most Godard specialists, from Jean Collet to Richard Roud, have noted the predominance of a marked dialectic in the French director's work—a dialectic that offers no answers, no solutions within either extreme. Instead, the only resolution offered by Godard (at least until his most recent films) lies in the quasi-Hegelian life and

movement created from the direct conflict between two opposite
poles on all levels within the work of art. Paradox and contradiction, of course, run thoroughly counter to the comfortable cause-
and-effect logic of the bourgeoisie, for whom every "why" can be
answered by a reassuring "because." But even the most deeply en-
trenched logic can take a certain amount of nonconformity, particularly if the latter is couched in a language and/or structure this
logic can follow; thus, for instance, a solid bourgeois can appreciate
an anti-bourgeois satire in the theater, provided the play is equipped
with a "well-made" plot and certain readily identifiable psychologies.
What is remarkable about Godard—and what has completely
alienated him from masses of people of all political persuasions—is
that this spirit of contradiction—this dialectic—totally and organ-
ically pervades everything concerning him, from his own personality
(which is inextricably bound up in his art) to his cinematic techniques, as is brought out by several of the interviews in this book.
It is in the devastating completeness of his debourgeoisification of
the cinema that Godard has been considered by many to be today's
most revolutionary filmmaker, and it is because of the almost
methodical thoroughness of Godard's anti-bourgeois art that he can
be considered, well before his explicit espousal of the Maoist left, to
be one of the most globally left individuals in the cinema, although
he has even been accused of being a fascist (through paradox, naturally). As novelist-critic Claude Mauriac has stated, in writing about
Made in U.S.A., "Do we finally have a great artist from the left?
Until Godard, we had been dealing either with political revolutionaries who created or liked the most conservative art, or else with
artistic revolutionaries who forced themselves as well as they could
to be political revolutionaries as well. And now we have Godard
looking approvingly toward China—that's his business. In the light
that comes from the extreme Orient, Waldeck Rochet can no longer
be particularly distinguished from Lecanuet, nor Kosygin from
Johnson. What is important is not what Godard is thinking—every
man to his own ideas—but the fact that he expresses what he is
thinking without saying anything about it in an articulate, logical
fashion; and yet his ideas are none the less obvious to us because of
that. What is important is that he proves to be a revolutionary by
means of an art that has finally been revolutionized." [1]

---

[1] Review of *Made in U.S.A.*, *Le Figaro littéraire*, 2 February 1967, p. 14.

As Marie-Claire Ropars-Wuilleumier points out in her article in this book, one of the prime ways Godard has broken most strongly with traditional filmmaking is through his avoidance of just about anything resembling a conventional storyline, narrative, or plot. It is the presence of a narrative in a work of art that can provide the internal event or events with an overall cause-and-effect justification so that, basically, there is eventually a reason for everything that happens. Thus bogged down in a temporality created by the necessarily logical chain of events, the purely aesthetic elements of a given work can rarely become independent enough to take on their full relief. The taste of the members of the "nouvelle vague" (of which Godard was one of the chief representatives) for the apparently plot-ridden films of Alfred Hitchcock and of such American directors as Samuel Fuller and Howard Hawks might seem paradoxical at first. But what these directors (and many more, including, for the French, Jerry Lewis) have in common is that they all use the narrative as the slightest of pretexts for justifying their films, thus allowing themselves the luxury of being able to concentrate on those more purely cinematic and aesthetic elements so admired by the New Wave. (It might also be added that the thread of a narrative, which depends greatly on language, will not be as obvious for a non-native speaker of a given language, thus affording foreign viewers of American films a certain "distantiation" from the very outset.) Although there may be a certain moral goal—the saving of a ranch or the recovery of a microfilm inside a statuette—the action that takes place in the attainment of this ultimate morality, which is usually stereotyped and represented by cardboard figures, overwhelms the goal and the narrative built around it to such a degree that most of the film can be said to grow out of a quasi-anarchistic state that is quite propitious to pure creativity. Certainly, few directors have ever buried the self-evident absurdities of a plot beneath a series of virtuoso actions-for-their-own-sake with more self-parodying relish than did Alfred Hitchcock in *North By Northwest*.

Godard's antipathy toward narrative has been summed up by André-S. Labarthe (who, incidentally, plays several small roles in Godard's films, including Paul in *Vivre sa vie*) in his brilliant article on *Une Femme est une femme*.[2] Here he compares Godard's attitude

---

[2] See "La Chance d'être femme," *Cahiers du cinéma*, No. 125 (November 1961), pp. 53–56. Large extracts reprinted in Jean Collet's book.

with that of French writer Paul Valéry, who steadfastly refused
throughout his life to write that classic first line of a novel, "The
Marquise went out at five o'clock. . . ." [3] If one could manage to
take apart Godard's various films and separate storylines from action, it would quickly be discovered that the narratives are of the
utmost simplicity (quite often being based on a sentence or two, as
in *Une Femme est une femme*) and/or that they are largely irrelevant
to what is occurring on the screen. Using neither a shooting script
nor any well-elaborated working plan, Godard's whole approach to
filmmaking remains completely anchored in the instant—the instant
the camera is turning—thus avoiding any links with a cause-and-
effect past or future previously determined by a narrative. The
project often changes radically as the film is being shot—*One Plus
One* was originally to have been a "parabole based around the
parallel themes of creation and destruction. A tragic triangle in
London—a French girl, who has at first been seduced by a reactionary Texan, falls in love with an extreme-left Black militant. The girl
(Anne Wiazemsky) is named Democracy. The Nazi Texan opposes
the Black, who obviously represents Black Power. . . ." [4] In the
end there is no Texan; the girl is transformed into a pastless, futureless creature whose language is reduced to "yes" and "no" (as Jean
Collet brings out in an article on *Alphaville*,[5] this "binary" language
represents the whole system of communication in a computerized
society; it also symbolizes the very essence of the Godardian dialectic); the theme of construction is still represented by the shots of the
Rolling Stones' rehearsal, but the final, completed version of the
song "Sympathy for the Devil" is never heard in the original version
of the film;[6] the theme of destruction is still represented by Black
Power, but in the form of a *group* of anonymous Blacks (pastless,

---

[3] Contemporary French poet-playwright Jean Tardieu, in *La Première personne
du singulier*, offers the following first line for a more Proustian type novel: "At
the age of seven or eight, I was not allowed to enter the salon when my mother
was receiving visitors. . . ."

[4] Guy Monreal, "Qui n'a pas son petit Godard," l'*Express*, 15–21 July 1968, p. 51.

[5] From *Télérama*, No. 851 (8 May 1966), pp. 79–80.

[6] As is generally known, Godard's producer changed the ending of the film,
allowing for the complete performance of "Sympathy for the Devil," also giving
the film the title of the song. Since this was done without Godard's consent, the
latter is said to have slapped his producer after the first public showing of the
film in April, 1968 (in London), and disappeared from sight, or at least from the
"official" world of the cinema. This date seems to mark the true beginning of
Godard's "Dziga-Vertov" stage.

futureless) who murder a *group* of anonymous white girls (pastless, futureless) in a junkyard near the Thames; one sees sequences in a cluttered bookshop (perhaps a direct allusion to a similar scene in *Deux ou trois choses que je sais d'elle*); one hears excerpts from a pseudopornographic novel and from *Mein Kampf.* All in all, the film might more aptly be entitled *One Plus One Plus One Plus* . . . , the meaning of the whole being greater than but inseparable from the fragments. Similarly, a projected *Emile* (after Rousseau) was at first to be "a modern film, the story of a boy who refuses to go to his high school because the classes are always overcrowded; he begins to learn outside of school, by looking at people, going to the movies, listening to the radio, or watching television. . . ." [7] What the film eventually became was *Le Gai savoir,* in which, as Richard Roud puts it, "there is, at last, no plot at all."

Godard usually works from scratch. When he does adapt a work (almost always a novel), he follows the Hitchcock tradition of using literature that is second-rate at best. Indeed, none of Godard's intended adaptations of literary masterpieces, from the *Emile* mentioned above to Balzac's *Lys dans la vallée* or Giraudoux's *Pour Lucrèce,* has ever materialized, for one reason or another. In this way, not only can the director avoid the almost inevitable sacrilege of forcing a great work of art into a medium for which it was not intended, he also avoids the a priori dictates of a creation that is almost always strongly bound to a narrative. And when Godard has adapted a novel, the resulting film has rarely been particularly identifiable with the original work. In the one Godard film in which he followed the structure of a novel with relative fidelity—*Le Mépris,* based on Italian novelist Alberto Moravia's *Il Disprezzo (Contempt)*[8]—the novel itself represents the story of the main character's attempts to discover the *cause* of a particular *effect* (the alienation of his wife). Even here, Godard has carefully buried the "solution" that is, after all, revealed in Moravia's novel—on the one hand, the ostensible reason for the wife's contempt is apparent to the spectator almost from the outset of the film (as it is in the novel); on the other

---

[7] See "Lutter sur deux fronts" (conversation with Jean-Luc Godard by J. Bontemps, Jean-Louis Comolli, Michel Delahay, and Jean Narboni), *Cahiers du cinéma,* No. 194 (October 1967), p. 70. This quote, and all others from this interview used in this book, reprinted by permission of Grove Press, Inc. Copyright © 1967 by Les Éditions de l'Étoile.

[8] The British title is *A Ghost at Noon,* no doubt suggested by the apparition of the wife near the end of the novel, a scene that is totally cut in the movie.

hand, the profound cause never becomes apparent to the main character in the film, or if it does, the audience is not aware of the change. In the novel, the hero, who seems rather incredibly blind, eventually arrives at a revelation; furthermore, the contempt-provoking act appears quite arbitrary in the film, since it is juxtaposed almost immediately upon a preceding scene poetically but objectively portraying marital harmony (through stylized dialogue and sculptural, monochrome shots of the couple making love), and since no prevailing psychology in the wife is ever brought out (as it is in the novel). Even this early film could bear the "One Plus One" title since it is, as Ropars-Wuilleumier mentions, both the story of the "contempt" and a quasi-documentary of a film being made. Godard also takes certain prose passages from the French translation of the novel (certain dialogues from the book are also used throughout the film) and has them spoken (off-camera) poetically by the main character and his wife during the apartment scene (thus turning the story back in upon its source, the novel); here, not only does Godard break up the first-person narrative and cause the wife in the film to say things about the husband that the husband says about *her* in the novel but also the passages quoted are taken from all over the novel and have no chronological bearing, no cause-and-effect relationship to the apartment scene in the film. Godard's narratives, when they exist at all, are more or less composed of a series of diachronic juxtapositions arranged within a chronology that is contained wholly within the structure of the film itself. (When French director Georges Franju once apparently asked Godard, during a debate, whether he would not agree that a film had to have a beginning, middle, and end, Godard's reply was, "Yes, but not necessarily in that order.")

It is important to note here that Godard's iconoclasm vis-à-vis the narrative could appear quite gratuitous and hollow were it not for the fact that this aspect of his art corresponds perfectly with a basic vision of life, an underlying philosophical outlook that pervades the director's entire work. For the one constant in Godard's films, from *A bout de souffle* to *Vladimir and Rosa*, is the presence—direct or otherwise—of a chaotic, neurotic, and essentially disemboweled society whose various actions have lost any possible contact with a raison d'être. To be sure, the specific manifestations of this social reality change from film to film and almost always correspond, in fact, with something quite relevant to the specific era in which a certain film was made; but a generalized negativism dominates all these particular forms of contemporary society. The fragmented illogicality of Godard's anti-narratives thus paradoxically represents a documentary technique for looking at a state of the world and civilization. Indeed, so inseparable are the rhythm of modern civilization and the cinematographic style used by Godard that the two appear to be mutually self-engendering in the director's films, and the importance and accuracy of Godard's work as unique social documentary has been stressed in a great deal of the criticism that has been written on him.

There is, however, another constant throughout Godard's work, wherein lies the other half of the dialectic. From one film to the next, one always finds a counter-current to the trends of modern society, a counter-current manifested both in the actions and the attitudes of the characters and, on the other hand, in the handling of pure cinematic technique. In other words, against a background of chaos and banality that is presented in all its blatant ugliness, Godard juxtaposes a varied layer of idealism that runs the gamut, throughout his oeuvre, from poetic involvement and even romanticism to radical political action. Generally, Godard seems to have a Rousseau-like vision of a civilization that has lost contact with an ideal through the progressive modernization, mechanization, "capitalization," and, ultimately, socialization of human life. Certainly, the dehumanization of man represents an important theme in many of his films, from *Alphaville* and *La Femme mariée*[9] to *Made in U.S.A.* and *Deux ou trois choses que je sais d'elle*. And one of Godard's apparent intentions in *Le Mépris* was to pit Homeric serenity against the neurotic state of contemporary man.[10] But what is brilliantly original about Godard here is that even this antithetical idealism is treated in a documentary style, and it is this particular paradox, perhaps more than any other, that has allowed Godard the enormous freedom to bring into his films "incongruous" elements that would be totally out of place in a movie with a traditional narrative and the accompanying psychological vicissitudes.

Obviously, much (but not all, as will be seen) of the idealistic side

[9] Since the title *Une Femme mariée* was imposed upon Godard by the French censors, the original title will be kept here, as it was in the English-language version of the title, *The Married Woman*.

[10] See Jean Clay, "Le Paradoxe de Jean-Luc Godard, nihiliste et créateur," in *Réalités*, No. 212 (September 1963). Title in English-language edition is "Jean-Luc Godard: The French Cinema's Most Negative Asset."

of the Godardian dialectic is represented by the characters. But these are characters who, unlike the director, are frequently not consciously aware of their idealism—at least Godard takes pains to avoid showing any such awareness most of the time. For one can note that Godard generally avoids an element that is normally extremely important in giving dramatic guts to a traditional narrative —namely, psychological development. Rarely does he offer a genuine *reason* for the actions performed by his characters, most of whom find themselves unable to progress logically through a civilized temporality—either they are confronted with the absurdity of an existence that is obviously not justified by any causative absolute, as in *A bout de souffle, Le Petit soldat, Bande à part, Pierrot le fou, Made in U.S.A.,* and so forth, or they become the innocent (*Les Carabiniers*) or not-so-innocent (*Weekend*) victims of their confidence in the system, which, in the most relativistic manner, eventually turns sour on them. Godard's characters remind one of Sartre's Antoine Roquentin, whose "nausea" is basically a reaction to the newly found awareness of the nonessential nature of everything that takes place within life (and therefore within time). But whereas Roquentin becomes aware from within himself of the basic condition of a universe that has always really been that way, Godard, more often than not, suggests a transformation from without—a kind of apocalyptic state with which various characters, some of them naively idealistic, must cope. Thus, in Godard's short *Le Nouveau monde,* the hero arrives at the conclusion that the destruction of a cause-and-effect existence has been occasioned by an atomic explosion.

What happens, then, is that Godard's main characters are more often than not play-acting—they become childlike individuals whose only raison d'être, whose only ideal, resides in a role they can play, either consciously or unconsciously, since no a priori justification for action manifests itself either within society or within the cosmos (the latter being of little concern to Godard, at least where his films are concerned). The source of the role played often corresponds to a certain idealistic or romantic nostalgia (see Ropars-Wuilleumier) that obviously stems from Godard's own penchants, especially the cinematic ones, such as the Hollywood gangsterism that pervades such films as *A bout de souffle* and *Bande à part.* In spite of their love, for instance, neither Michel nor Patricia, in *A bout de souffle,* can stop acting out a certain idealized life-style—Michel the Humphrey Bogart type; Patricia the all-American girl. (In an excellent early review of the film, Arlene Croce pointed out, concerning the role of Patricia, that "the writing, casting and playing . . . of this part, not to mention the whole psychological conception of the character and its function in the film's moral focus, are of such deadly perfection that, if we were as alert to the results of cultural export as we are to its necessity, picket lines and reprisals from the American Legion would be in order.")[11] Inasmuch, therefore, as Michel's murder of the policeman and Patricia's denunciation of Michel both arise from causes that are gratuitously juxtaposed upon both the context of the film's narrative (the boy-meets-girl story) and upon the broader framework of "normal" social behavior, both the murder and the denunciation can be said to be gratuitous acts. Even death is treated under the equivocal light of role-playing. In *Bande à part,* for instance, Arthur (Claude Brasseur) mimes the violent death in the beginning of the film that he eventually suffers at the end.

On the other hand, both love and political involvement (or both, as in *Le Petit soldat* and *Made in U.S.A.*) would seem to offer a more solid basis of idealism, rising above role-playing, with which to combat the meaninglessness of social existence. One of the principal themes of *Pierrot le fou,* for example, seems to be the Rimbaldian war cry, "Love must be re-invented." But even here, what appears to be one of the few truly motivated acts in Godard's films—Ferdinand's killing of Marianne and her lover—is caused not so much by a fit of jealous passion as by Ferdinand-Pierrot's eventual awareness that even love is a role that is superimposed upon social absurdity, on which it even comes to depend. (The clown-name "Pierrot," which Marianne uses for Ferdinand, is in itself indicative of the role-playing obsession in Godard's films.) Indeed, it is this rare type of awareness, particularly in its contrast with the usual unconscious or semiconscious role-playing, that occasionally gives a Godard film a startlingly dramatic relief. One of the most poignant moments in Godard's pre-1968 films occurs in *Made in U.S.A.* when Paula Nelson realizes that she can no longer take the quasi-political, quasi-amorous role she is playing seriously. Confronted with a situation in which all of her acts become basically gratuitous, Paula's only solution can be a more or less existential commitment to the

---

[11] Review of *A bout de souffle* (*Breathless*) in *Film Quarterly,* Vol. XIV, No. 3 (Spring 1961), 54.

present, to the instant—a commitment that characterizes, in fact, Godard's entire approach to the cinema: "Either this life is nothing, or else it has to be everything. By contemplating losing it rather than submitting it to the absurd,[12] I fix an absolute point of reference—that of morality—at the very heart of my existence. In this sense, the absolute is no place but here. No past can guarantee it, and no future can promise its existence. I choose to exist in order to become more and more present . . . for myself, for Dick and for other people." In a film such as *La Femme mariée*, on the other hand, this type of final, dramatic awareness never really takes place; the heroine plays her role out to the end. One senses that she is on the brink of intellectually discovering the gratuity of the love she is acting out (which is further emphasized by the fact that her lover is an actor—the last scene of the film, in fact, involves the lovers rehearsing a love scene from Racine's *Bérénice*); one also senses that such a discovery could unleash the type of madness, the type of alienation, alluded to by the very title of *Pierrot le fou*. Godard seems to stress this, consciously or unconsciously, through his use, as a musical leitmotif, of the opening of the second movement of Beethoven's third "Rasumovsky" Quartet, about which J. W. N. Sullivan wrote, "It makes on us the impression of something strictly abnormal. There is here a remote and frozen anguish, wailing over some implacable destiny. This is hardly human suffering; it is more like a memory from some ancient and starless night of the soul." [13]

This combination in Godard of documentary intentions and an essentially play-acting conception of human existence (in modern society) produces an approach to acting and the use of actors that is unique in the cinema. If one wonders why, for instance, Godard does not go all the way and use nonactors in his films, it is precisely because of the fact that nobody can play out play-acting better than an actor. Godard has pointed out on many occasions that what he wants from his actors is bits and snatches of gestures and speech that are characteristic of these actors *when they are not trying to act*. But the point is that an actor acting naturally will produce a different impression, due both to his own knowledge of his role in society and the spectators' knowledge of that role, from that of the man-in-the-

---

[12] In the translation of the film-script published in England by Lorimer, the French word *absurde,* which is not very distinctly pronounced by Anna Karina in the film, is mistakenly translated as "action."

[13] *Beethoven, His Spiritual Development* (New York: Mentor, 1949), p. 91.

street doing whatever he normally does. Godard, in fact, often deliberately disrupts the "suspension of disbelief" by having his actors address the audience. This is particularly shattering in *A bout de souffle, Pierrot le fou*, and *Weekend*, for example, in which the more involved narratives might tend to create an illusion of reality. Thus, the best way a potential Godard actor can prepare for a film is to plunge himself into the physical reality that represents the point of departure for a particular movie. When Marina Vlady, for example, asked Godard what she should do to prepare for her role in *Deux ou trois choses que je sais d'elle*, the director's answer was that she should walk to the place where the film was being shot each day, rather than taking a taxi. In this way, Vlady would become unconsciously assimilated with the reality of the apartment-complex background of the film in a manner that no amount of coaching could produce. It is the subconscious, nonintellectual side of actors that Godard wants to capture, which explains how Godard can call *A bout de souffle* a "documentary on Belmondo and Seberg," and which greatly justifies the quasi-improvisational shooting methods he uses. Thus, Godard effectively destroys the mythical purity of those two opposing poles of the cinema—the documentary and the adventure film—and, by playing these seemingly paradoxical elements against each other, forces upon the spectators an entirely new manner of approaching the cinema. The whole duality of reality versus fiction, of the film versus the world in which it is made, becomes buried in a general phenomenological ambiguity that has been ingeniously summed up by Godard in the following question: "When you see a photograph of yourself, is it fictitious or not?" In comparing Godard to Bresson, Claude Mauriac describes this ambiguity in the following manner: "In seeking to bring out the truest and most secret voices of his characters, the Bresson of *Pickpocket* seems to have desired a deliberate falseness. It is this same tone that thought would have were it possible to record the sound of its meanderings. Jean-Luc Godard proceeds in an opposite manner to arrive at the same result: one of the most original elements of *A bout de souffle* lies in the naturalness of its dialogues. We have the impression of hearing, for the first time, an authentic manner of speaking on the screen. But this naturalness is only an appearance. It has been totally recreated." [14]

[14] *Le Figaro littéraire,* 19 March 1960, p. 14.

Parenthetically, it might be noted that one of Godard's abortive projects, a film based on Giraudoux's play *Pour Lucrèce*, would have represented a high point of sorts as a manifestation of Godard's theater-within-life-within-theater aesthetic. As Godard describes it, the film would show ". . . the woman who plays Lucrèce getting out of a taxi to go to a rehearsal, or perhaps not even a rehearsal, but an audition. Then, the film would go further into the play by showing at various times either part of the audition, or of the rehearsal, or even of a scene actually being played. And, at certain moments, there would be a criticism of the play. Certain scenes would be played several times, either because of the actors or because of the staging. They could even be played by different actresses, each one trying out the role—Moreau, Bardot, Karina, and so forth. And the director, along with the entire troupe, would pass in review the seven or eight important theories of the theater—from Aristotle to the three unities, from the preface for Hugo's *Cromwell* to *The Birth of Tragedy* and up through Brecht and Stanislawski, but all the time progressing within the play. At the end, the audience would see the death of the actress who arrived at the beginning. This would be the last shot—at that point, one would be involved in fiction. A film such as this would also be intended to teach the audience what theater is." [15]

It is, in fact, principally this theatrical aesthetic that creates an almost perfect equilibrium between the two sides of the Godardian dialectic. For it is more often than not a mistake to see the enacted idealism—in love, politics, romanticized gangsterism, and so forth—of Godard's characters as having any more solid basis in an absolute reality than the quasi-nihilistic social structures and artifacts the director documents. What happens is that Godard, in offering a counter-current to the sterilities of modern life, is merely showing various ways in which this sterility, this brutal mechanization, is fought by various types of people. And the battles vary in convincingness from film to film. Thus, Nana's decision to become a prostitute, to play the role of a whore, in *Vivre sa vie* seems at least tenuously motivated by negativistic social circumstances. Juliette's downfall in *Deux ou trois choses* is more ambiguous, since it seems to represent both the heroine's desire to escape her surroundings and at the same time her need to be integrated into them. Obviously, the very fact that there

---

[15] "Lutter sur deux fronts," p. 68.

is a battle taking place will usually, but not necessarily, force people to take sides against modern society as Godard shows it. But this does not prevent the opposition from being shown just as objectively as is the society that is attacked. Thus it is not precisely Godard who is doing battle with the forces of mechanization, but the people and elements shown by him; this divorce between the personal involvement of the director and the involvement of his characters was one of the key elements in Godard's films until his Dziga-Vertov period, in which the link between the ideology of the director—or rather of the directing group—and the film is made explicit. But before the Dziga-Vertov period, the absurdities of the opposition are frequently made just as apparent as are the absurdities of that which is opposed.

In this manner, for example, the "knights in shining armor" in both *Alphaville* and *Made in U.S.A.* are detective-film heroes who are not intended to be believable and whose acts of violence are just as gratuitous as those perpetrated by the society they are combating. Just in case, for instance, the audience might be tempted to identify with the plight of *Made in U.S.A.*'s heroine and to construe a poetic message of sorts out of the relationship between Paula Nelson and the writer David Goodis, Godard has Paula shoot Goodis at the end of the film, an act whose only justification lies in the spy-thriller morality that Paula has already realized as absurd and meaningless. *Alphaville* is even more ambiguous in this manner. The role played by Eddie Constantine comes straight out of a comic strip (at one point in the film, "Lemmy Caution" even asks a dying colleague about Dick Tracy), out of the super-hero roles Constantine himself had played for so many years. Were the physical context of the film consistent with this role, it would be possible to fabricate some kind of message, at least on a campy level, from Lemmy Caution's heroics. As can be seen in the interview with continuity-girl Suzanne Schiffman in this book, however, the settings for *Alphaville* are entirely realistic and are given their science-fiction aura only because of their juxtaposition with the superimposed comic-strip narrative. Even the voice of the computer (from which, ironically enough, it is sometimes difficult to distinguish the mechanical narration style used by Constantine) is in reality that of a man with no larynx who is speaking from his diaphragm. Here Godard seems to carry on very much in the Cocteau tradition of transforming everyday reality into myth and myth into everyday reality, using unexpected combinations of elements to create this atmosphere rather than trick effects. Thus, reality becomes its own symbol, and the audience is forced to witness the combat as a whole rather than being afforded the cathartic luxury of identifying with one side against the other. It is a kind of Brechtian stylization that engenders inescapable intellectual reactions rather than forgettable emotional ones. For, emotionally, the two halves of the dialectic by necessity cancel each other out. One plus one equals zero. Even the discovery of "love" at the end of the film cannot be taken seriously, since this entire final scene is accompanied by a schmaltzy musical swell that concludes the film (the only Godard movie to end in this manner) in the best Alfred Newman-Hollywood tradition.

What Godard has done, then, is to sacrifice, in his films, emotional and psychological profundity—those essential building blocks of so-called bourgeois art—in favor of a more metaphysical depth and purity of form. (The latter element, which involves Godard's specific cinematic techniques, is treated in depth in the editor's article, "Nihilism versus Aesthetic Distantiation.") In being one of the first film directors to *consciously* favor these latter elements in a systematically applied aesthetic, Godard has helped revolutionize the cinema in much the same way other arts—poetry, painting, the theater, and so forth—were revolutionized before the cinema. And in his ability to translate what might be called the existential non sequitur into cinematic language; in his mélange of the various cinematic genres, from the detective film to the musical; in his dazzling array of film techniques and intraartistic allusions; and, perhaps most importantly, in his creation of a uniquely cinematic dialectic, Jean-Luc Godard has been one of the most controversial and at the same time one of the most influential filmmakers of the modern generation. As for this dialectic, the article-interview by Jean Clay has brought out what represents perhaps two of its deepest sources. On the one hand, Godard stated that it was through Sartre that he discovered literature, which was his first interest; on the other he also stated that he is a "believer." Indeed, the entire evolution of Godard and his work greatly resembles that of an early Sartrian hero such as Mathieu Delarue in the *Chemins de la liberté* trilogy. One sees the typically Sartrian fear of becoming frozen into a definition created out of other people's opinions; and there is thus the desire to remain free, which has frequently led Godard to provacateur tactics (Truffaut has mentioned this as one of the reasons for the anti-Camus remark in *Le Petit soldat*) in order to avoid becoming classified. But there also exists the desire to avoid the lack of direction implied by total freedom, the yearning to become involved (*engagé*), but involved in a cause for which there would be an absolute justification outside the immediate exigencies of the cause itself; and it is in the recognized impossibility of this absolutism, in spite of the desire to "believe," that there lies a second reason for noninvolvement. But finally, involvement in a cause does occur (Godard's espousal of the Marxist-Leninist left) growing out of a specific social occasion, and not out of an absolute. For Godard's cinema, this recent involvement has caused at least the temporary destruction of the dialectic that dominated his pre-1968 films—or at least the dialectic in the sense that it has been discussed here. Whatever one may think of such films as *British Sounds* or *Vent d'est,* these works are completely dependent on the exterior social cause that occasioned them. This is not the case for Godard's earlier works (as politically significant as they may be), which recreate, disanchor, and free the social reality that engendered them in order to give this foundation a timeless universality through a dialectic not limited to the Marxist variety. This same vitality, this same universality, is lacking (deliberately) in Godard's "Dziga-Vertov" films, whatever other merits they may have.

Sartre ended Mathieu's evolution with the character's first (and apparently last) pure act of involvement. Godard, before his recent near-fatal accident, showed signs of evolving beyond his initial *engagement.* He will no doubt always tend toward that ultimate gesture of liberty that is admirably summed up at the end of *A bout de souffle* when Michel, the instant before he dies, reaches up and closes his own eyelids. One can only hope and expect that Godard will continue to foil everybody's expectations of him. As one writer put it, "Jean-Luc Godard could be the Rimbaud of French cinema. It would be a shame for him to be satisfied with being the Cohn-Bendit." [16]

[16] Pierre Billard, "Jean-Luc Godard choisit le néant," *l'Express,* 19–25 May 1969, p. 111.

Chronology

1930   Born in Paris, 3 December, of Protestant parents, the second of four children. His father was a doctor with his own clinic; his mother came from the important Monod family of bankers.

1930–49   During the war, Godard became a naturalized Swiss citizen. From age 10 to 16 lived in the Canton of Vaud, attended school in Nyons. His parents divorced; he later attended the Lycée Buffon in Paris.

1949   Studied at the Sorbonne, preparing a "certificat" in ethnology. Began to frequent the Latin Quarter's "ciné-club" and then the Cinémathèque, where he made friends with such important cinematic figures as André Bazin, François Truffaut, Jacques Rivette, and Éric Rohmer.

1950   Founded, with Rohmer and Rivette, a *Gazette du cinéma* (five issues between May and November), for which he wrote a number of articles, sometimes using the pseudonym of "Hans Lucas." Played a role in and financed Rivette's experimental short, *Quadrille*.

1951   Played a role in Rohmer's *Présentation* (or *Charlotte et son steak*). Cut off from his money by his family, Godard began to lead a Bohemian existence, occasionally even resorting to stealing. Returned occasionally to Switzerland, where he held such odd jobs as delivery boy for a book-store, cameraman for Zurich TV.

1952   January: began writing for the *Cahiers du cinéma*. Traveled to North and South America with his father. During this voyage, Godard began to make his first film, of which only a tracking shot taken from a car was actually accomplished.

1953   Returned briefly to Bohemian existence in Paris after more than a year of traveling; later took a job as construction worker on the "Grande Dixence" dam in Switzerland.

1954   Having saved a certain amount of money, Godard decided to make a movie devoted to the construction of the dam at La Grande Dixence. Doing his own commentary and editing, he sold his short, *Opération béton* (Operation Concrete), first shown 2 July 1958 in Paris as a short with *Tea and Sympathy*. 25 April: Godard's mother killed in a motor-scooter accident in Lausanne.

1955   Backed by his own money, Godard filmed, in Geneva, a second short, *Une Femme coquette*, doing the scenario (after Maupassant), camerawork, and editing himself.

1956   After a long writing lull (October 1952 to August 1956), Godard began once again to do critical writings on the cinema, notably for the *Cahiers du cinéma* and *Arts*. Appeared in Jacques Rivette's *Le Coup du berger*.

1957   Once again penniless, Godard worked at odd jobs; took over Claude Chabrol's position as press attaché for Artistes Associés, where he eventually met Georges de Beauregard. Made his first French film, a short entitled *Tous les garçons s'appellent Patrick* (or *Charlotte et Véronique*).

1958   Shot *Charlotte et son Jules* (Charlotte and Her Boyfriend), an homage to Jean Cocteau (in the *Voix humaine* genre) in which Godard used his own voice to dub Belmondo's monologue. Using film shot and then abandoned by François Truffaut of a flooded region near Paris, Godard put together *Une Histoire d'eau* (A Story of Water), which he called an homage to Mack Sennet. Godard's silhouette used by Rivette in *Paris nous appartient*.

1959   Worked with Truffaut for the weekly *Temps de Paris*, for which Godard wrote a gossip column. Worked on the scenario for the Beauregard-produced *Ramuncho* (or *Le Pêcheur d'Islande*), which Godard eventually gave up. Wrote the scenario for *Une Femme est une femme*, and numerous critical writings, placing him in the vanguard of the "nouvelle vague" aesthetic. Appeared in Rohmer's *Le Signe du lion*. Offered Beauregard four scripts, including *A bout de souffle*, based on a Truffaut idea inspired by an actual event; Beauregard accepted *A bout de souffle*, which Godard shot on a very limited budget (400,000 francs) from 17 August to 15 September.

1960   3 March: Married Anna Karina (born 22 September 1940 in Copenhagen) in Béguins, Switzerland (near Lausanne). 16 March: *A bout de souffle* premiered in Paris, with triumphal success both with the critics and the public (260,058 first-run tickets in Paris); Beauregard eventually recouped more than 150 million francs on his investment. April–May: shot *Le Petit soldat* in Geneva. Although this film was to be released in the fall, the French censors banned it because of apparent references to the Algerian war; film was first shown 25 January 1963.

1961   Shot *Une Femme est une femme*, his first film in color and widescreen. September: participated in the collective film remake of *Les Sept péchés capitaux*. Appeared along with Anna Karina in a comic sequence in Agnès Varda's *Cléo de 5 à 7*. Began work on an adaptation of James Hadley Chase's *Eva* but abandoned the project. Began working on a film to be called *France la douce* ("the story of a woman from the right and a man from the left") for Pierre Braunberger, but likewise gave up the project. Appeared in Jacques Bourdon's *Le Soleil dans l'oeil.*

1962   February–March: shot *Vivre sa vie* in Paris; Godard's first commercial success since *A bout de souffle.* November: shot a sketch in the collective film *RoGoPaG* entitled *Le Nouveau monde.* Began setting up for *Pour Lucrèce,* which was to have starred Sami Frey, Pascale Robert, Nicole Bellac, Charles Denner, Michel Piccoli, and Marie Dubos; abandoned the project, paid off the crew by selling his share of *Vivre sa vie* back to producer Pierre Braunberger, and joined Anna Karina, who was working on Pierre Gaspard-Huit's *Sheherazade* (in which Godard appeared) in Madrid.

1963   January: finished shooting *Les Carabiniers,* begun in December 1962, and then spent many weeks editing it. Dedicated to Jean Vigo, *Les Carabiniers* was probably the most spectacular of Godard's commercial failures, and elicited violent polemics from the critics. In January, Godard also went to Marrakesh to film *Le Grand escroc,* an episode later cut from the collective film *Les Plus belles escroqueries du monde.* April–June: shot *Le Mépris* in Rome and Capri. Godard removed his name from the Italian version, produced by Carlo Ponti, who replaced Delerue's romantic soundtrack with a jazz score (à la *Breathless*) by Piero Piccioni; used the same color process for the entire film (whereas Godard has used two different processes, one for Rome, the other, more limpid, for Capri); reedited certain sequences; dubbed the entire film in Italian (thus rendering Giorgia Moll's role meaningless). December: shot *Montparnasse-Levallois,* a sketch in the collective film *Paris vu par. . . .*

1964   February–March: shot *Bande à part* (in 25 days) in Paris. During this same period, Godard also set up a production company called "Anouchka Films" with Anna Karina. June–July: shot *La Femme mariée* in Paris. Censors eventually forced the cutting of a sequence shot by Jacques Rozier at the Côte d'Azur (documenting the topless bathingsuit fad) and the changing of the film's title to *Une Femme mariée* in order to avoid the impression that Godard was showing a "typical" French wife. Later in the year, the French Federation of Ciné-Clubs (F.F.C.C.) devoted a series of "Rencontres," in which Godard participated, to the director's work. Two television programs were also made about Godard and his films.

1965   January–February: shot *Alphaville* in Paris. June–July: shot *Pierrot le fou* in Paris and southern France. Divorced Anna Karina. November–December: in Paris, between two rounds of the Gaullist elections, Godard shot *Masculin-Féminin.* The film represented a new, more politically involved direction for Godard.

1966 Published his letter to André Malraux, then "ministre de la 'Kulture,'" attacking Malraux for his weakness in the censoring of Jacques Rivette's film version of Diderot's *La Religieuse* (which starred Anna Karina). Shot, almost simultaneously, *Made in U.S.A.* (July–August) and *Deux ou trois choses que je sais d'elle* (August–September) in and around Paris. November: shot *Anticipation* (or *L'Amour en l'an 2000*), a "colored sequel to *Alphaville*," as a sketch in the collective film *Le Plus vieux métier du monde* (or *L'Amour à travers les âges*). This was the last Godard film in which Anna Karina was to appear. Godard appeared briefly in Raoul Lévy's *L'Espion*, the last film, to this date, other than his own, in which he appeared as an actor.

1967 March: shot *La Chinoise* in Paris. One of the principal actresses was Anne Wiazemsky, the granddaughter of French novelist François Mauriac; Godard married Miss Wiazemsky around this same period. Shot *Caméra-Oeil*, a sequence in the collective film *Loin du Vietnam*. Prevented by the North Vietnamese from visiting their country, Godard was one of two directors (the other was Resnais) to shoot his sequence in Paris. Shot *L'Aller et retour des enfants prodigues andate e ritorno dei figli prodighi* as an episode in the otherwise all Italian collective film *Vangelo 70*. September–October: shot *Weekend* in and around Paris.

1968 December (1967)–January: shot *Le Gai savoir* (the final editing of which was done after the May events in France), commissioned by French television, which later refused to show the film. In February and March, Godard's was one of the strongest voices in demanding the reinstatement of Henri Langlois, who had been fired as the head of the French "Cinémathèque." Although not particularly active in the debates led by the "États généraux du cinéma" during the May events, Godard sought out his own solutions to an ideological cinema, concerning himself particularly with the means for making production and distribution available to the proletariat. Afterward, along with other militants and filmmakers, filmed a series of unsigned "ciné-tracts." Formation of the "Dziga-Vertov" group with Jean-Pierre Gorin. Shot, apparently in May and June, *Un Film comme les autres,* including conversations between three Nanterre students and two workers from the Renault-Flins factories. June–August: shot *One Plus One* in Great Britain. In the autumn, Godard went to the United States to begin filming *One American Movie (1 A.M.),* which was done in New York, New Jersey, and Berkeley, California. Godard later abandoned the film—although he returned to the U.S. in September 1969 to finish it, he never completed the necessary work. September: trip to Cuba. Also traveled to Canada, where he began *Communication(s),* which remains uncompleted.

1969   February: shot *British Sounds* (or *See You at Mao*) in England.
        The film was to have been for London Weekend Television, but
        was refused after it was completed. March: trip to Prague,
        Czechoslovakia, where the Dziga-Vertov group filmed *Pravda*
        clandestinely. June: shot *Vento dell'est* (*Vent d'est*, or *Wind
        From the East*) in Italy. December: shot *Lotte in Italia* (*Luttes
        en Italie*, or *Struggle in Italy*) for Italian television (R.A.I.),
        which never showed it.

1970   February: filmed *Jusqu'à la victoire* (*Till Victory*) in Lebanon
        and Jordan. Devoted to the efforts of El Fatah and the Palestinian
        Liberation Front, the film has not been released to this date. In
        April, Godard made an eight-day tour of American universities
        to raise money for *Till Victory* (it was at the end of this period
        that the *Film and Revolution* interview in this book was made).
        Later made an advertising short for the Paris firm "Cinéma et
        publicité" to help finance the Al Fatah work. In Paris, Godard
        filmed *Vladimir* (or *Wladimir*) *et Rosa,* ostensibly based on the
        trial of the "Chicago Eight" and financed by Grove Press and
        German TV; was also to have made a second film, *18 Brumaire*
        (after Karl Marx), for Grove Press. (*Vladimir et Rosa* was at one
        time the subtitle for a projected Godard-Grove Press film to be
        entitled *Sex and Revolution.*)

1971   At the beginning of the year, Godard was working on recutting
        Till Victory. In April, he apparently went to Los Angeles to con-
        fer with Jane Fonda. 9 June: Godard seriously injured in an
        accident in Paris while riding on a motorcycle driven by his
        editing girl, Christine Marsollier, who was not as seriously hurt.

1972   After a long period of recuperation, Godard began shooting, with
        coworker Gorin, *Tout va bien*, with Yves Montand, Jane Fonda
        and Vittorio Caprioli. Film near completion as of the end of
        February.

Learning Not to Be Bitter:
Interview with Jean-Luc Godard
on LE PETIT SOLDAT
by MICHÈLE MANCEAUX

Jean-Luc Godard speaks in a low voice, with his eyes hidden behind dark glasses.

In *A bout de souffle*, his first film, the heroes also protected themselves . . . behind the smoke from their cigarettes. But from what are Godard and his characters protecting themselves? From the world? From involvement? From conformity? Jean-Luc Godard fears precisely these elements. He is hardly what you call politically involved.

"If the concepts of *right* and *left* have a meaning for you, where would you put yourself?"

"I feel that people on the left are sentimentalists. Those who are on the right have formal ideas. Since I am a sentimentalist, I would belong to the left, particularly with respect to my best friends, who belong decidedly to the right."

Obviously, Jean-Luc Godard does not have a political mind, and yet. . . .

And yet, he has just finished shooting his second film, *Le Petit soldat*, in Switzerland; in this film he dares to show, for around fifteen minutes, one of the anathemas of our twentieth century. Godard shows a man being tortured.

"Why this subject?"

"I've always wondered whether I would talk under torture, and why; no doubt I'd try not to talk. Because of a certain kind of human dignity, but what an absurdity! What is this burst of dignity that overcomes our strongest instincts? Why?

"I thought a great deal of Malraux while I was making this film. I had heard him say, during a speech, 'One day, I wrote the story of a man who hears his own voice, and I called it *La Condition humaine.*'

"In my film, the hero is forever trying to recognize his own voice. Even when he sees his face in a mirror, it doesn't seem to correspond with him. He keeps doing things he doesn't really want to do. He gives in all along the way. He's caught in a mesh.

"The story is about a member (Michel Subor) of an ultraconservative organization; his mission is to kill a Radio-Geneva journalist who has sympathies for the F.L.N. in Algeria. He gets caught by the F.L.N. and tortured, but he escapes. . . . There's a girl informer for the F.L.N. (Anna Karina) who wants to follow him, but that doesn't work either. At the end, the hero simply says, 'You have to learn not to be bitter.'

"I could just as well have imagined the opposite. That the French were doing the torturing. Furthermore, in the film, it is mentioned that the French do the same thing. I found the whole thing more complex that way. Torture is abominable, but I realized that it is also comprehensible. Especially modern torture. You're completely removed from other people's pain. It's the same thing when somebody tells you he has a toothache. At the very most, you can feel sorry for him, but you absolutely cannot imagine his pain. In torture, it's even worse. You put somebody in a bathtub. It's not horrible to see. When you turn off the water and see him gasping for air, it's then you realize his suffering, and it's precisely at that moment that the victim is happy, since he can breathe. The whole thing is idiotic.

"Turning the crank of an electric battery and watching a man jerk with the shock isn't horrible either. I think you can torture simply through lack of imagination, and this happens to be a very current phenomenon.

"Will my film be censored? I doubt it. It's an adventure film. I could just as well have invented a story based on the theft of Sophia Loren's jewels. But why not choose something current, why do you have to consider present events as something taboo? A film is out of date when it doesn't give a true picture of the era it was made in. *Quai des brumes* or *Quatorze Juillet* will never be outdated. But I would consider it indecent to make a film today about the resistance. If Jean Rouch had shot his film in the French underground in 1943, that would have been right. But I find that doing it now is dishonest, impure, and fabricated. Why not use the word F.L.N. since it exists? It doesn't help matters any to use the initials P.B.Z., for instance. My film might also just as well be called 'Tintin, Secret Agent in the Country of Milk Chocolate.'

"Tintin would like to find an ideal. He would like to have the strength of purpose to cut a path for himself, even with a dagger. But he can't do it. He says that his parents were arrested because they were friends of Drieu La Rochelle, and also that he would like to die like Pierre Brossolette. He also says, 'Ethics is the aesthetics of the future.' That's a quote from Gorky; but in the film I have him say it's Lenin, because I like Lenin better."

"Technically, did you work from day to day, as in *A bout de souffle*, writing your dialogues in snatches?"

"Yes, but it didn't work as well. In *A bout de souffle*, I could say everything I wanted to say. Anything went. Everything went into my main character. This time, there is a precise storyline. The characters have to say the right thing at the right time, and something else won't work. So quite often I went for two days without shooting, without ideas. On the whole, I shot one day out of every three. There are moments when I let myself go. Subor speaks about Brittany, or about the *Confessions* because he is passing near the Ile Rousseau in Geneva. But that was rarer than in *A bout de souffle*. There are especially a lot of silences, stammerings, as in a TV interview. I really made this film under the influence of Bresson (*Pickpocket*) and Malraux.

"What a beautiful work *l'Espoir* is; it's really 'funny' how Malraux has changed so much at present."

Godard says "funny" because he really finds that "funny." [1]

[1] The following footnotes accompanied the stills that appeared in *l'Express* with the interview of 16 June 1960: 1) The first picture shows a car with Bruno hiding behind a copy of *l'Express* whose cover shows a picture of Hitler; the note reads: "For this shot, which shows the agent of the extreme right taking aim at a member of the F.L.N., Jean-Luc Godard said: 'The week I was shooting (22 April), *l'Express* came out with this cover. It was perfect timing! Furthermore, it was confiscated by the authorities. I thought it would be funny to have a rightist secret agent reading this magazine and hiding behind the title, *Twenty Years Later*, which indicated the rebirth of Fascism. I imagine the public will see this only as a gag, at best; but for me, every detail is always filled with little hidden meanings.' In another shot, one can see a photo of two young Budapest partisans in the background of the scene showing the two young heroes kissing. Godard explained: 'It's the same couple, the same fear, the same frontiers to cross. This shot from Budapest is there to get the audience involved, to keep it from leaving its era. People always tend to try and take refuge in fiction.'" 2) The second picture shows Bruno being tortured in the bathtub; the note reads: "Jean-Luc Godard hired Michel Subor (. . .) at the time Subor was understudying Serge Reggiani in Jean-Paul Sartre's play, *Les Séquestrés d'Altona*. I saw Subor with scars from electrodes on his wrists and ankles. It was Godard himself who *really* tortured him for the needs of his film." 3) The third picture shows Anna Karina; the note reads: "She has the only female role in the film. Jean-Luc Godard found her by putting the following ad in a trade paper: 'Wanted: very pretty young woman, 18–20 years old, to become my star and my friend'" [editor's note].

A Movie Is a Movie:
Interview with Jean-Luc Godard
on UNE FEMME EST UNE FEMME
by MICHÈLE MANCEAUX

"Pardon me, sir, but would you like to get this young lady pregnant?" The bewildered little man, who had been peacefully walking along the Boulevard Strasbourg, turns on his dignity. "Now
there's a stupid way to behave," he answers, eyeing his questioners
from head to toe.

Another passerby: "Pardon me, sir, but would you. . . ."

"Sorry. I don't have the time."

And still another. "I'd be delighted, but I'm sure the young lady
wouldn't want to. . . ."

Jean-Claude Brialy, dragging Anna Karina by the hand, crosses
the Boulevard.

Hidden in the corner of a gateway, Jean-Luc Godard and his
cameraman, Raoul Coutard, are filming the scene and breaking up
with laughter. Godard rarely laughs, but here he has pulled off a
beautiful joke on the busybodies of the big boulevards, and the
scene may very well be just as hysterical in his film *Une Femme est
une femme.*

He taps Jean-Claude Brialy on the shoulder: "That was very

*From l'Express, January 12, 1961, pp. 36–38, and July 27, 1961, pp.
32–34. Copyright © 1961 by l'Express. Reprinted by permission of the
publisher. Translated by Royal S. Brown. This selection represents the
conflation of both interviews, which were made before the film's public
premiere, although the second took place after the film was shown at
the Berlin Festival on July 1. The title used here is that of the second
interview.*

good." Godard rarely says much more than that. Godard is an enigmatic character. *Une Femme est une femme* is a comedy, in cinemascope and color, with an extremely simple, undeveloped subject that can be summed up in the following sentence: "A woman wants to have a baby, just like that, all at once, the way you feel like having a piece of candy." . . . Around this subject, Godard has embroidered a musical comedy. If you want to call it that. Godard himself is not quite sure—in the titles, he haphazardly throws about the names of his actors and producers, while in the middle of all this he adds words such as "Lubitsch, July 14, Comedy . . ." anything at all. . . .

"That's all there is to it, but it's very funny," says Godard (meaning "If you don't agree with me, you can leave"). "It's an excellent subject for a comedy à la Lubitsch. In fact, the film is dedicated to Lubitsch. Belmondo's name is Alfred Lubitsch. Brialy's name is Ernest Récamier. I did that just for fun, so that Anna could want to become Mme Récamier. . . . I don't know whether it's a comedy or a tragedy. At any rate, it's a masterpiece."

But then, later, Godard admits that this masterpiece really isn't one. "There's a basic weakness in this film. It's a color film . . . theoretically made to be shot à la Visconti. By that I mean with a great deal of care, and with a taste for details. A set-designer's film. I deliberately shot it in a manner that was the opposite from what it should have been. By going fast, by rushing over things, by improvising. But in the end run, I'm happy with it because I shot it in one sitting, as it were, just as I had written the scenario, two years ago, in a half an hour. Nobody has ever shot a film like that. It's almost automatic writing.

"What interested me was to alternate, almost systematically, a sad scene with a happy one. To use gags à la Jacques Tati or Mack Sennett and then, all at once, mix things up by showing a realistic, serious situation. In short, I wanted everything to be constantly unstable." . . .

As Godard had announced, he has made Anna Karina his favorite actress. In *Une Femme est une femme,* she plays a striptease dancer. She lives with Brialy, but he does not want to get her pregnant because he does bicycle racing on Sundays and does not want to be out of shape; so she asks Belmondo to do this favor for her.

In the film, Belmondo works for the city, putting traffic tickets on car windshields from dawn to dusk. Godard chose this particular

job because it is quite typical of our times, and Godard is constantly
interested in showing what is current. "I hesitated. I had at first
thought of making him a car-switcher, one of those guys who, every
hour and a half in a regulated parking zone, moves cars to a different parking spot and gets small tips from the drivers. But a guy
who gives out the tickets offers all sorts of gag possibilities."

Godard does have ideas. No doubt the most original are born
either at four o'clock in the morning or else in the car that comes
and gets him and drives him to the spot where the film is being shot.
He scribbles down notes on a piece of paper, and he follows these
indications religiously throughout the entire day's shooting. Or else
he doesn't make any notes, and there is no shooting for that day.

Godard shot *Une Femme est une femme* in five weeks, with the
subject mentioned above and using not a single word of written
dialogue. He invented the situations each morning and read to the
actors what they were supposed to say. The actors never knew what
they were doing, or where their various actions fit into the film.
"Furthermore, it didn't matter," explained Brialy. "He made us
play false situations in a realistic way, and realistic situations in a
false way. The phonier it was, the more it had to seem natural; on
the other hand, when things went on normally, then we really bore
down and overdid it."

"What I try to do," Godard said, "is to maintain the independence
of the artist, of the painter who can leave his canvas to go get something to drink if he feels like it, or to seek inspiration for that matter. I can do this because I work fast and the producer knows that
I'm conscientious and that I won't go over the film's budget."

For Godard, adapting a novel, or even working on a well-elaborated scenario, offers no interest.

"My basic principle is that if I manage to express myself on paper,
to tell my film, to set up the editing, then I no longer need to make
the film itself.

"When you want to make a movie at the age of seventeen, of
course, the first thing you say to yourself, after you've read a book,
is 'That's great. I'm going to make a film out of it.' Even essays. Even
philosophy. I remember I wanted to make a film out of Camus' *Le
Mythe de Sisyphe*. Now, the only adaptation I might like to make
would be of Bernanos' *Nouvelle histoire de Mouchette*. And even
here, I would be ashamed of myself, because I know that the book
is so extraordinary and that the cinema can offer it nothing further.
If someone has written a book, it's because he is an author. If

Faulkner had wanted to make films, he would have been a director. It happens he wanted to write books, and I don't see why they should be transformed."

Godard makes films as if he were writing. You always see Godard through his films and, like a writer who is always rewriting the same book, Godard always makes, to an extent, the same film. Godard was obviously aware of this when he said, "In my three films, there's always the same subject. I take an individual who has an idea and who tries to follow through on this idea.

"I also like the very principle of a journal. I'd like, for instance, to make a film on myself, showing my life during, say, two weeks, during which time I would be looking for an idea, the idea for a novel. Yes, that would be it. I'd try to write a novel. I don't know whether I'd manage to or not. It would be my life while trying to write a novel. And the people I would see and talk with. And then me in the process of trying to write a novel. I would go ask Sartre what you have to do to write a novel, there would be a conversation, etc.

"I'm not a true movie director. Neither is Clouzot, for that matter, because his only example of 'film-vérité' is not *La Vérité* but his shipboard journal when he was married, when he went to Brazil . . . and he never succeeded in making it into a film. Rossellini made *Voyage to Italy*. You can tell a story in the movies, but you can also tell the story of an idea."

Godard makes a mockery of all the rules. One day, Brialy played a scene without a coat on. The preceding day, for the same scene, he had worn a coat. Brialy pointed this out to Godard. "That doesn't matter. You'll simply have forgotten it."

In the same way, when the weather changes and overexposes a film or underexposes it, Godard has his actors say, "Look, there's less (or more) light than there was a while ago." He says that his film is either "a musical comedy without music," or else "a fascinating mistake."

A musical comedy without music because he has music play whenever he feels like it, without it being in the slightest way justified by the situation. "If I feel like hearing a Charleston, I'm certainly not going to put a juke-box in the corner just to be realistic."

A fascinating mistake, "because it's a mistake to shoot an unprepared comedy in exteriors, in the winter, in cinemascope and in color. But it's fascinating because it's difficult, because your brain is really working for five weeks."

Godard creates both adjuvants and restraints for himself. To help himself, for instance, he asked Faizant to interpret in gag form some of his comic strips, and it would seem to be an excellent idea to use comic-strip artists as gagmen. To hinder himself, on the other hand, he had the apartment where he wanted to shoot reconstructed in the studios. Including the ceiling. Studio sets are never constructed with a ceiling. But Godard had a real apartment constructed so that nobody could "cheat" with the lighting. In the evening, the apartment was locked shut and not opened until the next day; and the light, which always came through the windows just as real daylight would, never varied for two weeks. Also, the walls were painted white, which is never done in the cinema.

Raoul Coutard, who has been a revelation as a cameraman, explained, "Godard breaks all the rules of the cinema. He never looks into the camera. Occasionally he will ask, 'Do you have a full-length shot?' 'No,' someone replies, 'it's a mid-shot.' He answers, 'All right. That doesn't make any difference.' It's unbelievable. Occasionally somebody tells him that such and such a person should not be in such and such a spot. So he automatically does the opposite of what has been suggested. Sometimes he even asks what should be done so he can do the contrary. When he gives an order, he says, 'Cut it off there,' and he indicates a distance which goes, for instance, from the knees to the shoulders."

Coutard has done three films with Godard. He was formerly in Indochina, an amateur photographer, a former photographer-correspondent, finally becoming a photographer-reporter in *La Passe du diable,* which was done by Dupont and Schoendorfer in Afghanistan. *A bout de souffle* revealed Coutard, just as it revealed all those who participated in its making, from Belmondo to Jean Seberg. Now, everybody wants Coutard as a cameraman.

All the directors tell him, "I want the kind of photography you did for *A bout de souffle.*" But they don't understand. Each director has his own style, and Coutard has quite precise ideas on them.

"Jacques Demy, in *Lola,* wanted to work without artificial lighting, as did Godard; but he also wanted broad camera movements. Instinctively, Godard knew this was impossible.

"My best relations have been with Truffaut. I've made three films with Godard, but we've never really talked to each other.

"Valère is the most precise. Before shooting began for *Les Grandes personnes,* everything was written down on paper. And he's the only director who still uses low- and high-angle shots. With all the others, the camera is fixed once and for all at the same height, the height of a man looking at things. When the characters sit down, I sit down. But that's it." . . .

Shooting *Une Femme est une femme* in color was hardly a monotonous undertaking, however. Strasbourg-Saint Denis in the winter is certainly not the gayest or most colorful region you can find. Godard simply spread splashes of color against this grey background. But even the brightest colors remained rather dull when it rained.

Coutard said, "It's not because of the film's color that people will come knocking at my door. But it's going to be an amazing film."

Brialy said, "I'll accept anything from Godard. You can't treat him like anybody else. Nobody else has the same criteria."

Indeed, Godard acts only the way he wants to. He is deliberately impertinent, self-righteous, ill-bred . . . but he always surprises you and could care less about the impression he makes.

His films are very much like him. They are both sophisticated and intellectual while at the same time being striking; he captures reality, life, everyday language in a manner that no one has ever done before. He has a formula for that. He says, "I will have managed to do what I want when I've used a scenario à la Hitchcock and filmed it à la Jean Rouch."

In *Une Femme est une femme,* there are several attempts in this direction. For example: in order to get even with Anna, who has gone off with Belmondo, Brialy goes to get a whore on one of those "specialized" streets. Godard had warned the real whores who were usually there so that they would leave in order to avoid difficulties with the vice squad. In their place, Godard used actresses. As he was shooting the scene, an old man came by and thought the actresses were the genuine item. Godard shot the whole scene. Too bad for the old man. But so much the better for humor and sociology.

What is amazing about Godard, and several others, is precisely that he has created not only a new form of cinematographic expression but at the same time a new audience to understand it.

He says, "There is certainly no reason why the films I make should not displease some people. I don't know why people say that a film has to be liked by everybody. Nobody's ever said that a book, or a painting, or a piece of music has to please everybody. It should please those who like it. Of course, you're unhappy if your work isn't liked. Especially after having made two or three films, because you feel even more responsible than with the first; but I no longer believe that cinema should be aimed at the masses. In the past, the masses used to go see average films. There was an average mass, and there were average films. Today, all these average films are being directed bit by bit toward television, and the masses of people see them on their television sets. Now, all you have left are either big, enormous productions, such as *Lola Montès* or *Ben Hur*, or small productions. In that way, you can make either marvelous films or lousy films."

Godard writes his dialogues directly, from day to day, and he shoots chronologically. But between what he wants to say and his own self the cinema nonetheless imposes an intermediary—the actors. What does Godard think of this situation?

"I don't feel, the way Stanislawski did, that an actor has to put himself completely into the character he's playing; instead, the character changes according to the personality of the actor who plays him. At first, for instance, *A bout de souffle* was supposed to star Charles Aznavour and Bernadette Laffont, and then Sacha Distel and Annette Vadim. I didn't really care. But in the end, it was done with Seberg and Belmondo, and I was quite happy with it. I would have shot—perhaps not the same film—but I would have ended up shooting *A bout de souffle* one way or the other.

"The actor intercedes, but he doesn't know it. All he has to do is be himself. 'Real' actors bring nothing to the film; they wait to be told how to move, to speak, and so forth. For me, I would rather the actors keep, in the film, certain gestures I like to see them make in real life. A way of holding a cigarette, or of combing their hair. I tell them my thoughts, but their thoughts also remain, since they remain themselves. I try never to make more than two takes. The more you repeat, the more mechanical things become. The more withdrawn the whole film becomes from life."

Godard also has his own ideas on directors. "There is a certain snobbery about directors these days. The director is now well received in the 'best' circles, whereas before he was considered as a simple worker. Before the war, people such as Duvivier and Carné were artisans. They received no consideration, unlike a Proust or a Malraux, even if they were worth something. Today, directors are interviewed and invited to all sorts of important gatherings. I know from exeprience. I rented a villa on the Riviera from a lady in the wealthy Passy district in Paris. 'Ah!' she said, 'a director!' It was just as good as being a banker.

"But there are the artists, and then there are the others. Personally, I'm in favor of the word 'artist.' It's a very beautiful word which used to be frowned upon. Artists were people like Alphonse Daudet, people with big hats, Windsor ties, and so forth.

"Today, directors almost always dress like everybody else. But to me, an artist always belongs to the left. Even Drieu La Rochelle belonged to the left. It's a state of mind. And on the other hand, Khrushchev and Kennedy both belong to the right, they're both totalitarian.

"Belonging to the left doesn't mean showing a man working. A film like Reisz' *Saturday Night and Sunday Morning* is what I would call a rightist film. Reactionary, paternalistic, in the sense that the director has imposed an idea on the film that the audiences will be quite fond of. Everybody speculates on the film's receipts at the box office. Like *A Taxi for Tobruk*, it's dishonest."

Godard often appears paradoxical. In his film *Le Petit soldat,* torture is practiced by Algerians; and in his three feature films, you keep running across informers and stool pigeons. Why?

"You should make a film only when you're directly concerned. Making a film today about the concentration camps is dishonest. It should have been made in 1943. The only person to have succeeded in making such a film recently is Resnais, because he didn't make his film on the camps themselves, but on the memory of them. For me, for instance, honesty, in *Le Petit soldat,* is showing that one's friends, at least people I would fight with, if I had to, even if I weren't from their country—let's say the Algerians—honesty is showing these people torturing. I feel that, in this way, the accusation against torture becomes stronger, since you see your own friend torturing. And yet I'm accused of being dishonest.

"Stool pigeons? Perhaps; yes; you find them in life. Anybody can turn a person in. An apology for the police? Oh . . . yes. Yes and no, since I'm against the police, and then I'm in favor of them. In the Balzacian sense, to the extent that it's mysterious. . . ."

Godard prefers to talk about Balzac. Why not Husserl?

"Balzac represents philosophy plus adventure. That corresponds quite well to the cinema. Of course, you don't go adapting Balzac novels just for that reason; but I mean that the cinema is just that— an adventure, with the philosophy of this adventure at the same time.

"Directing is like modern philosophy, let's say Husserl or Merleau-

Ponty. You don't have words on one side and thought on the other. You have thought and then words. Language is not something in itself, nor is it a simple translation. Directing is the same thing. When I say that directing is not a language, I mean that at the same time it is also a thought.

"It is life and a reflection on life. That's why, in my films, I have my characters talk about everything. I capture them 'live.' "

Is it this "capturing 'live' " that Godard tries to attain over and above everything else?

"Yes and no. I like to mix up a certain kind of fiction with a documentary. Without being as documentary as Rouch, although *La Pyramide humaine* seems to me to be the most beautiful film of the year.

"Rouch began by making documentaries and now he's become a true filmmaker. He discovered the cinema by practicing it.

"There are some marvelous touches in *La Pyramide humaine,* some completely dramatized scenes that he would never have made before. For instance, there's a scene, where the guy is playing the piano for the girl in the deserted house, that is pure *East of Eden.* You tell Rouch that and he is delighted, because he loves Kazan.

"Rouch is an ethnologist caught in the trap of cinema. He still calls himself an ethnologist, but I don't really think he is any more, at least most of the time. Now, he has become a filmmaker interested in ethnology.

"Obviously, it's not the same thing with me, since I create my characters.

"The most beautiful thing that takes place in the cinema is when fiction enters into the documentary. The most beautiful film is *Nanook of the North,* which is a documentary. But Flaherty staged his documentaries. When he filmed the Balinese and Polynesian dancers, he didn't let them do just anything.

"Now, the documentary is being discovered, people are shooting things 'live,' 'Cinq Colonnes à la une,' [1] and things like that. That's fine, and it's interesting; but in the cinema, there's something else. There's a way of looking at things."

---

[1] French expression roughly indicating sensationalistic reportage; i.e., something that would take up all five columns of a newspaper's first page [editor's note].

Shipwrecked People from the Modern World:
Interview with Jean-Luc Godard on LE MÉPRIS
by YVONNE BABY

. . . As everybody knows, Le Mépris *is based on a novel by Alberto Moravia, just as a fight between Godard and his producers was based on this film. Since* Le Mépris *also shows misunderstandings and discord between filmmakers and businessmen, "the imaginary has completely flowed over into life." The latter words came from Godard himself, who ran into unpleasant difficulties, both before and after the shooting of the film.*

"I had read the book a long time ago," *he told me;* "I liked the subject a great deal, and since I was to make a film for Carlo Ponti, I proposed a chapter-by-chapter adaptation of *Le Mépris.* First he said yes and then, out of fear, no; and when I suggested using Kim Novak and Frank Sinatra as stars, he refused. He wanted Sophia Loren and Marcello Mastroianni. But I didn't want them, and so we remained at an impasse until I found out that Brigitte Bardot was interested in the project and would accept to work with me. Thanks to her, everything suddenly became easy and everybody was delighted, including the Americans, or to be more exact, Joe Levine,[1] who partly financed the whole affair and who had been guaranteed by Ponti that the film would be 'very commercial.'

"Therefore, we shot in complete freedom for six weeks in Italy. I showed the film to Ponti, who liked it and found it more normal than my other films. But the Americans didn't have the same opinion: 'It's very artistic,' they declared later on in Paris, 'but it's not commercial, and you'll have to change it.' Ponti then asked me to add a scene. He didn't really have any idea what kind of scene, and neither did I. All I knew was that I couldn't do it, and I told

From Le Monde, *December 20, 1963, p. 18. Reprinted by permission of the publisher. Translated by Royal S. Brown. The title used here is an abridgment of the original.*

[1] Joe Levine is the world-wide distributor for the film.

him: 'Take my name out of the credits and do what you want with it.' Time went by, and after a few months, the Americans began to complain that they were losing money. From their throne room—you can see that even the most worn-out clichés are occasionally true—they almost cried in order to get two more scenes, including one in which the audience would see Michel Piccoli and Brigitte Bardot without any clothes. They wanted a love scene which would open the film and which, to an extent, would explain and justify the contempt.

"Basically," *Godard added, thoughtfully,* "the Americans had realized that they had paid more for Brigitte Bardot than she was going to bring in for such an endeavor—an 'art film' based on a difficult novel. The problems did not come from Brigitte Bardot herself—from the very beginning, she assumed responsibility for all the risks she had taken, and she always backed me up. Rather, it arose from what she represents today in the cinema and in industry. So when I called up the Americans and told them they could have 'their' scene, they were quite happy; it was as if I had given them a Christmas present. . . ."

Are you sorry you shot this scene?

"Not at all. The simple presence of nudity was not foreign to the film, which is not erotic. On the contrary. But it was possible, even fitting, to show Brigitte Bardot that way at the beginning of the film since, at that moment, it is she who is undressed; she is not yet the moving, intelligent, and sincere wife of the scenarist Paul Javal (Michel Piccoli), who at one point in the film—through sheer coincidence—says, more or less, 'In life, you see women dressed, whereas on the screen, you see them naked. . . .' Under other conditions, I would have refused this scene; but here, I shot it in a certain way, using certain colors—I used a red lighting, and then a blue lighting so that Bardot would become something else, so that she would become something more unreal, more profound and more serious than simply Brigitte Bardot on a bed. I wanted to transfigure her, because the cinema can and must transfigure reality.

"It was especially important for me that Brigitte Bardot seem as natural as possible. For the rest of the film, I wanted to show shots from the *Odyssey*, speak of Ulysses, take shots of the sea, of colored Greek statues, of Fritz Lang . . ."

. . . who plays himself?

"Yes, to the extent that he represents the cinema, for which he is both the director and the voice of its conscience. From a more symbolic point of view, however, particularly since he is shooting a film on the *Odyssey*, he is also the voice of the gods, the man who looks at men. On a more banal level, you might say that he is the old Indian chief observing his anxious warriors. Just like Brigitte Bardot and like the producer Jerome Prokosch (Jack Palance), Fritz Lang is a prototype. I like to think that in Jules Verne you have the scientist, the child, and the captain, and that in my film you have the young wife, the adventurer, and the old man. I wrote the dialogues and the ideas spoken by Fritz Lang, who agreed on the principle, although he occasionally changed a detail or improvised a line; but he left things up to me. Just by his presence in the film, anyone can have the idea that the cinema is something important; and if I played the role of his assistant, it was out of respect, so that I wouldn't lend him shots—as short as they may have been—that weren't his own.

"*Le Mépris* is the story of a misunderstanding between a man and a woman. I feel that misunderstandings represent a modern phenomenon. You have to try to either control them or run away from them, so that they don't end up—as in the film—in tragedy. There are moments in life when you can't turn back, when something breaks definitively, which is neither the fault of one person nor the fault of the other; each one, however, suffers and feels both bitter and remorseful. I tried to make this break more tangible by reducing the length of time the film takes place to two days, whereas the novel takes place over a space of six months. The sentence, 'She looked at me tenderly,' takes up very little space in a book; but to give it its true depth in the cinema, you need five minutes—in other words, you have to film a quick glance over a long space of time. Before I made the film, I noticed that I had both my dislikes and my hates, but that I had no idea of contempt, that evasive, difficult feeling that acts like a microbe. Now, I don't know whether or not you can 'see' contempt or scorn. Perhaps one can only capture the instant during which it exercises its force—after a certain gesture, after a misunderstanding.

"*Le Mépris* is a simple film about complicated things, and it is more of a reflection than a document. This time—and this is new for me—there is no main character, but rather groups of people, shipwreck victims from a modern world landing on a myserious island, Capri, where the water is blue, where there is sun, and where everything has to be reinvented, including the cinema."

No Questions Asked:
Conversation with Jean-Luc Godard
on BANDE À PART
by JEAN COLLET

J. C.: Bande à part is based on a novel called *Fool's Gold*, by
D. & B. Hitchens, which was published in France as *Pigeon vole* in
the "Série noire" collection. I haven't read this book. Why did you
use it as a point of departure?

J.-L. G.: What I liked in this novel was a certain tone in the
narrative and in the dialogues, and I tried to maintain this tone in
the film. Of course, the tone may have come from the translation,
which is bad. But at least the translation created a certain style that
interested me. I even kept it in the commentary that accompanies
certain scenes in the film.

The book is like a novel that I've always wanted to make into a
film—*Banlieu sud-est*, by René Fallet. It's the kind of story in which
you have two guys, a girl, and a bicycle race. You find that in most
of the pre-war French novels. In the film previews for *Bande à part*,
I call it "A French Film With a Pre-War Atmosphere."

J. C.: Like *Quai des brumes*?

J.-L. G.: No, more like the novels that weren't filmed before the
war but which were already films. Certain novels by Simenon or
Raymond Queneau. Like the latter's *Loin de Rueil*, for instance.

I tried to recreate the populist, poetic climate of the pre-war
period, and I don't mean this in a derogatory way.

J. C.: In seeing your film, which is after all a pure Grade B story,

From *Télérama, no. 761 (August 16, 1964): 49–50. Reprinted by permission of the publisher. Translated by Royal S. Brown. The title used
here is a free translation of the original.*

it seemed to me that you were able to hide your allusions and quotations with much greater ease. You've often been reproached for your love of quotations. It seems to me that they won't even be noticed this time.

J.-L. G.: Yes, I wanted to make a simple film that would be perfectly understandable. For instance, when distributors see *Muriel* or *Le Mépris,* they can't manage to decipher them. Whereas *Bande à part* is completely clear.

But that didn't stop me from putting everything I really like into the film. I took advantage of every situation and every instant in the film. For instance, if a scene takes place in a car, the two guys talk about the cars they like. And in the choice of names, in certain dialogues, and in various parts of the commentary, I also managed to slip in everything I like.

J. C.: In this way, doesn't your film have certain keys to it, just as you have *romans à clefs?* For instance, Arthur gives Odile a Queneau novel whose title is *Odile.* Why? Can you give any other keys to the spectators?

J.-L. G.: I chose Odile for the heroine's name as a reminder of one of Queneau's first novels. It's part of the film's atmosphere, part of the climate I was mentioning earlier.

But the Queneau novel entitled *Odile* is itself a *roman à clefs.* It's a novel in which the author relates, in a humorous vein, his experiences with the Surrealist movement. At first, I wanted Arthur to give Odile the André Breton novel called *Nadja.* But it bothered me to have him give her a book called *Nadja* when her name was Odile. So I chose Queneau's *Odile,* in which you can find all of the Surrealists scarcely camouflaged behind pseudonyms—Aragon, Soupault, Breton, and so forth. Breton's name in the book is Anglarès. And it's for that reason that I have Arthur open the Queneau book and read, "Anglarès related. . . ." At that moment, he has the right to tell of a passage from *Nadja,* since Anglarès is Breton.

In that way, I hid all of these quotes, and I was therefore able to use a lot more of them than in my other films. For instance, Arthur has the same first name as Rimbaud, and so I used a text by Rimbaud in one of my commentaries on Arthur.

J. C.: You managed to live up to the challenge you set for yourself by shooting this feature-length film in twenty-five days, which is a record. Why this rapidity?

J.-L. G.: I always like to have a balance between the shooting of a

film and its financing, between the budget and the subject, or at least
what I think of as the subject. When you go to a certain party, you
dress one way and not another. Even if what you wear has no relationship to what you are going to see, say, or do. You prepare yourself. . . . For instance, you pay the extra money for a taxi because
you're going to a very "chic" party, whereas normally you'd take the
subway.

It's in that vein that I shot the film in twenty-five days. I always
like to impose restraints upon myself. The freer I am, the more I
feel I must force certain basic conditions and rules upon myself. I
never agree with the conditions my producers set up, simply because
these are never the right conditions with respect to the film's subject.
Therefore I try to find the right conditions and then live up to them.

For instance, people have always told me that I rush through my
films. They're very happy if I finish in four weeks instead of six. But
let me finish in three weeks, and they're no longer happy—"Ah, even
so, you shouldn't do a rush job. . . ."

But it's not a question of that. It's a challenge I set up for myself.

In *Le Mépris*, the challenge was to shoot in Italy using direct
sound. That's never done, because the Italians shout at the top of
their lungs and their motorbikes make a lot of noise. So all of their
films are dubbed over. You might think that this challenge has nothing to do with the film. But that's not true. It's a discipline. It's like
doing gymnastics every morning so that you can be in shape throughout the day.

J. C.: You also don't allow yourself to write dialogues. Why?

J.-L. G.: I write them at the last minute. That's so that the actor
won't have any time to think about his dialogues and get himself
prepared. That way, he has to give more of himself. He's more
clumsy that way, but also more total. I leave my actors quite free.
I correct them every once in a while if they do something that
doesn't work or doesn't have anything to do with the subject. Simply
because they can't realize as well as I do what the film is all about.
But there's little rehearsing. Only two or three takes are ever made.
Usually, it's the first or last that works. I explain how they're
supposed to act the way Mack Sennett probably explained things
to his actors: "You come on, you do this and we start rolling. . . ."

On the other hand, for the dance scene in the cafe, we rehearsed
for two weeks, three times each week. Samy and Claude didn't know

how to dance. We invented the steps. It's an original dance, and we had to perfect it. It's a dance with an open, line figure. It's a parade. They dance for the camera, for the audience.

J. C.: In this film, then, the subject is the three characters, a trio that forms a "band of outsiders." It's almost a psychological film. But the camera always keeps its distance with respect to these characters.

J.-L. G.: Yes. When the Americans saw it, they said to me, "It's an impressionistic film. . . ." The fact is that I began the movie with the idea of making it a pure piece of reportage. But as you watch people, you begin to get interested in them, you get closer to them. You can't help getting closer to them.

J. C.: . . . Until you reached the point of the commentary, which you wrote after the fact and which shows us the souls of these characters.

J.-L. G.: Yes, and it makes you feel at the same time that you are quite removed.

J. C.: When did you really discover these characters?

J.-L. G.: When I saw the finished film. Before that, they escape you. Everything you do is staggered and contradictory. For instance, Arthur, when he goes off to rob the house, looks quite disguised, artificial, and theatrical. With his black mask, he looks as if he's playing a gangster. That's why, immediately afterwards, the theft scene is treated with a great deal of violence and brutality. It had to be realistic, you had to see the scene as somewhat true to life.

J. C.: In this trio, you left the sensitive character, Franz, in the background; yet he seems to be the foil to the cynical Arthur.

J.-L. G.: That's what the film is all about. Odile is obviously attracted at first toward the more brilliant of the two. And then afterwards, she discovers Franz, who is more solid, but who doesn't have appearances in his favor.

J. C.: Arthur is quite harsh and scornful towards Odile.

J.-L. G.: It seems to me that he's the kind of guy who goes to wait in line on Sundays to see Johnny Hallyday; or you find him playing the coin machines at the Bastille. When this kind of guy meets a girl, he feels that insulting her is the only way to court her. He's like that. . . .

J. C.: This kind of character, who resembles a beast of prey, seems to turn up in all of your films. One might say that the theme of your entire work is "the instinct to capture." Arthur thinks only of taking.

And as fast as possible. Taking money, seducing Odile. We don't seem to be far here from *Les Carabiniers* or from the character played by Belmondo in *A bout de souffle*.

J.-L. G.: It's true that I have always had a tendency to want everything all at once. You see it in my habit of shortening the action of my films. The novel that inspired *Bande à part* takes place over four or five months. In the film, it's three days.

It seems to me that the rapidity and the rapaciousness you see in the character of Arthur ought to arouse sympathy. He represents a precise type. He doesn't know how to discuss, so he acts. People who speak have to find beautiful things to say—they recite Shakespeare for instance—or else it's not worth the trouble to speak. You're better off keeping quiet.

The characters in *Bande à part* don't know how to discuss. They're little animals. Instead of being the wild animals of *Les Carabiniers*, they're domesticated animals, you might say. They're also the little suburban cousins of the Belmondo of *A bout de souffle* and of *Une Femme est une femme*. Furthermore, *Une Femme est une femme* almost had as a title *On est comme on est* [You Are What You Are].

J. C.: Why the title *Bande à part,* which you finally kept after having tried several others?

J.-L. G.: I like it precisely because these three characters really do form a "band of outsiders." They're not like other people. They're more honest with themselves than with other people. They're people who lead their own lives. It's not really they who live outside of society. It's society that is far from them. They go everywhere—you see them in the Louvre, in the bistros; they're no more withdrawn from society than the characters of *Rebel Without a Cause*.

J. C.: You say that they're more honest than other people. But they're thieves. . . .

J.-L. G.: I mean they have natural reactions. These are characters right out of Jean-Jacques Rousseau. They're just the opposite of the hero of *Le Mépris*, Paul Javal, who is a bad offspring of civilization.

But none of that was premeditated. I shot the film quite fast. When you shoot fast, you don't have the time to think about things. Things take place and become organized all by themselves. For instance, I found myself at a loss for the end of the film. I didn't know how I was going to end it. It had to end harmoniously. It's a quartet—one of the instruments has disappeared, so the rest no longer have much to do. Finally, after having tried several overly complicated solutions, I came up with that last shot of Samy and Anna leaving. It's one of the shots I like the best. Because they finally seem to be *natural*. It's a 'resolution.' They've found themselves. You don't know what's going to happen to them. They won't necessarily be happy. But they are 'resolved.' They are finally what they are. They have accepted themselves. They needed to have Arthur come into their lives to arrive at this point.

J. C.: The last shot of *Bande à part* shows the world turning.

J.-L. G.: Yes, that could be the moral of a film by Bergman: after all the catastrophes, the world keeps on following its course.

J. C.: At the end of *Le Mépris*, you might say the same thing— the characters have touched off a catastrophe, but the world keeps following its course.

J.-L. G.: Yes, absolutely. But in *Le Mépris*, the catastrophe comes from the fact that the characters are too "civilized." They are carried away because they have invented their own ideas, their own techniques, and so forth, by themselves. On the other hand, the characters in *Bande à part* are not dominated by any technique or by any preconceived idea. They know it's wrong to steal money. They have neither the mentality of thieves or of capitalists. They're like animals. They get up in the morning. They have to find a bird to kill so they can eat at noon, and another for the evening. Between that, they go to the river to drink. And that's it. They live by their instincts, for the instant.

The danger would be to make a system of it. Whereas these characters correct themselves. For the moment, they're happy because they're not asking themselves any questions.

A Leap into Emptiness:
Interview with Suzanne Schiffmann,
Continuity Girl for ALPHAVILLE
by MICHEL COURNOT

"Godard begins his films by leaving his crew in the dark. Nobody knows what he is going to do. Neither does he, or not exactly, at any rate. *Alphaville* is the first film whose story he told me before he started shooting it. Charles Bitsch, his assistant, who already knew the story, would occasionally interrupt him: 'But you had told me . . .' Godard would answer, 'I know, we'll see,' and he would go right on.

"When everything was finished, I told him that the film lasted two hours. That was too long for Godard; he doesn't like to make long films. And so he cut out a bunch of things—fights, chases, anything that was spectacular or even . . . visual. The things you usually find in a movie. After all the cuts, all that was left were the bones.

"I timed the film more or less on rough estimates. You can't time Godard. He writes three lines and they last a quarter of an hour. He writes three pages (rarely, however) and they last two seconds.

"Occasionally Godard times himself. He says ahead of time: 'Sequence 1 will last two minutes; sequence 5 will last thirty seconds, and sequence 4 has to last three minutes; I don't know what will happen—people will talk, we'll see. . . .' He works out a sketch for the rhythm; he invents following blocks of time.

From Le Nouvel Observateur, *May 6, 1955. Reprinted by permission of the publisher and Georges Borchardt, Inc. Translated by Royal S. Brown.*

"Godard lives in constant fear of ending up making a film too short, of not having a movie of sufficient length. He didn't worry about *La Femme mariée,* but for *Bande à part* it was terrible. In *Les Carabiniers,* you occasionally get the impression that he was deliberately drawing the film out. . . . It's the work of a lazy man. And it's the one I like the best. It took *Alphaville* quite a while to get off the ground. Godard is always late getting started. He doesn't feel like shooting, he feels that it is better to wait. He searches. . . . He spent five days retaking the first shot of *Le Petit soldat.*

"For *Alphaville,* he fluctuated for three days—no, four. He would tell us to meet him in a café, at La Villette. Then he would leave with Coutard and Constantine in a car. He wouldn't go anywhere. He would telephone us to go and wait for him in another café, at the Quai de Javel. Then he would come there and tell us to go to bed. Godard *cannot* shoot the first three minutes of a film. Each time, it's a leap into emptiness. And then it's done . . . he has jumped, he lets the crew follow him, and everybody sets off in two cars.

"He's not easy to follow, because he invents as he is shooting. A man like Franju writes out his films completely; you might almost say that all he does is *supervise* his films. Godard invents as he shoots, and you can't do anything about it. I manage to tell him, 'A while back, Constantine's collar was turned up,' but it doesn't do any good. Godard doesn't believe in this kind of logic, he believes in the logic of rhythm, of feelings.

"Godard directs his actors by indicating with extreme precision certain gestures, certain looks, and the placement of certain syllables that are pronounced. He doesn't give psychological explanations, ever, except to Anna Karina; but what goes on between the two of them is so mysterious that you never really understand it. For the others, no psychological explanations. I remember an actor, in *Vivre sa vie,* who was supposed to take off his clothes in a room, next to Anna Karina. Godard told him, 'Put your foot there, like that, and take off your shoe.' The actor asked him, 'What attitude should I have?' 'What do you mean "what attitude"?' 'My shoe. What attitude should I have when I take it off?' Godard grabbed hold of a bed to keep himself from falling.

"I remember the scene very well, because the same actor, at an

unexpected moment, had said 'yes.' The cinema is quite strange
—this totally insignificant 'Yes,' which was barely audible, made
the scene a bit 'smutty.' Godard cut it immediately. I don't know
a more puritanical person.

"Kazan was there, that day, squatting in a corner of the room.
He had come to see Godard shoot. It was a long shot, a fixed shot.
The camera didn't move, the actors came and went out of the
field, and they played around and talked as soon as they were off
camera. Kazan asked me, 'What angle is he going to shoot this
same scene from when he retakes it?' 'None. He never shoots a
sequence from more than one angle.' Kazan didn't understand.

"Godard is the only director who never shoots a sequence from
more than one angle. He takes the shot, and that's it—he goes on
to the next one. He edits in the same manner, almost end to end;
he doesn't make twenty different shots in order to have twenty
different solutions. He has only one solution. During the editing,
he reinvents certain solutions.

"He is obsessed by truth, by reality. He wants to keep to the
greatest degree possible everything that has taken place during
the shooting . . . unless something comes from the equipment and
not from 'reality,' either a camera noise or a noise made by the
tracking dolly.

"In *La Femme mariée,* there is a fairly long tracking shot that
takes place during the husband's arrival at the airport. The rails
had been badly laid, and during the shooting, Godard heard the
noise of the wheels moving along the rails. It wasn't much; it
covered up the voices once or twice. If any other 'real' noise—a
truck, a plane—had covered up the voices, he would have kept
it. The sound engineer said to him, 'You don't have to retake the
shot just for that; an airport is filled with noises, the sound made
by the tracking dolly could be anything, nobody will know the
difference.' No, he retook the shot.

"Obsessed with the truth, Godard is annoyed by the fact that
the film seen by the public is not the original, but a copy. He is
jealous of painters, because you can see their original paintings.
He often says, 'A film doesn't exist. A painting exists.' If he were
left completely to his own devices, he would splice end-to-end the
various shots from the original, from the first print. He wouldn't
correct the printing imperfections, and he would show this copy
in the theatres. Then his movie would 'exist.'

"The same thing happens during the editing. Godard doesn't 'correct' during the editing, in order for the various cuts to create a certain order without being felt.

"He does 'real' editing. In *Vivre sa vie*, there is a tracking shot that moves along the counter of a bar—you see the fugitives being shot at outside by the police, and then the actor enters the bar, his face covered with blood. The tracking shot was too long. Any other director would have been satisfied to shorten the tracking shot at the beginning or the end, and nobody would have noticed anything. Godard said, 'Let's make use of the machine-gun volleys; we'll cut out so much film for the first volley, so much for the second, and so forth.' The tracking shot takes on the rhythm of the scene, and the cuts are *felt*.

"You might say that *Alphaville* was shot without any light, in darkness. Coutard had said, 'We'll add a little light and I'll close the lens; it will amount to the same thing, we'll have darkness.' Godard refused, forever concerned with the 'truth.' He shot without lights, using a special film that was quite rapid . . . but even so! . . . It became the big joke of the film. 'Nobody will see anything! —Yes, but we shot the film!' Result—3000 meters of useless film. Godard did not retake everything. Certain shots were cut out, others were left in the film unaltered. What's really wild is that they are good."

Film and Revolution:

Interview with the Dziga-Vertov Group

by KENT E. CARROLL

Why did you decide to call yourselves the Dziga-Vertov group?

Godard: There are two reasons. One is the name Dziga Vertov itself, and one is the group Dziga-Vertov. The group name is to indicate a program, to raise a flag, not to just emphasize one person. Why Dziga-Vertov? Because at the beginning of the century, he was really a Marxist moviemaker. He was a revolutionary working for the Russian revolution through the movies. He wasn't just an artist. He was a progressive artist who joined the revolution and became a revolutionary artist through struggle. He said that the task of the Kinoki was not moviemaking—Kinoki does not mean moviemaker, it means film workers—but to produce films in the name of the World Proletarian Revolution. In that way, there was a big difference between him and those fellows Eisenstein and Pudovkin, who were not revolutionary. (. . .)

Is he more than an historical example? Can those same principles be applied today? And if so, how can you apply them to the very different circumstances that exist?

Godard: First we have to realize that we are French militants dealing with the movies, working in France, and involved in the class struggle. We are in 1970 and the movies, the tool we are working with, are still in 1917.

Would you term that a contradiction?

Godard: Yes, this is a contradiction. We have to deal with and be aware of this contradiction first. The group Dziga-Vertov means that we are trying, even if we are only two or three, to work as a group. Not to just work together as fellows, but as a political group. Which means fighting, struggling in France. Being involved in the struggle means we must struggle through the movies. To make a film as a political group is very difficult for the moment, because we are more in the position politically of just individuals trying to go on the same road. A group means not only individuals walking side by side on the same road, but walking together politically.

Is it necessary to work as a group? Could an individual, independent filmmaker make films politically?

Godard: It depends. First you have to try and be independent from the ruling class economy. You have to realize what it means to be independent. It doesn't mean just to be a hippie on a campus. They think a place like Berkeley is a so-called liberated area, but when they go to the border of this liberated area they see that the bars on the prison remain, only they're more invisible. You have to be independent first from the bourgeois ideology, and then you can move toward a revolutionary ideology. That means you have to try to work as a group, as an organization, to organize in order to unite. The movies are simply a way to help build unity. Making movies is just a little screw in building a new concept of politics.

Gorin: What we are trying to make are revolutionary movies that will promote revolutionary change. You will have to break all the old chains. The first notion to disappear is certainly the notion of the *auteur.*

Godard: The notion of an author, of independent imagination, is just a fake. But this bourgeois idea has not yet been replaced. A first step might be to simply gather people. At least then you can have a free discussion. But if you don't go on and organize on a political basis, you have nothing more than a free discussion. Then collective creation is really no more than collective eating in a restaurant.

Does it demand certain talents or certain kinds of knowledge?

Godard: Yes, but you can't speak of kinds of knowledge or talent, only of social use of knowledge and social use of talents. Of course, to handle a gun you need a certain capacity, a certain ability. To run fast, you need to have good legs and good training. Not to be out of focus when you photograph something, you need a certain capacity. But then there is the social use of that certain capacity. That technique or that capacity does not just exist in the air like the clouds.

You imply that your purpose is to break down not only an esthetic, but also the whole history of film. Then, is it more advantageous to be first a radical before becoming a filmmaker and attempting to make revolutionary films, or the other way around?

Godard: I was a bourgeois filmmaker and then a progressive filmmaker and then no longer a filmmaker, but just a worker in the movies. Jean-Pierre was a student and then a militant, and then he thought he had to go to the movies for a moment, just because it was an important part of the ideological struggle which is the primary aspect of the class struggle today in France. So we joined And he had to learn techniques a little more than I, and I had to learn political work as a duty, not as a hobby.

Is it possible to take advantage of expertise? Could you, working among yourselves and knowing what kind of film you wanted to make, use someone like Raoul Coutard?

Godard: Why not? For example, at the moment we still need an editing girl or boy, not because we can't do it, or we don't know how to do it, but because we want someone better trained. That way it goes faster, and we have to go as fast as possible. I mean, Lenin can take a taxi because he has to go fast from one place to another and he doesn't necessarily care if the taxi driver is a fascist. The same is true with editing. We are hesitating for the picture we have done for Al Fatah between two girls who are politically involved in a different way. They are at different stages of the revolutionary process, and we have to choose which one is best for the movie from a political point of view. One of the girls belongs to a group which has a very precise political program we agree with for the moment. The other one is much less militant, but it might be that to work on this movie could be progress for her and, because of this progress, we might have a more productive political relationship together. . . .

. . . We made a step forward when we tried to reduce all those so-called technical problems to their utmost simplicity. When you read a book on photography, whether by Hollywood photographers, whether by Kodak, it looks like building an atomic bomb, when it is not. It's really rather simple. So we are trying to make only a few images, work with no more than two tracks, so the mixing is simple. For the moment, most movie makers, except some underground movie makers, work with ten to twelve sound tracks and mixing lasts one week. The mixing is only three or four hours for us. We just work with two tracks and possibly later with one track, because with one track, we can really have simple sound again. But for the moment, we have not the political capacity of working with one track. This is the political stage, not simply a problem of techniques.

Is See You at Mao *the first film you attempted to make by the kind of revolutionary political process you've described?*

Godard: The first one was called *A Movie Like the Others.* It was done just after the 1968 May–June events in France. But it was a complete failure. So the real first attempt, with a bit of thinking, is *See You at Mao,* which is still kind of bourgeois, but progressive in many aspects of its making. Like the technical simplicity of it.

For example, in *Mao,* the shot of the nude women can generate a real progressive discussion. Just yesterday evening in Austin, a student said there was no difference between *Zabriskie Point* and *Mao.* I said, "Okay, but after seeing *Zabriskie Point,* what do you do?" "Oh well," he said, "I'm thinking more." I said, "Okay, what are you thinking more of?" He said, "Well, I don't know." Conversely from *Mao,* he asked why instead of a woman's body we didn't use a man's body? And I said, "Because we were actually discussing how to try and build an image for women's liberation." And then we had a real political and progressive discussion which you absolutely do not have the capacity of having with *Zabriskie Point.* That's what we mean by saying that simple techniques generate progressive political ideas.

Is that how you determine if another step has been taken? Is the success of each succeeding film based on the reaction from the people who view the film, on your own attitudes about the film, or on a combination of the two?

Godard: Mostly our own attitudes determine progress because, until now, there have been mainly negative aspects in our films. But the fact that those negative aspects can be transformed into positive aspects in succeeding films is because they were nevertheless achieved in a progressive way. There was a basic cut from the other movies. This cut was progressive, and although the results were mainly negative, we can dig out of that some progressive things. . . . You see a movie like *Amerika* by Newsreel, which I saw two days ago with the Newsreel people in San Francisco. They themselves say it is only feelings and that it is not good. They realize that, but they only feel; they do not have the capacity of saying what is not good. In *Mao* we realize that it's not good that on the assembly-line shot we are still obliged to use Marx's quotations instead of the voice of the workers. Yet, because of that, we can begin to deal with the class problem in England. But Newsreel can't do that. They can't because the next picture will be the same. But if it is not the same, it is not because of them. It is because there is some change in America and the changes in America are not coming from inside America but from the struggle *against* America *outside* America.

Is Pravda *a step beyond* Mao?

Godard: Yes, but only because *Pravda* differs in the negative aspect; we made the effort to finish it, and not to quit and say it's just garbage. But having made that psychological effort, we must also put a notice on it. This is a garbage Marxist/Leninist movie, which is a good way of titling it. At least now we know what not to do anymore. We've visited a house in which we'll never go again. We thought it was a step forward but we realized, how do you say, a jump into emptiness. It was a learning process. And the first thing we learned was that it was not done by group work, but by two individuals.

You continue to use the metaphor "step forward." Does that imply that at some point there is a final step, a full-blown revolutionary film with no negative aspects?

Godard: No. Only revolution again. People think we are aiming at a model, and this model you can print and then sell as a revolutionary model. That is shit. That is what Picasso has done and it is still bourgeois.

Gorin: Precisely. What is the difference between the two conceptions? One is saying, finally, art is art, which means things are things, and they hope to stay the way they are. We are saying that art is revolutionary art, art is a sensation of movement, and movement doesn't exist with a Greek urn. Only specific movements can exist with specific situations. That means that revolutionary art is a very wide open country, and there is not one form, but hundreds and thousands of them that, like political revolution itself, will never stop.

At the very beginning it's likely that it will be easy to gauge steps forward but, after the initial departure, how will you measure progression?

Godard: At a certain point you go from quantity to quality. Until *A Movie Like the Others* I was a moviemaker and an author. I was only progressing from a quantity point of view. Then I saw the job to be done, and that I had the possibility of doing this job only with the help of the masses. For me this was a major advancement. You can't do it as an individual. You can't do it alone, even if you are an advanced element of the good militant. Because being a good militant means being related, one way or another, with the masses.

Does it then follow that other revolutionary filmmakers, or would-be revolutionary filmmakers, have very little to learn from your own experience and that, secondly, at a certain point, each separate film can only be judged in its own specific context? That it can't even be related to the film that went before or the films that come afterward?

Gorin: No, I think that all revolutionary filmmakers have to meet at a certain point. They must confront the same problem we did. First they will be engaged, in their own way, in a war that will be quite similar to our struggle. But you have to work on general principles because each step of the revolution is trying to produce a parallel approach. There should be different types of revolutionary moviemakers, and sometimes we have to fight with them ideologically because that is one way we analyze our principles.

Godard: For example, the Newsreel people are fighting the Underground moviemakers, and both Underground and Newsreel are fighting Hollywood. This is a contradiction within the imperialistic system. And then there is Dziga-Vertov. We are fighting Hollywood, Newsreel, *and* the Underground. But sometimes we work on a united front with the people of Newsreel because it is important at a certain point to work with them to fight both Underground and Hollywood. For example, we took a movie made in Laos (we think it is a revisionist picture, even if they call it a Marxist picture), and brought it to the Palestinian fighters just for them to see others in another part of the world fighting against imperialism. So at that moment we were working on a united front. It is like when you make a demonstration in the street. Sometimes you must coordinate it with a group you are fighting ideologically. You do this to concentrate on the main enemy at the moment. To have a revolutionary form does not mean a discussion between two intellectual old ladies in front of a cup of tea. Having a revolutionary form is part of being related to the struggle and an expression of that struggle. An example of the contradiction we are dealing with is the laboratories. Except perhaps in China, when you are doing movies, even revolutionary ones, you are absolutely not related to the people who are processing the films. Not at all. You just go to them like you go to the grocery. This is the situation. And this is the trouble with the movies. The economic reality is the lab and the studio. But they are just objects.

But aren't they objects which you must presently use?

Godard: And we use them. We exploit them. For example, if

you do fast editing, you know, a lot of shots, you have to be aware of the negative editing girl who is working at the lab. The boss of the lab is obliging her to edit as fast as if there were a very few shots. You see? She's just a worker on an assembly line and this assembly line is just a movie, frame after frame.

Is one of the contradictions the distribution of the film?

Godard: Yes, one of the contradictions is between the distribution and the production. This contradiction has been established by imperialists who put distribution in command, who say, "since we have to distribute movies, we have to produce them in such a way that they can be distributed." So we, Dziga-Vertov, have to do the exact opposite. First we have to know how to produce, how to build a picture, and, after that, we will learn how to distribute it. It means that with the very few films we have, the very little money, we must try not to distribute always the same way. The old way was to make it to sell it. To make another one to sell it. To make another one and to sell it. Now, this is over. It might mean that we will be obliged to stop making movies for economic reasons or maybe from political decisions. At a certain historical point we will know if it's more important not to make a movie.

How do you see the possibilities of distribution, via EVR or video tape in home cassette form?

Godard: I don't believe in EVR from the class point of view, because EVR is just a new name of 20th Century Fox or M-G-M. It's run by CBS. It has been invented by CBS and it's used by CBS exactly the same way they use the network. The result is that EVR is only distribution, it can't produce a movie. So if you want to work on tape, the video cassette is probably the future. It will have a significant effect on the future from both a technical and social point of view. With Sony for example, or Ampex, you have both the producing capacity and the distribution capacity. So there is a huge fight today between Sony and EVR. Because they are very well aware that if they sell tapes to workers like English muffins, then it means the end of the old imperialist form like CBS.

Gorin: We must make a real study of the possibility of the video tape because video tape is taken for movies but it is not movies; it is a very specific thing with its own political meaning.

Are there any examples of people making genuine revolutionary films, political films by political means?

Godard: Maybe, but if there are, they must be unknown; and they have to be. Maybe there are one or two in Asia, and one or two in Africa, I don't know. In China they are probably working like that, but related to the Chinese situation. It's easier for the Chinese because there have been twenty years of dictatorship of the masses, and now the masses are taking over the ideological super-structure. This means that they have the capacity to really begin to work on art and literature in a true, revolutionary Chinese way.

How do you evaluate films like Battle of Algiers *and* Z?

Godard: A revolutionary film must come from class struggle or from liberation movements. These are films which only record, they are not part of the struggle. They are just films on politics, filmed with politicians. They are completely outside the activity they record; in no sense are they a product of that activity. At best, they are liberal movies.

They claim they attack when they're just what the Chinese call a bullet wrapped in sugar. These sugar bullets are the most danger-ous ones.

They advance a solution before analyzing the problem. So they put the solution before the problem. At the same moment they confuse reality with reflections. A movie is not reality, it is only a reflection. Bourgeois filmmakers focus on the reflections of reality. We are concerned with the reality of that reflection. But, at the moment, we must deal and work with only a few resources. This is a real situation. This is a ghetto situation. Our commissioned movies have been rejected by British, Italian, and French tele-vision because they were fiercely attacking them. And they feel us out the same way as the FBI. And we have not a possibility of having an Oscar or selling to CBS. We absolutely have not.

Gorin: Movies were invented about the time that the old bour-geois arts were declining. Movies were used to reinforce all the implications of the other arts. In fact, Hollywood movies are really from the same old psychopolitical form as the novel.

Godard: You have a very good example with Emile Zola. He began as a progressive writer, dealing with mine workers and the working-class situation. Then he sold more and more copies of his books. He became a real bourgeois, and then photography was invented. Then as an artist, he began to make photographs. But what kind of photographs was he making by the end of his life? Just pictures of his wife and children in the garden. In the begin-ning, his books were dealing with a coal workers' strike. You see the difference? He could have at least begun again to photograph strikers. But he did not. He was shooting his lady in a garden. Just like the Impressionist painters were doing. Manet was making pictures of the railroad station. But he was absolutely not aware that there was a big strike in the station. So one thing that can really be proved is that the development of movies and the invention of the camera did not mean progress, but only different kinds of tricks to convey the same stuff already in the novel. That's why the relationship between novels and moviemaking, the way a script is written and the way the director casts the film, why all those things are really a reinforcement of the same ruling-class ideology. The narrative line has brought the novel to death. Novelists became incapable of transforming progress into a revolutionary movement because they never analyzed where the narrative line was coming from. By whom was it invented? For whom and against whom? In a movie, there is no pure technique, there is nothing like a neutral camera or zoom. There is just social use of the zoom. The social use of the camera. There could be a social use of the 16mm camera. But when it was invented, there was no analysis of the social use of this light, portable camera. So the social use was controlled by Hollywood.

Do all art forms have as much possibility as film as ideological elements in revolutionary struggle?

Godard: I think it is much more difficult for painters and sculptors, much more difficult for arts like theater and music, because there is no science of music, and absolutely no social use of music except by imperialists. Look at the Rolling Stones. A year ago they were considered the leading hippies since the Beatles. Look what happened. Those Rolling Stones did a show at Altamont and allowed a situation where people were killed. There is nothing more to say.

Gorin: It is very hard to define a main form of art that is most representative of the current political movement. But on this political line, for the integration of the struggle, film is far more useful than music. But that doesn't mean, for instance, that in China, all forms of art cannot be revolutionary.

Godard: We think that the music in China is, for the moment, less revolutionary than theater, just because the Chinese tradition of theater is more Chinese than music. For example, the blacks here have a problem with their music because it has been stolen by the whites. So first they must recover it, and afterwards they must transform it, because now the whites have black sounds in their music. And this process is really very difficult. (. . .)

Could there come a point when you decide that there is no point in making more films? Might you decide to devote your energies entirely to a different kind of revolutionary activity which would not allow you to make films?

Godard: Well for the moment, we can't say because we are still dealing with movies. Some look to Che Guevara because he died fighting, and think they must do the same, but that is a very romantic notion. We speak of organization as outlined by Marx and especially Lenin. It means to change your life, even your personal life. To be related in a new way. For me, it means being able to work with Jean-Pierre, in the films. It means being able to work with the workers we are related to. But also to organize my own life, related to all that, to change it with my wife too, for example.

That seems extremely difficult. It seems that many people, although radical, are involved in a political activity only in relation to their primary social identity or the work they do while their personal life remains quite separate.

Godard: Yes, of course, and it is as difficult for the bourgeois as it is for the workers. The student or the bourgeois has to do the main effort, because they are in the position of having the possibility of doing it faster than the worker. And that is where the real difficulty is now.

What about the problem of financing films? As more and more distribution outlets become aware, like the television stations, of the kind of films you want to make, and the reasons you want to make them, won't most of the regular sources for finance be entirely unavailable?

Godard: This is why we may have to work just in a suburb or in a certain factory with the video tape. The only possibility might be to ask two hundred people for ten cents every week in order to deliver to them their information. Information *from* them *to* them. And this will be political work. But still we have the four pictures we are going to do for Grove Press. Grove Press has already bought two pictures in advance. What does it mean for us? It means we can control the picture except inside the States. It means, since it is more money than we have had in the last two years, that we have a capacity to think and work on the picture for six or seven months. It means we have no bread and butter problem for six months, and we have more creative possibilities. It means to pay people on the same basis that we are paid. But still we know

what Grove Press is, more or less, and we know, more or less, what
we are. So the first picture, *Vladimir and Rosa,* will deal with sex-
uality. We know Grove Press is interested in erotic things as well
as politics and avant-garde art. And since Barney Rosset is interested in that, we have tried to work within that, and to deliver
the best picture we can. But at the same time, militants will be able
to learn something from the movie. And if they are angry that it's
handled by Grove Press, which is a contradiction, at least it is
progressive to deliver a picture that will upset people. So if they're
really angry, that may lead to political action. That a contradiction
exists is obvious, but the answer is quite clear: we are far more
realistic in our approach than those who act as if the revolution
had already occurred.

*If a major film company came to you and said they'd give you,
say, $500,000 to make a film on a property they had selected, how
would you respond?*

Godard: We'd take it immediately, at least today we'd take it
immediately. Tomorrow we don't know. We need money badly.
Even when I was a bourgeois movie maker I was never offered
such an amount of money. Even when I was making *Pierrot le fou,*
or *The Married Woman.* But now, no one would offer such a sum.

*Could you make a commercial film intending to use your share
of the profits for other more political projects?*

Godard: That was just about the deal I had with United Artists
a year ago that was broken by United Artists. I had a deal to
make a picture called *Little Murders* by Feiffer. We had two screen
writers, Bob Benton and Robert Newman, deliver a script on our
indication, and then United Artists said to Bob Newman, 'Okay,
your script is good, but we don't want any more Godard.' I think
those two screen writers are honest liberals—they gave back the
money, and then UA broke the deal without even telling me. I
didn't receive the remaining $5,000 on my contract. Apparently,
United Artists had heard that we made a movie that Italian TV
turned down and they too were afraid to be attacked in their own
house.

That doesn't really answer the question.

Godard: If they had said what we must do we would have
done the movie, and tried to spend the money in a good way. We
would have tried to work politically with the union people, to
use some of the money with ads in *Variety* in a political way. It
would be almost nothing—but at least to fight that fight—and to

get money. The only people who can give us money now sometimes may act just out of charity.

These two films, Vladimir and Rosa *and* 18th Brumaire, *will they be fictional films?*

Godard: With *Vladimir and Rosa* we will try again with fiction but it will be very difficult. We were just on the beginning of that in Palestine because the Palestinian situation became very clear. The road leading to fiction is not yet clear—it's still bushes and trees.

Is that a specific goal—to make a revolutionary fictional film?

Godard: We think that movies are fiction and that reality is reality. That's all. We don't think documentaries are reality. Fiction is fiction, reality is reality and all movies are fiction.

The only problem is to try to make revolutionary fiction. To have made bourgeois fiction and to go into revolutionary fiction means a long march through many dark countries.

Do you consider the Al Fatah film Till Victory *your most successful attempt?*

Gorin: I think it is. Every political movement is a national liberation movement, and we have moved to our own point of liberation.

Godard: Now we have to convey this liberation movement into a class struggle.

Is there a true revolutionary situation in the States, a situation that is in any way comparable to the Palestinian situation?

Godard: You can't compare that.

So the film can only be a function of your own political involvement as you relate to a specific political situation?

Godard: It's like between man and woman. You can only work together when each one is the outside and the inside of the other one. If not, it's just a bourgeois marriage. For instance our contract with Grove Press is a bourgeois marriage. But it is correct because this is the way people are married today. . . .

How do you now consider your older films, especially those like La Chinoise, *which are pointedly political?*

Godard: They are just Hollywood films because I was a bourgeois artist. They are my dead corpses.

At what exact point in time did the break from bourgeois to revolutionary filmmaking occur?

Godard: During the May–June events in France in 1968.

Are there any of these earlier films that you now consider to have any positive merit?

Godard: Perhaps *Weekend* and *Pierrot le fou.* There are some things in *Two or Three Things.* Some positive things in those films. *One Plus One* was my last bourgeois film. I was very arrogant to make that, to think that I could talk about revolution just like that—just to take images thinking I knew what they meant.

What about One A.M., One American Movie, *that you shot two years ago during your last trip to this country? Will you ever complete it?*

Godard: No, it is dead now. When we first arrived, we looked at the rushes. I had thought we could do two or three days' editing and finish it, but not at all. It is two years old and completely of a different period. When we shot that I was thinking like a bourgeois artist, that I could just go and do interviews with people like Eldridge Cleaver and Tom Hayden. But I was wrong. And Tom Hayden was wrong to allow me to do that because it was just moviemaking, not political action. When we were in Berkeley I talked to Tom and apologized and told him I thought he was wrong. But Cleaver was correct. We paid him a thousand dollars and for him to take that money was correct. His was a political decision—he needed the money to escape America.

Do you still maintain any relationship with people from the bourgeois days, people like Truffaut or Coutard?

Godard: No, not really. We no longer have anything to talk about. We are now fighting one another, not as persons, but they are making bourgeois garbage and I have been making revolutionary garbage. *(laughter)*

Some people may be put off by the voice tracks of both Mao *and* Pravda *and the color quality of* Pravda. *Were these technical problems a question of time and money or in some way intentional?*

Godard: Mao should be projected very loud, especially during the long tracking shot at the BMC factory that opens the film. The movie was originally made for TV and that terrible noise in it is important. For bourgeois people to be uncomfortable with that scene for only eleven minutes may make them think that those workers must deal with that screeching every day all their lives.

We had some technical problems using only two tracks and very little mixing. But it is not important that every word be understood. On *Pravda* we used poor raw stock, but the washed out look is correct. Politically Czechoslovakia is a washed-out country. But the American boy who was doing the voice track in *Pravda* was inexperienced and we did not have the opportunity to make many takes. But, again, every word is not meant to be understood.

You've referred to certain filmmakers who, perhaps without them being aware that there were progressive elements in their work, had the capability of being Marxist filmmakers. Can you explain?

Godard: Yes, when we speak of the social use of techniques that is true. I just said that people like Jerry Lewis or Laurel and Hardy, if they were in the Russian Revolution, could have delivered Marxist movies because they had the biological capacity of doing those things. Or if they were in China now the Chinese Revolution could use this capacity in a revolutionary way. Just think of Laurel as a political commissar, and Hardy as a peasant. In their techniques, in their image and sound, is the possibility of a political analysis. They dealt with concepts, bourgeois concepts, but nevertheless, concepts. Even the Marx Brothers did not do this because the Marx Brothers are more the Jerry Rubin type. They are not dealing with concepts. Jerry Lewis and Laurel and Hardy are scientific.

Gorin: There are no feelings. Absolutely no feelings in Laurel and Hardy, and only a few in Jerry Lewis. In Chaplin, there is only feeling.

Godard: And what feelings there are could be transformed, with the help of the masses. . . .

Gorin: They demonstrate an attempt to at least see what a movie really is—nothing is considered reality.

Godard: So to say that was not a joke statement.

I think I understand what you mean, but many people dismiss what Jerry Lewis does, because he seems to deal with middle-class American values in comic-strip form.

Godard: You must see that it's because Jerry Lewis and Laurel and Hardy are really making a blackboard of the movie. A bourgeois blackboard, but it's a blackboard nevertheless. Not a university blackboard, but on this blackboard you can construct things.

Blackboard implies learning and understanding. Is there some potential efficacy in using film to rouse feeling and then use those feelings?

Godard: Of course, but you have to put feelings in their place. But until now, feelings have been put in command. Feelings first and then concepts. We have to do the reverse, and so for the moment when we say we don't believe in feelings it's just for a certain time. This certain time can be for a hundred years, but, for the moment, we have to use feelings only after concepts. For example, in the Palestinian movie, at the end we try to use feelings, but only because we have the possibility to use them correctly. We can use a song, and with the song comes some warmness, but because there is the concept of the armed struggle before, you get the warmness in the right way. It doesn't make you forget things. On the contrary, it reinforces.

An interesting concept is your distinction between taking a picture and building a picture, and secondly, the relationship between sound and image. How do these concepts relate politically?

Godard: Because you belong to a certain society today in America, or we in France, you just think that when you are speaking that your words and your structure, that they go together, that there is a complete unity. But there is no unity. There is a continuous struggle between what you say and what you think and the way we are living in a certain social condition. You are not a unity. You are trying to be a unity, but the fact is you are not. And the movie represents that in a very simple way—it's just image and sound—it's not just adding together—it's a struggle. Hollywood wants to just add them together there on the screen, just like you put a stamp on a letter.

Exactly what do you mean by a film as a unity?

Godard: Well, to build it economically and aesthetically, as an ideological product for a different purpose. What is a bourgeois moviemaker doing? He is dealing with image and sound. He's building too. But for what? To achieve a truer presentation of reality, he's using hundreds of sound tracks, so that when you step on this carpet, you have the very sound of your foot on this carpet. But it means no more than that. He thinks it is real, but of course it is not. We are using the same elements, but in the way we use them we are transforming them. Our purposes are quite different.

REVIEWS

JEAN COLLET

(Les Carabiniers)

❖❖❖

No doubt Jean-Luc Godard's *Les Carabiniers* will be less well re-ceived, less well understood than Fellini's *Eight-and-a-Half*.[1] It is much easier to communicate joy than horror. *Les Carabiniers* must be examined at close range, because, more than any other, this film invites all sorts of misunderstandings. It must at least be admitted that *Les Carabiniers,* like *Eight-and-a-Half*, represents a "free" cin-ema in which all the rules of the art are broken. It might be added here that this liberty is made up of insolence, provocation, and casu-alness.

Les Carabiniers is a fable—two couples live in poverty on a piece of vacant land. One day some riflemen come and lead the two hus-bands off to fight the king's war. It does not take much to convince them—"In war," they are told, "you can do everything that is ordinarily prohibited. Kill, rape, steal. In war, everything is per-mitted. You can take everything. . . ." One of the two men is a kid who has not quite grown up, a brat you might say. Jean-Luc Godard has found one of those faces (Albert Jurosse) that the cinema has lost the secret of finding—a glutton's face with overly soft cheeks, the face of a disquieting, overgrown, hardened baby.

So, our hero and his companion go off in uniform to seek freedom. With the innocence of animals, they begin to live by their instincts, spreading the horrors of war everywhere. They return home with a loot consisting of postcards—the cities, the factories, the monuments, the women they conquered. But they don't have time to revel in

From Les Signes du Temps, *July 1963, p. 33. Reprinted by per-mission of the publisher and the author. Translated by Royal S. Brown.*

[1] *Eight-and-a-Half* opened in Paris around the same time as *Les Carabiniers* and was reviewed in the same issue by M. Collet. (editor's note)

these paper treasures. Yesterday's enemies have become today's friends, and the overly conscientious little soldiers are shot.

The interesting thing about this fable is that it hides an experiment—how far can one go in the instinct of possession? Because it is certainly a question here of instinct. These are not men one usually sends off to war; they are bums who live from day to day, human beings who are still the prey of childlike impulses, primitives who are simply trying to live, live off of the death of other people. You cannot judge them. To do so would be to misunderstand the whole point of the film and divert it from its true meaning. To begin with, these are two completely amoral human beings. Furthermore, the way Godard looks at them—and the way we look at them through Godard—remains completely outside these characters. He neither blames them nor justifies them. He looks at them. From a distance. Always from the same distance. With a steady eye and an impassive camera.

Impassive? Of course not, for heaven's sake! War is a game, a sophomoric prank, a picnic on abandoned property. This farcical style, which will provoke the anger of some people and make others think, is definitely the style of Father Ubu. *Les Carabiniers* is Ubu all over again. And isn't doing what you want, precisely when you want to do it, immediately, exactly what leads Ubu down the path of war? For Jean-Luc Godard, whose critical attitude shows up even in the way he makes his films, *Les Carabiniers* is a commentary on *Ubu roi*; it is the rebirth of Alfred Jarry.

And it is also the rebirth of a certain kind of cinema. When one says that a certain filmmaker "captures something live," one forgets what a bellicose connotation this image can have. This filmmaker, like the riflemen in this fable, takes only pictures, postcards. But don't both kinds of "capturing" give rise to death and blood? If this idea seems excessive, all you have to do is read Edgar Allen Poe's *The Oval Portrait*, that novelette which represents the whole moral of the film and is used by Godard toward the end of *Vivre sa vie*— the artist takes life to produce his work; he kills in order to create.

No doubt this extremely profound reflection on the cinema by a filmmaker will escape most spectators. The most explicit scene in this respect will no doubt appear irrelevant to most—at one point, the young soldier goes into a movie theatre, sees a film by Louis Lumière and a film showing a pin-up girl taking a bath. People will probably not be very amused when the young barbarian rushes towards the screen and rips it in order to seize this dream creature. Yet this image is one of the most admirable that the cinema has ever given us—it is the whole parabole of the artist and his creation, and it represents perhaps the first time that modern art has turned quite so vigorously back towards itself, hesitating to recognize that it is an art of capture and not of offering; the artist trembles as he touches the sacred roots of his art, of all art.

This first moral of the film, which concerns the filmmaker, guarantees, it seems to me, the purity of the second, which concerns war. And the second gains considerably by its closeness to the first. Thus, in *Les Carabiniers*, Godard puts on trial not only war, violence, and bestiality but also all elementary appetites, starting with the appetite of the eye—a sin shared both by the filmmaker and the spectator. The long, unpleasant scene in which the young warrior lifts up the skirt of a young woman (in front of a Rembrandt painting) and remains frozen, his eyes shining, should make the audience think before it arouses its righteous indignation. It is the voracity of the eye that is on trial here, as is, of course, through this first voracity, the power hunger which is life itself.

Where then is freedom when art is just as criminal as war, and when life becomes a necessary war? It seems to me that in this film, only the camera confronts a moral and therefore a kind of freedom. I mentioned "the impassive eye" of the camera; but it is more than this, I feel. It is a respectful eye that Godard aims towards his tragic universe. The distance he maintains vis-à-vis his characters, the withdrawal created by the use of the fable, the rejection of an outmoded picture style—all of these are signs of an artist who refuses to possess his universe and offer us the illusory key to it. It is precisely an album of faded postcards that he forces us to skim through rapidly. "You see," Godard seems to be saying, "in war just as on the screen, there is nothing to take, and you have to kill a lot. Whether you make films or war, you're always taking pictures, 'titles.' Therefore it's better to take pictures, from a distance, and pretend. There's no way out." You can't kill to be free. Can you if you're creating a work of art? It is difficult to "live your life."

These thoughts of an artist on his profession lead us quite far away from Fellini's joy. But what does the end point matter when it's the path taken and its harshness that count. Godard performs an

experiment on creation in a state of death, Fellini in a state of exalta-
tion. But don't this death and this happiness represent the two sides
of a same truth?

CLAUDE MAURIAC
(Masculin-Féminin)

❖❖❖

Scarcely has Jean-Luc Godard finished one film than he begins and
soon finishes another. An unusual pace in cinematographic creation.

Godard has been able to bend the rules of production and use
them toward his own means; he has sufficiently demonstrated, on
the whole, that his methods bring in money; and thus he has always,
up until now, been able to find money when he needs it.

Filmmakers are not the only ones to dream of such fertility.
Godard's talent is always there, always peremptory, just as stunning
in *Masculin-Féminin* as in his preceding works. Occasionally, we
find ourselves reticent, we refuse to give in, we balk; but we are soon
caught, and caught again. We hail the success of the work, and we
try to understand it.

Our first reaction is perhaps to say to ourselves that it is no doubt
not so difficult, when one has the skills and when one has given up
carefully constructed works and well-planned dialogues, to direct
such films.

But to feel this way is to forget that Jean-Luc Godard learned
to use a camera by enforcing his own style of production and creation. It is to forget that this was no easier for him, at the beginning,
than for anybody else, and that he must, with each new film he
makes, fulfill his challenge yet one more time. It is to him that

From Le Figaro Littéraire, *April 28, 1966, p. 14. Reprinted by permission of the publisher and the author. Translated by Royal S. Brown.*

French cinema owes its escape from sterility. Most filmmakers before Godard seem academic to us. Those who have followed him owe him a great debt.

For there is a cinema according to Godard, the cinema of Claude Lelouch, which was born from the same creative liberty, with one additional conquest: the director has no other cameraman than himself. The happy thought of a camera-pen, once dreamed of by Alexandre Astruc, has finally become a reality. At first Claude Lelouch groped around without turning out anything interesting; but now he has given us a finished work with *Un Homme et une femme,* which will represent France at the next Cannes festival.

Godard will go down in history as the man who exorcized the cinema, who gave the camera its liberty. Before him, the camera was a sacred object that only a particular kind of priest was allowed to operate. There were certain rites that nobody, not even the high priest responsible for the film, dared to question. There were many "thou shalt's" and "thou shalt not's"; the lighting had to be set up in such a way at such a moment; a lot of time and a lot of money were spent. The uninitiated admired the ceremonial and participated in the cult from a distance; but the idea never even entered their heads of one day being able, even if they were called to the cinematographic vocation, to be admitted among the holiest of the holies. What is amazing is that even the initiated seemed to be hypnotized. The camera, a magical object, frightened them. And it is for this reason that they surrounded its use with so many rules and restrictions.

Along came Godard, and with him the great desanctification. If he treated the cinema with great disrespect, it was because of his great love for it. There was a reality to be captured, a world to describe, and there were things to say—that is what the cameras and microphones were there for. In using them, he thought less about the tools he was working with than about what they should allow him to see and hear.

No matter what the profession, the worker is not really qualified until that moment when he is able to use his instruments without thinking about them. The artist likewise must control his means—there is no question of aesthetic accomplishment without technical mastery. The person who is in perfect control of his art can work quickly and well. Godard directs his films the way Picasso draws—with a single stroke of the pen. But Godard does not shoot his films the way Picasso paints (or the way anybody else paints, for that matter). His films are sketches. He could no doubt not give them any greater depth without ruining them.

Masculin-Féminin is precisely dated. The film was shot in Paris during the last presidential campaign. The young men and women he shows us in complete freedom belong so much to their era that we have the impression that we have scarcely noticed them in the streets, in the subways. And we would never have had the chance to hear them if Godard had not been there. In five years, these characters will have grown less old than the image of youth they offer us. In fifty years, thanks to Godard's investigation, they will be the witnesses for their era. Every film Godard makes will be an invaluable document, and I doubt that they will ever show their age. There is too much warmth, too much despair in the way Godard sees them. The effort of an artist to capture and the effort of a man to understand will always be timeless.

Of all those girls, for whom love is apparently no longer a problem (or at least, this is the way they act; only one leads us to understand that she is still chaste, and she is not the least charming), of all these young women whom we want to believe on their word (the word of Godard more than their own; they make love without comment—in order for us to know what they are thinking, what they are really feeling, we would have to have a female Godard), in the midst of these girls who apparently have no complexes, and in the midst of a few other young men who are more or less, like the girls, seen from the outside, Jean-Pierre Léaud stands out as the image of the young man for all times—nervous, worried, unhappy, despondent. No doubt he also represents the image of Godard himself, who already belongs to another era—but the difficulty of being knows no season.

And it is perhaps here that we can get a glimpse of Godard's secret, of what makes his works so moving and beautiful, as rapid and incomplete as they are—perhaps even because of their rapidity and their incompleteness. More care, more tension would perhaps have blurred the message that comes from the depths of solitude, a message we do not need to decode, as we can clearly read it before us on the screen—it is the same story moving from generation to generation. As removed as these young persons must already appear to Godard, he is like them; and as old as I may be, I am like Godard.

By suppressing the various solemnities of the cinema, Godard has made us even more aware of its basic mystery. It is because he was able to free himself from all the usual complexes vis-à-vis the camera that his inhibitions, his sadness, his personal distress are so simply and so seriously expressed. A Mirror-Screen. A generation is there that tells us directly its secrets.

But, passing these images of the instant, the man of every instant; behind these young men, a man who is still young. Despair has no age.

JEAN-LOUIS COMOLLI

(Anticipation)

❖❖❖

It is no doubt fitting to explain to our readers the reason behind the scathing note appearing in our last issue and concerning the collective film, Le Plus vieux métier du monde ("A film to avoid, five of its six sketches being worthless, while the sixth has no relationship to what Godard filmed"). The copy of Anticipation such as it is shown in the theaters is the result of the joint efforts of the producers and distributors of the film, and it no longer represents the work of Godard. For those who have seen the film as it is being projected commercially, Godard's sketch is shown with a uniformly yellow wash, except for the last shots, which are in color. Why in the world was this uniform used? In order to uncover the origins of this jaundice, it is necessary to go into a few technical details which here, more than ever in Godard's cinema, represent an important part of the film's raison d'être. Godard shot the whole work, with the exception, once again, of the last shots (showing the kiss), in black and white. But this was done with the intention of having these sequences

From Cahiers du Cinéma, no. 191 (June 1967), pp. 67–68. Copyright © 1967 by Les Éditions de l'Étoile. Reprinted by permission of Grove Press, Inc. Translated by Royal S. Brown.

developed with monochrome washes—certain sequences were printed by the laboratory entirely in red, others in yellow, others in blue. Furthermore, the film's commentary still makes allusion to these uniform colors ("Soviet color," "a European color," "a Chinese color"). But in addition, by making use of effects afforded by various counterprints, negative prints, and certain laboratory treatments augmenting the contrasts, and so forth, Godard managed to totally obscure certain shots, and even entire scenes—that is, the contours both of people and objects melt away completely, leaving a kind of blur that overwhelms the entire shot, erasing even the features of the actors. As on the screen of a poorly adjusted television set, in which the contrasts are excessive, one no longer sees (in Godard's version) anything but protoplasmic forms moving about ambiguously; it is impossible to make out the physical characteristics of the actors—so much so, in fact, that Charrier (and it was this aspect that upset the foreign buyers), who was already wiped out in the sound track by the mechanical and chopped-up diction he was forced to use, was demolished to the same degree in the pictures; a shadow among other shadows, a blurred form moving about, a negative of himself. Throughout the sketch, when the relationships between the passenger and his hostesses are still "normal," the shots are excessively abnormal (and this is stressed in the commentary, which regularly notes "positive" precisely at the moment the shot is negative); at the moment of the kiss, on the other hand, the shots become positive and burst into color (while the commentary says "negative"). A game? No doubt, but one that has definite consequences.

For the first time, Godard has anchored an entire film in the quicksands of "experimental cinema" and the latter's laboratory effects. Of course, Godard could say, like Antonioni, "All my films are experimental." In that case, the experiment lies in a domain other than that of the very act of filming—the attempt and the temptation to *destroy* the picture itself, which is to say the vital raw material of the cinema. It is of course impossible to completely destroy pictures *through* the cinema; that is, by using pictures. But the experiment may very well be that of determining precisely how far a picture can go in destroying itself, and just what its resistance threshold is; of finding out, by printing a film in negative, in monochrome, in a system of false values of light and dark, and by pulverizing the shot in all possible manners, whether something would remain even so, something that would represent the very heart of the cinema, the soul beneath all the surfaces and all the appearances. The result of this experiment is, of course, that the more one hampers and paralyzes the function of the picture (which is to *show*), and the less, therefore, it shows precise forms, the more it becomes matter and movement, returning to grain, to textures, to fusions, to elementary drawings—the more, in other words, the cinema becomes painting. But through what mysterious convergence do three of the most brilliant filmmakers of our time—Bergman in *Persona*, Godard in this film, and Antonioni in *Blow-Up*—persist in trying to discredit the cinematographic picture, in trying to make it betray and destroy itself? Blind cinema. . . . Needless to say, none of this remains in the commercial copy of the film. Deeming that Godard had gone too far in anticipating, the producer-distributors had a normal, positive copy of the film printed from the original negative, so that everything becomes again "clear" and "plain": the actors' faces, the forms of the settings. . . . Also liquidated were the monochrome colorings of the sequences and the plastic deformations of the shots. It is only thanks to the Festival d'Hyères that a few privileged persons have been able to see the film as Godard conceived it.

ROGER GREENSPUN
(Weekend)

About half way through Jean-Luc Godard's "Weekend," Emily Brontë and her poetry spouting fairy-tale buddy, Gros Poucet, wander through and offer some riddles, a few cloudy answers to

From New York Free Press, *1, no. 41 (October 17, 1968): 8. Reprinted by permission of the author.*

solid questions, and a little lecture in natural history. Our hero and
heroine, Roland and Corinne (Jean Yanne and Mireille Darc), are
on their way to her parents' house to grab her dying father's money
before her mother can grab it for herself, and their car has been
smashed up, and all they want are some directions. Because they are
pragmatic types, and all Emily will give them is metaphysical crap,
they prove their own philosophical point by setting fire to her and
letting her burn up, while Gros Poucet sits at her flaming feet and
recounts the woes of Bertolt Brecht in Hollywood. But before and
during her consummation, Emily makes a couple of interesting
points.

One, obviously, is that she burns very well. For a movie so basically
involved with the violation of the human body at various levels of
civilized indifference or savage intent, at least one personal immola-
tion could not be dispensed with. The other point has to do with
that natural history lecture, actually a meditation upon a stone—a
pebble looking a little like a human skull, but predating man, perhaps present at the birth of the universe, now tossed aside. The stone
is compacted of matter so unfeeling that one must do it the utmost
violence to work a change upon it. Of course the two illustrations are
not unrelated, and after contemplating an inviolate of stone, who
would not be instructed by a demonstration of how well people
burn? But to keep the illustrations separate for a moment, consider
a) the fragility of human life, and b) the immensities of the geologic
eras and of cosmic time. If you keep these two unremarkable notions
in mind, you will have a useful pair of coordinates for mapping your
way into Godard's latest epic masterpiece.

Several reviewers have praised "Weekend" in the New York press
—most notably Pauline Kael in the New Yorker, where her comments on what she calls "Godard's vision of Hell" conclude among
ads for clocks starting at $195, cigarette lighters ending at $800, and
Canadian whisky holding steady at $9 a fifth. But each, including
Miss Kael, has drawn back from certain moments in the film that
they consider inappropriate interpolations. The forest ramble with
Emily Brontë and Gros Poucet is one such interpolation. A farmyard
Mozart recital involving three agonizingly slow 360 degree camera
pans is another (perhaps the most brilliantly boring moment in re-
cent movies—and, incidentally, a chance to reintroduce Blandine
Jeanson, previously burned to death as Emily Brontë and now turn-

ing pages for pianist Paul Gegauff). And a third, most blatant, interruption allows a pair of garbage collectors—one black, one North African—to harangue the audience with threats of revolution.

The argument is that these interpolations, a kind of funky display of virtuosity on Godard's part, interrupt the fiction with a form of direct address that is, even in this wild movie, inartistic. I'm inclined rather sharply to disagree. In Godard, direct address, whether by actors or by the camera calling attention to itself, is usually highly artistic and, as in "Weekend," may serve as a major dramatic balance to the fiction.

Godard always introduces stories into his movies. In "Alphaville," Lemmy Caution is taken prisoner by the secret police when they get him to let his guard down by telling him a funny story. In "Contempt," one of the great sources for "Weekend," nobody moves without an aphorism or a tale to explain his actions. But except for a sick creation story concerning the hippopotamus, "Weekend" replaces stories with riddles, with audio-visual instruction, with quotations from history, and with more or less intellectual harangues.

Since the whole movie, on one level, moves toward an understanding of the style of revolution (just as "La Chinoise" argued about the content of revolution), it seems entirely appropriate that revolutionary threats should be held up to view. And since, at a deeper level, revolutionary style becomes a means to the end of making a journey through interior time and space, those threats are ultimately a part of the exceptionally complicated dramatic and symbolic process of the fiction.

"Weekend" accomplishes a number of significant dislocations as it moves from bourgeois to anti-bourgeois, from advanced technology to primitive technology, from mass culture to barbarism, from the present to the future—which is no more than a memory of the prehistoric past. Between the rhetoric of black power and the warfare of the cannibalistic hippies of the FLSO ("Seine and Oise Liberation Front") with which the film ends, it is only a matter of time, or of degree of alienation, since the whole film is concerned with showing that the impulses of both groups are present now and in all of us. Godard views his angry Africans in the context of anthropology and the systems of barbaric organization of the Iroquois Indians studied by Lewis Henry Morgan (American ethnologist, 1818–1881, and a favorite of Engels, the movie tells us). From them he cuts to his hippies, all dressed in beads and Indian headbands. But of course he remembers at the same time a bratty kid at the beginning of the film—the kid wore an Indian suit and attacked a car, and called for help from his basic protective unit—dad with a rifle and mom with a fighting tennis racket.

"Weekend" actually keeps moving in and out of its fiction—which is essentially a shaggy-dog story anyway. No character can be taken seriously, no character takes himself seriously, one scene's corpse may be the next scene's revolutionary—and in the midst of a supernaturally dense green world, Godard has mounted his most resolutely artificial action. But because that action is so sensational, because it has a recognizable beginning, middle, and end, and because it makes such an acceptable and intellectually digestible point with its battling cars and its monumental traffic jam, each obvious interruption seems like a lapse of taste and a failure in invention. But each obvious interruption is in fact an involution of the fiction. For its pause at the side of a yellow garbage truck, "Weekend" emerges richer, fertilized, and somehow refreshed.

I assume that everybody knows the film's story and general progress —how it moves from casual killing to purposeful killing, from merely poisoning your loved ones to eating them, from erotic abuse of bodies to murderous use of bodies, from civilization and its discontents to totem and taboo. "Weekend" continually enters new phases of regression, sinks into a primitivism of the future, mediates between junkheap and cosmos, relates man and animal, and explores time from minutes to hours, to weeks, months, the seasons, the ages of man, the epochs of mankind, and finally the eras of the earth. But to make its extraordinary leaps in time and in imaginative awareness it seems to need the help of dialectic—whether casually integrated into the plot or seemingly segregated from the plot and even from the principal characters, who are as bored by the voice of Africa as the critics have been.

I treasure those moments of true speaking because they are such bold dramatic lies and because by breaking the fiction they wonderfully redirect it. Essentially they invoke curses, and then the film opens up to show that each curse has already come to pass as part of the story. As for that underlying curse of human brotherhood, that recognition of his "semblable" that horrifies Godard as much as it did Eliot and Baudelaire in the Puritan tradition before him; without its superb intellectualizing, its symbolic profundities, its breathtakingly energetic world view, I'm not sure that "Weekend" would be saying much more than another movie around town—that we are what we eat.[1]

RICHARD ROUD
(Le Gai Savoir)

◆◇◆

After he got back from that trip to Damascus, old Saul-called-Paul must have been something of a drag to his old drinking companions. "What's gotten into him?" one can hear them say, just like most of Godard's admirers who have been bitterly complaining about *Le Gai Savoir* (which although begun in December 1967, was only completed after the apocalyptic Month of May, 1968). And a possible reaction to this film—indeed, it was mine the first time I saw it—was one of nearly total rejection: it just wasn't like the others; one felt almost cheated. Here we had a young couple sitting in a TV studio for an hour and a half: talking, just talking. To be sure, there was the occasional shot of a street, but by and large the film could be seen as a masochistic exercise in which Godard systematically—almost religiously—stripped himself of all his aesthetic trump cards, all his aces. The screen actually goes black for minutes at a time, which is about as self-effacing as you can get.

Of course, another reaction was possible: to try to find in this film those elements which *are* like the earlier work. To examine it as an aesthetic object, picking out the good bits. And there are quite a few. The first image, for example, of the orange-ribbed transparent umbrella, is as beautiful as anything he has ever done. The photography of Jean-Pierre Léaud and Juliette Berto is good enough for a shampoo commercial, so lustrously does it render their hair,

From Sight and Sound *38, no. 4 (Autumn 1969): 210–11. Reprinted by permission of the publisher.*

[1]Allusion to Barry Feinstein's film, *You Are What You Eat* (1968), which starred, among other people, Tiny Tim (editor's note).

shining with mysterious highlights. The Cuban revolutionary hymn with which he ends most of the episodes; the piano sonata which turns up as punctuation; the extraordinary mask effects, now with Léaud's face hidden behind Mlle Berto's, now the opposite, and, most effectively, with her lips synching his words spoken behind her; the remarkable camera movements going from left to right to pick up Léaud, then Mlle Berto, and in the same shot, Léaud again. The list is, if not inexhaustible, then at least long: her yellow gown with its purple peignoir, seen against the figures of Batman and two other comic strip heroes; the nearly invisible construction of what looks to be a formless film.

But such an appreciation would run totally counter to Godard's intentions. He did not want to make an "aesthetic object," the "work of art," all too easily assimilated by the very society it is attacking. The work of art can be isolated, defused, reabsorbed by society. He has not totally avoided this danger, but from the disastrous reactions at Berlin, at least, he came pretty close.

The most intelligent way of approaching the film would seem to be to take it *sui generis:* given Godard's career, and *assuming* he has not completely cracked up, what did he think he was up to?

Godard always was a critic as well as a film-maker, so one should be neither surprised nor upset if *Le Gai Savoir* (Kestrel) is something of an essay; a pamphlet, even. One could say that he should in fact have *written* a pamphlet. But this would be fatally to misunderstand his new position. Film must be made for that enormous portion of the globe (60%, some say) that is illiterate. He is too clear-headed to think that *this* film is for the Cambodian coolie or the Peruvian peon; and his final disclaimer is neither false modesty nor masochistic self-beratement. When he says, "This film didn't want, couldn't want, to try to explain the cinema, nor even constitute its object. More modestly it tries to give several effective means of so doing. This is not the film that should be made, but rather it shows that, if one has a film to make, one would necessarily pass by some of the paths trodden here."

But film is valuable not only for illiterates: it can *show* what is being hidden. It is both practical and theoretical. It's more fun, says Godard, than an equation or a blackboard demonstration. Accepting this, we must now examine what this blackboard demonstration is about, what this equation stands for. Originally the commission from the French television network was for a film about education, and *Le Gai Savoir* was announced as being a modern version of Rousseau's *Emile*. But it turned out otherwise: the film is really about language.

The recently rediscovered writings of the German critic Walter Benjamin shed much light on Godard's development, not as a film-maker, but as a critic who uses film instead of paper. Benjamin's great unfinished work (*Paris, Capital of the 19th Century*) was to have been a study of the complex links between economic evolution and cultural facts. Benjamin, before his untimely death in 1940, began to feel certain that this was in fact the essential task of the critic. Like Godard, he was prey to more and more frequent psychological depressions, and this, combined with the growing Fascist threat, brought Benjamin's work to an ever more exacerbated state. Like the flame between two carbon arcs, he was stretched, almost to breaking point, between Marxist politics and the metaphiysics of language. "The most worn-out Communist platitude," he wrote, "means more than the most profound bourgeois thought, because the latter has only one true sense, that of apology."

Godard has always been as sensitive to cultural climates as the most intellectual barometer, so I doubt whether the comparison with Benjamin is fortuitous; equally important is the whole recent French interest in linguistics, and, most recently, in the American writer Noam Chomsky, whom Godard actually cites in *Le Gai Savoir*.

This does not mean that Godard has pored over the works of Benjamin or Chomsky; he doesn't have to. He is like the bookstore employee he talks about in *Le Gai Savoir*, who over the years had had just two or three seconds between the time he took the books from the customer and the time he wrapped them up to glance at their contents: over the past thirty years he has educated himself, beginning with the alphabet and the multiplication tables. Now, says Godard, he is launching into Faulkner and Chomsky. It would appear that Godard has a magpie talent for picking up a book, mechanically leafing through it, and maddeningly coming up each time with its essence.

From his leafings through Chomsky and the other linguistic philosophers, he has reached the conclusion that language is the key to our problems; it is the enemy. As Juliette Berto says at the beginning of *Le Gai Savoir*: "I want to learn, to teach myself, everyone, to turn back against the enemy that weapon with which it attacks us: language."

"Yes," replies Léaud, "we have to start again from zero." "No," she answers, "before starting again, we have to go *back* to zero," and going back means disintegrating man and his language. Thus also Chomsky: The renewal of the study of language should lead to a liberation from all our behavioristic conditioning, and should ultimately lead to a political criticism of our alienation. All thought has been consciously or unconsciously bound up with the conditioning of bourgeois society of the past hundreds of years; it takes a great effort to look at everything afresh, questioningly, and *Le Gai Savoir* is an attempt at this most arduous of intellectual exercises.

However, it has to be admitted that often the effort proves too great, and Godard spills over the edge of common sense into intellectual dishonesty. To the unsympathetic, much of the dialogue will sound like naive gibberish; on the other hand, it is not easy to divest oneself of the preconceived ideas of a lifetime; and Godard must be allowed something for having made the effort.

He has, in a sense, left the film unfinished. The sequence of Juliette Berto's song he assigns to Bertolucci to do; the analysis of an "honourable family" is willed to Straub, and so forth. Although Godard might not like it (he isn't too partial to Bach) one might usefully compare *Le Gai Savoir* to *The Art of Fugue*. Both are didactic, methodical; both unfinished; both have little overt emotional subject matter; both are grandiosely simple in means; finally, both have their boring moments. If this is to be the cinema of the future, God help us. And yet, it seems to me certain to exercise a profound influence on younger film-makers. Just as Bach's audience dwindled to nothing in the early 19th century (*The Art of Fugue* was actually given its first performance only in the 1920s), but continued to have a great influence on the composers of the period, so *Le Gai Savoir* will never be a popular film, but it might well turn out to be an extremely important one.

ROGER GREENSPUN
(One Plus One)

❖◇❖

An English-language movie by Jean-Luc Godard, opened theatrically yesterday at the Murray Hill. If you go on Monday, Wednesday, Friday or Sunday, you will see Godard's film, which is properly known as "1 + 1." On other days, you will see a film popularly advertised as "Sympathy for the Devil," which exactly resembles "1 + 1" except that in the latter part of the last reel a complete version of the song "Sympathy for the Devil," which the Rolling Stones have been rehearsing and recording in cuts throughout the film, is played on the soundtrack. Several monochromatic stills of the film's last shot are added to fill out the song's time. The changes and additions are the work of the producer, Iain Quarrier.

Why anyone, given the choice, would prefer a producer's version of a movie to a director's escapes me. The movie to see at the Murray Hill is "1 + 1." Not only does the use of the song impose a sense of emotional fulfillment (and, I think, the wrong sense of fulfillment) upon a conclusion that does not ask for it, but also the use of the song's title for the movie suggests a meaning that is less interesting in context than, say, the proposition "1 + 1 equals 2."

For "1 + 1" is a heavily didactic, even instructional, film, like much recent Godard, and it builds upon repetition, or, if you will, addition. The Rolling Stones' repeated assays upon "Sympathy for the Devil" in their recording studio, the rote repetitions of passages and slogans passed back and forth among black-power revolutionaries in their riverside automobile junkyard, the mere adding up of questions and answers in the interview sequences, juxtaposing words to make new combinations (such as "So-Viet Cong") and finding new words in old combinations (such as SDS in "Sight and Sound"; LOVE in "All About Eve")—all suggest a concern with ways of putting things together, and the film seems determined to be the prospective text of some ultimate, infinitely complex collectivism.

Whatever its intentions, "1 + 1" contemplates rather than advocates revolution. It collects evidence and examines texts—including a by now famous pornographic political novel read on the sound track (" 'You're my kind of girl, Pepita,' said Pope Paul as he lay down on the grass . . . ," and so forth)—records interviews ("The Occident is fighting communism because the Occident is Faustian?" "Yes."), and observes the forces preparing the apocalypse.

In "1 + 1" the camera comes alive on its cranes and tracks. As if lost in a precise meditation it moves deliberately among the persons and places of the Stones' recording studio or from wreck to wreck in the fantastic black power junk heap.

The chief delight of the film lies in this precision and in these scenes. At the end, when it martyrs its one named character, Eve Democracy (Anne Wiazemski), it spreads her body across a mighty camera crane on a seashore. The crane lifts her in a great sweeping movement, red and black flags flying in the wind, across the sky. And at this moment, and not until this moment, it seems possible that the meaning of Godard's film depends not only upon a cause but also upon the camera's eye: not only in sympathy, but in objectivity as well.

PENELOPE GILLIATT

(See You at Mao and Pravda)

◆◇◆

Godard's voice carries. He has finished two new films, "See You at Mao" and "Pravda," each about an hour long, in a style going toward the most didactic and thorny destinations, yet he can't for the life of him suppress the force and grace of that singular delivery of his. Even these raw first works of a new stage that is now tough going seem likely in the end to reach the ears of people out of sympathy with his radical politics, not because of the yelling powers of polemics but because of the carrying powers of a poet's voice. Godard can make a silly film or an endearing one, but he can't make an ineloquent one. His path now goes away from narrative completely, and it isn't exactly a paved highway. "It will be a process—a road—eventually leading to fiction, but it's still not a road, it's bushes and trees," he said lately in an interview by the Grove Press film distributors. Some people will have a bumpy ride through these films. But the radical young will recognize a comrade, and other people fond of Godard—of the company of this gifted, taxed man who is always pitted against some difficult new problem set by himself—will sit out the jolts and trust the driver.

The voice of the two films is political and speculative, raised to a pitch of slightly mysterious tension because of Godard's own urgencies. There is a faint trill in the air, the unmistakable upper harmonic of somebody at work on something original and hard to do. Godard is intent now on making "revolutionary films" in which everything will be concrete and nothing suave. He calls himself and his comrades the Dziga-Vertov Group, after the Russian whom he regards as the only true Marxist filmmaker. "We took his name for our group not to emphasize one person but to indicate a program, to raise a flag," he said in April of this year. (Later, with his own half-secret sense of ridiculousness, he said very seriously that there are, for the moment, just two people in this group, the other being a comrade called Jean-Pierre Gorin. Gorin added that there is sometimes only one.) Godard now wants to make films that are as dogmatic as possible. He wants to strip them of the emotionalism that he obviously finds wheedling and mechanical in traditional movies, including his own early ones. He wants to pound people with language. Godard is the most literary of filmmakers, in a sense that is different from the usual one, with his way of plastering words even across images—on posters, in graffiti, on children's blackboards—as well as pouring them into the sound track by the bucketful. In these new movies, it is almost as if he wanted to attack people with so much repetition and so much claptrap that they will be whipped into hauling themselves, bleeding and half-concussed, across some threshold of boredom into another way of seeing things. And yet, in spite of his irate theories and his intentness on creating the texture of a gaudy, comfortless, grainless present where what is to come is somehow more palpable than what is current, he keeps arriving at moments of film that are agelessly composing.

Godard has always been obsessed with the energy that can be released by pitting opposites against each other: kindergarten colors, world-worn reflexes; pious mottoes, godless mishaps; computer voices, real blood; windbag commentaries, suffering people; clever creator, simple-minded creation. This, say his films as they perpetually tug apart in the middle, is what it's like to be living merrily when something is terribly wrong, to be in a jet filled with air-hostess smiles and the sound of the "Wedding March" on the Muzak system when no one in the plane can recover the feeling of what it was ever really like to grin and when no one there believes in marriage. Our jet—capitalism, industrialism, revisionism, the whole shooting match —is going nowhere, say the films, and some expert pilot had better hijack it.

In "Mao" and "Pravda," Godard is pushing documentary to a place it has never been. The sound nearly always plays against the image. "Pravda," a newsreel collage of Czechoslovakia just after the Soviet invasion, has a commentary that sometimes lets slip some unslippable sardonic remark about the getting of the photograph, which has an effect rather like the relief of suddenly hearing a technician being mutinous on the air on TV by accident. Often the "Pravda" commentary goes into an extended pastiche of a conversation between Lenin and Rosa Luxemburg, deliberately unconvincing and batteringly trite: "That's what we've got to do, Rosa," says fake Lenin earnestly. "We've got to organize these causes and sounds along antirevisionist lines." Which practically makes you want to thump the screen with fury that such a bright filmmaker can talk such garbage to contrary-minded purpose—except that he then goes even further and becomes peculiarly soothing with his morganatic marriage of overbred sound and simple image by linking the high-flying talk to an inexplicable and beautiful shot of a red rose lying in a puddle. Or there will be sermonizing about politically meaningful work, delivered in the most shop-soiled, most politically drained words, but going with touching photographic attentiveness given to a factory worker who is a very evident victim of political meaninglessness, undermined by work done for an unknown boss in the

cause of wages, and not of the thing produced. The words are intentionally not acted; they sound generally as if they were being
parroted by people who didn't understand what they were saying,
often going back over a sentence or mistaking a word. "No, Rosa,
no longer be satisfied with true texts over false images," says the
enacted Lenin, in this film in which Godard puts a phony-sounding
text over images that are unquestionably true: third-hand text,
spontaneous images; ungainly text, graceful images; fidgety text,
serene images. The commentary will gabble through theories about
production and wealth while there is a Gainsborough shot of people
loading hay onto a cart. And always there is this Brechtian dislocation somewhere, reminding us that a movie is not real but only an
aping of the real, and that while traditional filmmakers are concerned with the reflection of reality, Godard is concerned with the
reality of the reflection. In both these films, it is clear that something slightly cracks Godard's heart—mad stranger though he will
be in most people's experience of what is saddening—about the
ebbing of a man's vital energy when he sells it to an unknown
employer and when his capacity for work is a piece of merchandise
up for bidding. "Mao," made in England, begins with an amazing
tracking shot to the right that lasts about ten minutes through an
English car factory. The shriek of saws and lathes is frightful. It
becomes more than you can put up with. But it does last only ten
minutes. What happens to the men in the shot, who are working a
forty-hour week? The commentary mutters, barely audible in the
din, that what a car-factory worker produces for himself is not the
thing he assembles but money. One grows fond of Godard's way
of talking to himself about his political worries. It sounds very like
him. A cracked whisper, urgent. Sometimes one that can hardly be
made out. "Organize." "Strike." Notes to himself. In "Mao," he
varies it sometimes by having a little girl's voice repeat bits of a
Marxist history lesson after a teacher. Or there will be theories
spouted about Women's Lib, and awkward, groping interviews about
it, over a placidly repetitive shot of a naked girl going slowly in and
out of doors, and then over an endlessly held closeup of another
girl's naked hips and thighs. The tiny shifts in the position of a leg
or a forearm are mesmerizing, and weirdly brilliant in their aesthetic
justness. I can imagine that there might be an uproar from some
Women's Lib hard-liners about the exploitation of nudity, but
Godard is the hardest-liner of them all and he is out on his own.

This study of a bit of a torso is classical art, and it's protective of women in some very far-out, moving way. The film ends with a magnificent and, again, endless shot of a bleeding arm feeling with its fingers into the soil, clenching into a Maoist fist, and then groping slowly toward what turns out to be a red flag—halfmade revolution —in a slow tracking shot that goes in the direction opposite to the one in the car factory, with its opening study of a blood-red, half-made car. "Mao" is quite a picture, tense and shapely, with Cruik-shank's or Hogarth's attention to the bony English face, and torn apart aesthetically in order to reflect a struggle that Godard deeply minds about. The fight he sets up between words and images is a metaphor for political struggle and for our own sense of concrete reality, where there is always a disjuncture between what we say or think and what we experience. You are not a unity, say these films. You are trying to be a unity, but the fact is you are not.

ESSAYS

Form and Substance, or the Avatars of the Narrative

by MARIE-CLAIRE ROPARS-WUILLEUMIER

From *A bout de souffle* to *Pierrot le fou*, a number of similar elements allow us to reconstruct the plot of a similar story, in which the same type of anarchistic adventure briefly unites a man whose internal sureness makes his strength and an uncertain woman who eventually betrays him and thus casts him toward death. From one film to the next, however, one form has been broken, another has tried to take shape, while a changing world molds itself in its own image. The same type of confrontation can serve as a basis for comparison—and contrast—between the grey, secret (or parallel) police forces of *Le Petit soldat* and the red, white, and blue ones of *Made in U.S.A.*; on the other hand, from the prostitute in *Vivre sa vie* to the young woman in *Deux ou trois choses que je sais d'elle*, the twelve tableaux have exploded into a few pieces, and the study of an individual has been expanded within the framework of an apartment complex and a city—"elle" (her), which is to say Paris. And if this cyclical return of similar themes and characters traces obsessive variations on a universe belonging only to Godard, who has always belonged to a "band of outsiders," the perpetual changes in form which, in a few years' time, have rendered abstractly identical elements unrecognizable, force us to seek elsewhere—and precisely within these very forms

From Jean-Luc Godard au dela du recit, *Etudes Cinematographiques, no. 57–61 (Paris: Lettres modernes, 1967), pp. 17–34. Copyright © 1967 by Lettres modernes. Reprinted by permission of the publisher. Translated by Royal S. Brown. This essay also appeared in the author's anthology* L'Ecran de la memoire, *coll. Esprit "La Condition humaine" (Paris: Seuil, 1970).*

—the meaning of an artistic output whose evolution seems to follow quite closely that of its basic language.

Indeed, starting from the means of expression in order to understand the meaning becomes, with Godard, even more necessary as a technique than for any other director. The prime reason for this is that Godard, in referring explicitly to the phenomenological point of view that refuses to see language as the simple translation of a previously conceived idea, has himself defined the directing of a movie as a creative form of thought;[1] and it is only this form that allows us to comprehend and fully appreciate a thought which, if one were to be limited to the professed concepts or declarations of Godard himself, would seem singularly evasive and rather impersonal—nothing is more deceptive than taking literally either what Godard has to say himself or the antithetical ideas he gives to his characters: the incoherent brilliance of the former is belied by the fragmented banality of the latter, thus offering both the nonbelievers as well as the hagiographers fertile ground in which to exercise their respective functions. But if form constitutes the best introduction to Godard's work, it is particularly because, throughout his career, form has sought its own way and manifested itself, rather than remaining in the background, thus bringing about a different manner of considering it. For if this phenomenon characterizes all of modern art and not just Godard, it takes on a special resonance in the latter's work inasmuch as it allows for an investigation into the effectiveness and present-day chances of the means of expression. And since this investigation goes to the very heart of Godard's creativity, it orients the general direction of his work and gives authenticity to its meaning.

The starting point of everything in Godard is a break with a certain means of communication. Godard's earliest intentions, in *A bout de souffle,* were to tell a story while at the same time opposing the traditional (at least in France) ways of handling a plot;[2] his most recent intentions to date can be seen in *Made in U.S.A.,* in which an attack on America is accomplished through a violent

---

[1] The statement referred to here can be found on pages 33–34 in this book in the interview from l'*Express*, 27 July 1961 (editor's note).

[2] "What I wanted to do was start with a conventional story and remake, but in a different way, all the movies that had ever been made." Quoted by Jean Collet, *Jean-Luc Godard* (Paris: Seghers, 1963), coll. "Cinéma d'aujourd'hui," p. 61.

destruction of American cinema,[3] which is annihilated by its own weapons through the simple marriage (Godard style) between Walt Disney and Humphrey Bogart. Between these two extremes, one finds all of the constantly broadening stages of an adventure in which the cinema is seeking to define itself; each stage is always broader than the preceding; for Godard is the first to break with his own methods—the audience is invited to follow a storyline in ways that are always different from the established ones—even if they have been established in only one film—in which the only raison d'être for a given subject would be to simply take place as it is being told. If Resnais brought radical innovations to the narrative potential of the cinema, it was by transforming this potential from within, by causing its expressive impact to be transferred from one aesthetic system to another through distention, confrontation, or distortion. Godard, on the other hand, began to attack this potential from the outside with his first feature film, never hiding his destructive intentions. This is most evident in *Une Femme est une femme,* in which a parody on musical comedies is repudiated through the use of particularly obvious theatrical techniques; the latter, however, are themselves attacked in the circus scenes, which in turn remain without any support at all: here, a deliberate effort is made to play the cinema against itself in a series of satirical shots and reverse shots, as it were. This deliberate undermining is already at work, in a more covert but more profound manner, in *A bout de souffle;* but it is in *Vivre sa vie* that it reaches, in a first stage, its high point. For when Godard suppresses, in *A bout de souffle,* all of the dramatic links not only between scenes but also *within* the scenes and even within a single sequence, he is tearing down logical continuity and therefore the very finality of the storyline. By cutting out all transitions and explanations, Godard is able to bring the audience's eyes and its attention back to the image itself, which he preserves in a kind of pristine state by divorcing it from the role of intermediary it usually plays vis-à-vis the succession of shots. What was at first attributed to casualnesss

---

[3] "It seems to me that everything needs to be rediscovered about every problem. To do that, there is only one solution, and that is to avoid American cinema. If you wish, my own way of denouncing the Soviet-American collusion is to deplore the fact that the present dream of the Soviets is to imitate Hollywood at the very moment the Americans no longer have anything to tell us." From *Le Nouvel observateur,* 12 October 1966; interview with Sylvain Regard.

on Godard's part (on the part of his characters) must actually be ascribed (as it soon was) to the invention of a new aesthetic.

In *A bout de souffle,* which is filled with holes, allusions, and interferences, and in which Godard emphasizes the high points and the low points while using elliptical techniques to slough off the preceding actions as well as the consequences of a given event, a storyline takes shape in opposition to a narrative tradition that was originally invented in order to overcome the inherent discontinuity of cinematic expression by establishing an invisible continuity in which the theoretical logic of a narrative superimposed its own syntax over the true language of the cinema.[4] All the old habits of the eye, which had been trained to forget the breaks between the shots in order to reconstruct, through the succession of images, the linear evolution of a character or an action, are therefore totally upset. But in deemphasizing the abstract continuity of the images in favor of the concrete presence of each individual shot, Godard is aiming at a new form of montage, rather than at eliminating it. From a series of clashing shots, which are thus liberated from their function as transitions, is born a new kind of narrative whose continuity depends on the subjective attention that links them together, and not on any exterior events which might unite them. And if the characters take form suddenly, in a precipitous style in which every bit of "dead air" has been eliminated, it

---

[4] Christian Metz (in "The Cinema: Language or Means of Expression?" in *Communications,* No. 4, 1965), giving a scientific basis to various ideas that had remained scattered until then, has strongly demonstrated how the cinema cannot be a language, inasmuch as its smallest unit of expression—the shot—is the equivalent of an entire sentence, and not of a word; therefore, cinematic linguistics can only be of the syntactic variety, and not the morphological; and it is stylistic organization which constitutes the cinema as a language.

Nonetheless, it would seem that the stylistic implantation of certain forms creates certain paralinguistic habits in the audience. Thus, it is not difficult to conceive that the initial efforts of directors to cover up the breaks caused by editing and to give to their "language" a logical continuity created a narrative tradition that causes the audience to forget the passages from one picture to the next and leads it to substitute the thread of a plot for the actual succession of pictures proposed by the director. It was not until certain novelists, such as Raymond Queneau, that great forerunner, came along and literally imitated cinematic editing, that directors became aware of the discontinuity inherent to their form of art. And it is no doubt because of the influence of these novelists that modern filmmakers are tending to restore to the cinema this *acquired* discontinuity. In order to accomplish this, they have to completely overthrow the narrative patterns familiar to the audience so that the perception elicited once again belongs to the domain of aesthetics.

is because the content of the shots is less important than the long race that gives life to certain shots (and in which even the conversations take on the form of a march, a dance, or a piece of music) and which, in the midst of the occasionally accelerated editing, causes them all to rush toward the end of the voyage, which is reached in the film's last shot.

It is no doubt with *Vivre sa vie* that Godard completely mastered for the first time the fundamental building block of his art: that precise, isolated, and superbly composed shot whose autonomy is further accentuated in *Vivre sa vie* by the division of the film into a series of subtitled tableaux.[5] But, in one part of the film which foreshadows *Made in U.S.A.*, all the forms of a new type of narrative, whose meaning grows entirely from the means of expression, depend on the movement given to this type of shot by the camera, and on the editing. The long takes in *Vivre sa vie* are animated at each instant by precise and repeated camera movements, which tirelessly trace in space the geometrical surroundings of a presence through which Godard tries to capture, as do the title shots with a face, the identity of a woman who wants to give herself only to herself. In *Une Femme mariée* and *Alphaville*, these fixed takes are broken by a whirling montage of lights and sounds, the reflections of a world of mutants. If paintings seem to win out in the central portion of *Pierrot le fou*, at the beginning of this picture they seem to be hurled against each other, changing all the surroundings into pure, colored vibration. And in *Made in U.S.A.*, Godard alternates the recitativelike immobility of a pensive face, which soon dissolves into nothing but eyes and a mouth, with lacerating flashes of a few telescoped shots in which people are thrown against a wall and nailed there, along with freedom.

---

[5] Jean Collet has particularly emphasized the autonomy of the shot in Godard's work, but he tends to attribute this to the aesthetic of dramatization. In truth, it is to the invention of a new style of editing, quite simply liberated from narrative conventions, rather than to a denial of editing, that one can attribute such a revolution. Quotations given by Collet himself in his book *Jean-Luc Godard*, pp. 83–84) show the importance Godard placed, as early as 1956, on reintroducing editing into the shot sequence: "It is possible, then, that it is not the job of staging to express, with as much precision as evidence, the existence of an idea or of its sudden bursting into the midst of the narrative, but that it is the job of editing to do so." This demand is justified by the presence of a new way of looking at the film and by the subjective role this plays in "destroying the notion of space in favor of the notion of time" (*Cahiers du cinéma*, No. 65, December 1956).

1. Jean-Luc Godard around 1967. Photo by Georges Pierre.

2. Godard and Brigitte Bardot (with black wig) during
the shooting of *Le Mépris*. Copyright 1963 by Jean-Louis
Swiners. Reprinted by permission of *Réalités*.

3. Godard, sans dark glasses, during the shooting of *Le
Mépris*. Copyright 1963 by Jean-Louis Swiners. Reprinted
by permission of *Réalités*.

4. Albert Juross in *Les Carabiniers:* "One of those faces the cinema has lost the secret of finding." Reprinted by permission of *Cahiers du Cinéma.*

5. Anna Karina in *Bande à part:* "The camera always kept its distance with respect to these characters. . . ." Reprinted by permission of *Cahiers du Cinéma.*

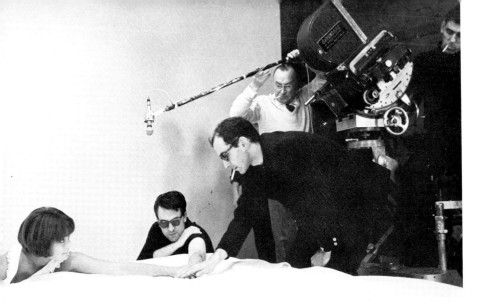

6. Macha Meril, Jean José Richer (hand stand-in for
Bernard Noel), Godard, and (at far right) Raoul Coutard
during the shooting of *La Femme mariée*. Photo by Georges
Pierre.

7. Claude Brasseur and Sami Frey in *Bande à part:* "The
little suburban cousins of the Belmondo of *A Bout de
Souffle*. . . ." Reprinted by permission of *Cahiers du
Cinéma*.

8. Eddie Constantine in *Alphaville:* A face, a "serie noire" novel *(The Big Sleep),* and a gun. Reprinted by permission of *Cahiers du Cinéma.*

9. Anna Karina in *Pierrot le fou.* This still appeared on the front page of *Les Lettres françaises* along with Aragon's "What Is Art, Jean-Luc Godard?" and was dedicated by Godard "to *Les Lettres françaises,* the only newspaper to publish poetry on its first page." Reprinted by permission of *l'Avant Scène.*

10. Anna Karina and Eddie Constantine in *Alphaville:* "A universe in which light makes holes in the night the way poetry interrupts silence or noise." Reprinted by permission of *Cahiers du Cinéma.*

11. Godard, Karina, and Jean-Paul Belmondo during the
shooting of *Pierrot le fou*. Photo by Georges Pierre.

12. Godard burying Belmondo and Karina in the sand
during the shooting of *Pierrot le fou*. Photo by Georges
Pierre.

13. Jean-Pierre Léaud in *Masculin-Féminin:* "The image of a young man for all times—nervous, worried, unhappy, despondent." Reprinted by permission of *Cahiers du Cinéma.*

14. Godard and Anne Wiazemsky during the May 1968 events in Paris. Reprinted by permission of *Cahiers du Cinéma.*

15. "The body of Eve Democracy across a mighty camera crane" in *One Plus One*. Reprinted by permission of *Cahiers du Cinéma*.

16. Anne Wiazemsky and Yves Alphonso in *Vladimir and Rosa*. Reprinted by permission of Grove Press, Inc.

Thus, the linear continuity of the exterior narrative totally disappears. But at the same time it is replaced, through the rhythm imparted by varied montages to these separated and essential shots, by an internalized order perceived by the audience in proportion to its ability to forget the dramatic content of the shot and to take notice of the form that makes it exist. Nonetheless, this form—and here we arrive at the beginning of a second stage—becomes more and more complicated as it becomes freer. The freeze "snapshots" [6] that appear for a second, well-surrounded by the space in which they are inserted, and which still leave their dazzling mark on *Le Mépris,* become instants that are both pregnant with meaning and totally ambiguous. In Godard, space becomes less and less a manner of expressing the temporality of the individual; instead it becomes more and more the image of a piece of time, of a fragment of life containing an inexhaustible totality whose slightest movements must be captured and put together. Therefore the abstract elements composing the traditional storyline are replaced by a symphonic recomposition of their discernible parts. Thus one finds in Godard's films a proliferation of expressive elements that are presented simultaneously to all of the senses—posters, letters, colors, neon signs, songs, airplane noises, and muddled voices, names, faces, music, paintings, films by Dreyer or Lang, quotations that are either spoken, written, recited, or shown, absurd puns, and shaggy-dog stories: all of these elements pile up alongside Vietnam, newspaper columns for the lovelorn, the Ben Barka affair, or *Eighteen Lessons on Industrial Society.* Autonomy is thus restored to each instant, which is thereby able to take on the full force of what existence offers to the perception in an instant, a season, a crisis. To reproach Godard for overusing quotations and for his predilection for long speeches is to ignore the fact that these sentences are used as objects and not as meaning, the latter taking form only through the global confrontation between all the discernible objects noticed by the audience, which finds itself located at the point where all of these objects converge. "I am a painter with letters," Godard says of himself. "I want to restore everything, mix everything up and say everything." [7] Life does not speak for itself, and it is only in bringing music and painting into the cinema, in add-

[6] Collet, p. 46.
[7] *Le Nouvel observateur,* 12 October 1966.

ing colors to pictures and sounds to words, that it becomes possible to express life.[8] More so than any other, Godard's means of expression represents an attempt to integrate all means of expression into the cinema. Thus, in order for the spectator to fully grasp this unique language, it is important for him never to concentrate on one expressive element at the expense of another, but rather to accept globally all the elements without trying to understand each one separately.

In order for this immediate communication of totality to take place, a guiding rhythm must be present to blend together all the themes that pile up and to draw them into a movement which, through confrontation, allows only the end result to emerge. Thus, the confusion created by the editing and the sound-mixing is essential to the final clarity of the main idea; and this confusion becomes all the more meaningful when one notes that it becomes the very matter of the narrative, which is defined both through this confusion and in opposition to it. "Velasquez, at the end of his life, was no longer painting definite things, but what is to be found between definite things." This quotation from Élie Faure, which opens *Pierrot le fou*, sets the tone for an itinerary whose markedly polyphonic orchestration is intended to lead to the communication of the undefinable. And if, early in his career, Godard's critical writings turned out to be categorical, they provided the springboard for another, *positive* form of expression which became rooted in a meaning invented from its own means—a break with the traditional forms of communication provided, bit by bit, the basis for a methodical investigation into the means of communication.

It is in *Le Mépris* that we see clearly, for the first time, that double aspect of the means of expression that permits the fulfillment of language by talking about language. If Godard's earlier films emphasized the difficulty of communication between two people who revolve undecidedly about the core of an impossible dia-

---

[8] "For us, with the cinema, it's another matter, and first of all life, which is nothing new, but difficult to express . . . all you can do is live it and die it, but talk about it . . . well, there are books, yes, but in the cinema, we don't have books, all we have is music and painting, and these things as well, as you know, are lived and hardly ever talked about. With *Pierrot*, then, perhaps you understand why there is what there is to be said about it? . . . because life is its subject, with cinemascope and color as its attributes, because I am, after all, broadminded." *Cahiers du cinéma*, No. 171 (October 1965).

logue; and if *Le Mépris* is the story par excellence of a misunderstanding, in which the break between two persons is neither expressed nor explained, the latter film also turns the problem around
by presenting the problem of the very possibilities of speaking. In
as early a film as *Vivre sa vie,* Nana listens in silence as Brice
Parain explains language to her; and even before that, in *Une
Femme est une femme,* titles of detective novels provide the super-
structure for the marital quarrel. But *Le Mépris* offers a new step
toward the discovery of this meaning—from this film on, the theme
of the couple becomes secondary while the solitude of the individual becomes the solitude of a being whose own language
escapes him.

For *Le Mépris* offers, simultaneously with the story of a couple
breaking up, the story of a film being made. The mediocrity of
the one story is set against the Homeric grandeur of the other, in
which mental lucidity is combined with the blue splendor of the
sea. It is an absurd splendor, however, since the seascape is inhuman in its triumph: the world of Homer, the world of blossom-
ing intelligence and controlled language no longer belong to our
time; the scriptwriter, who is the victim of the inexplicable contempt of his wife, is also scorned by Fritz Lang, the director. For
the scriptwriter opposes Lang's version of the *Odyssey* with a psy-
choanalytical version which would communicate, behind the harmonious universe of the Greeks, impotence and chaos. The cinema
—that *art which has no future and which substitutes for our eyes a
world that corresponds to our desires*—is denounced as it is in the
process of exercising this illusion, which is emphasized by the false,
made-up statues, the buxom sirens, and the victorious Ulysses
running across the dispossessed scriptwriter, whose wife dies in a
setting whose red and blue colors are those of the myth. Nothing
is left, at the end of *Le Mépris,* of the false symmetry that is occasionally established between the myth and the present-day story;
and the formal beauty of each shot is belied by the narrative itself,
while the tragic overtones of the work arise from the difference
that is perceived between the chaotic state of the real world and
the polished, ordered language of the forms.

It is here that Godard's early love of the cinema as a critic can
be put into its proper historical perspective. The clash between
Godard and his era takes place because of the discovery that the
world has changed, since former means of expression are no

longer sufficient to communicate its meaning; and if the world is perishing because of its inability to find a language, the only chance it has left lies in the invention of a new art form, an art form stripped of traditional logical structures and receptive at each instant to everything contained in an instant. It is therefore easy to see a correspondence between a means of expression that takes in all the means of expression without settling on any one of them, on the one hand, and that search, which with *Le Mépris* becomes a central theme, that leads Godard toward the definition of his era through an attempt to find the language of his era.

It is this direction that gives the three films following *Le Mépris* their true depth, since it allows us not to confuse the subject with the meaning of each film. To see *Une Femme mariée* as a satire on advertising and *Alphaville* as a mildly futuristic forecast of the technocratic era is to not see in these films the same point of departure that marks *Pierrot le fou,* in which a Rimbaud-like effort is made to rediscover poetic eternity. Even Godard's attempts at sociology should not lead us into misconceptions. For Godard lacks both the sociologist's rigorous methods of investigation and his ability to scientifically delineate the fields to be explored. The description of the married Woman would be little more than a superficial investigation spread out over a rather unrepresentative milieu if the film did not literally burst with that dazzling inventory of "signs of the times," through which Godard's cinematic language takes form and through which a language for the modern generation tries to define itself. This is the first time such a language has been used with such force. Wavering between Racine and body-building advertisements, looking at television and listening to Purcell, snowed under by radio commercials, magazines, illuminated signs, arrows, posters, graffiti, and records; trapped in the center of a whirlwind of words, gestures, things, and noises, the married Woman, in the space of a single day, turns to newspapers and to men (her husband and her lover) with equal devotion in an effort to find anything that can tell her the truth. Moving with her, but in the most chaotic state, is a kind of stream of consciousness monologue, of which the audience can hear only occasional, almost inaudible bits and snatches. Of this attempt at a kind of awareness, of this woman who notices at each instant the discord between what she perceives and what she is—a discord that is just as profound as the one that separates the beauty of nudity in love from the lewd-

ness of advertisements for women's underwear—Godard makes it a
point of showing only the itinerary; not once does any kind of
coherent language, any kind of controlled thought win out, in the
universe of this modern Bérénice (Racine), over the disjointed
review of all the means of expression that "unform" the modern
world. "In the theater, there's a text," says the actor (Bernard Noël).
But not in the cinema. The theater belongs to yesterday, the cinema
to today. The wrong approach to this film would be a literal and
isolated interpretation of the conversations that are held at each
stage of the investigation. On the contrary, these attempts at speech
must be appreciated in all their absurd and pompous inadequacy,
of which the maid's monologue, taken from Céline's *Mort à crédit*,
offers the best example in the form of a self-parody. But this inadequacy is also stressed by each appearance of the commenting voice,
which takes no shape and which becomes fulfilled only when the
director is able to capture and gather together, in a single melody
produced by the camera, all the sensations capable of translating
this voice. For the victory of the cinema resides in the defeat of
coherent language, in the triumph of disorder, which only on occasion becomes, in those rare moments of joy during which the
editing becomes lyrical, the inexpressible goal that is sought:
lyricism, that harmony between being and language, can today be
only instantaneous and ephemeral. The greatness of *Une Femme
mariée* is that it shows the difficult search for this lyricism, and not
the fulfillment.

If the married Woman moves within the universe of language,
within its prosaic elaboration, *Alphaville* plunges outside it to the
very heart of its poetic rebirth. Once again, the meaning of the
film is established in opposition to its subject—with this mythical
city where poets are hunted down and computers are omnipotent,
Godard offers less a foreshadowing of a dead world of the future
than the present-day discovery of an extremely ancient era in which
poetry had an absolute existence. Surrounded by the destruction
of their language, which is breaking down bit by bit and becoming
less expressive, while at the same time human gestures become more
and more mechanical and voices become less and less personalized,
the inhabitants of Alphaville become carriers of the very "germ"
they are trying to wipe out or ignore; for when certain words
disappear and the syntax is broken down, these same words emerge
in a freed state from the censored dictionary. In this pure state, they

are learned afresh and are thus restored to their poetic state. It is these words that Godard seeks out, snatching from immense sonorous masses—just as the lights from headlights, lamps, and fires snatch the city from the night—isolated fragments of an Éluard poem, bits of poetry, islets of ancient terms which have been conquered and renewed, thus creating through the cinema a series of harmonious instants in which Éluard's poem, instead of being illustrated, seems to be recreated.

Alphaville—and there should be no doubt about it—suggests the opposite side of the world of *Une Femme mariée*. Out of the banal greyness that uniformly dominated *Une Femme mariée* but which, in *Alphaville*, is seen in only a few anachronistic shots suggesting the "outside countries" (actually the ones we live in), grows a galactic universe in black and white, a universe in which light makes holes in the night the way poetry interrupts silence or noise. Across from the impossible language of *Une Femme mariée* arises the other side—the rediscovery of song. In order for this to take place, one must accept color—white as well as black, both of which are unreal—and insert into this different world a dancelike rhythm, a prolonged echo of those rare happy moments which occasionally accelerate the harsh progress of the married woman. The recording of pictures and the recording of words, therefore, take place within a same movement that changes words into pictures and pictures into words through a similar type of montage that had rarely, before this film, attained such intensity and such richness; the film is edited in a manner that invents, shot after shot, an unknown country, separated from its surroundings, projected far ahead of the present (but in order to return just as far into the past) into the sources of myth and poetry—Lemmy Caution, in snatching Natasha from the night, becomes a new Orpheus. But it is at the moment of this victory, at the moment of the return, that the film stops, leaving us at the borders of those "outside countries" whose dismal nature is well known to us. What has happened is that the world of *Alphaville* itself inspired poetry—for if poetry transforms the night into light, it is only the night that can permit the birth of light. Once it has been rediscovered, poetry can only become lost once again, and it is precisely because it had been lost that it constantly shines in the night of *Alphaville*, in which Godard proposes the only poetic dimension that is accessible to our times and to the cinema, namely a kind of nostalgia. The true subject of *Alphaville* revolves around a new version of the orphic quest, in which, no matter what variations are made within the myth, only Hell permits the possibility of song, only death the illumination of life. But in *Alphaville,* for the first time, it is in seeking out his own song that Orpheus has begun his voyage.

Poetry that is rediscovered by dint of its loss—poetry that is lost as soon as it is rediscovered: *Pierrot le fou* is the film of poetry possessed, of an impossible poetry. It is a film that finally brings the voyage to a close. The impasse of *Pierrot* is represented by a particular construction which transposes two poems by Rimbaud—the one (the opening of "l'Éternité") is murmured at the end of the film and materialized near the middle: *The sea gone away with the sun . . .* ; the other is never spoken, but it inspires the entire first part of the film, in which the *crossing of France by its rivers* brings strongly to mind the unmooring of the *Bateau ivre,* which flees towards the sea once the *haulers have been nailed naked* (those topless and semitopless women of the advertising reception at the beginning) *to colored stakes* (red, green, and yellow walls against which heads and busts are brought cruelly into relief). The opposition of these two poems illustrates the abyss which, in the cinema, separates the search for poetry from the imitation of its structures. Just as the first part of *Pierrot le fou* is animated by the rhythm of a feverish departure, each incident of which is reduced, for the audience, to a colored sensation, so is the central part of the film, the "Eden," frozen into long, fixed shots in which immobilized space seems to be enclosing time within eternal images, whereas actually each of the component parts of this poetic language, whose poetry can spring only from the instant and dies from being trapped by the movement of time, reappears, distinctly separated and perceived in isolation. Thus, dance is no longer a vibration of space simply adding the perception of movement to the perception of a body, but a spectacle; language is no longer words snatched from voices and confronted by colors, but a type of speech; and while the characters are reduced, almost like simplistic archetypes, to their essences, thought affirms its heavy presence, both signifying the intention of the film and annihilating it: "The problem is one of poetic continuity," reads a fragment of a journal written by Pierrot, the writer. If the last part of the film, destroying this impossible continuity, returns, in a slower rhythm, to the movement of the beginning, it is because Pierrot has withdrawn bit by bit from this impossible world, from this "anywhere-out-of-this-world" where life cannot last.

Here, one runs into a contradiction that arises between the attempts to understand Godard and the very existence of these attempts, and it is a contradiction which, henceforth, will be resolved only through division and separation. *Pierrot le fou* marks both a new departure and a limit—basing the narrative around the search for a means of expression, Godard ends up destroying this narrative when the nature of this means of expression is revealed. From *Le Mépris* on, this essential nature always turns, in one way or another, about poetry, whether it be through Homer, Racine, Éluard, Rimbaud, or, henceforth, Queneau. For it is the nature of poetry to reveal in an instant the absolute, to give an immediate possession of totality. There is no such thing as a long poem of pure poetry, since poetry is created outside time and seeks immobility. The central portion of *Pierrot le fou,* in which only space reigns and in which the moving signs of *Une Femme mariée* and the flashing signals of *Alphaville* are replaced by artistically composed cine-paintings, represents the impossible image of this stoppage of time, of this projection into a world that escapes, once and for all, from history.[9] It is an impossible image, since the success of this search implies the failure of the cinema: to stop time, one has to destroy the narrative; poetic immobility is the opposite of cinematic temporality, whose structure, determined by the very movement of the pictures, each one evoking, in its own mobility, the movement of the next, is based on this necessary succession and implies the preservation of a narrative, even a fragmented one. If there is an art in which poetry can only be born as a surplus taking place at the outer limits of the adventure, it is the cinema, which is, more than any other, a moving art. From his collaboration with André Breton, Georges Franju had already arrived at the conclusion that true cinematic poetry lies not in the systematically shocking images of surrealistic films but in those minor moments when it floats and tends to come to the surface in spite of the desires of the director.[10]

[9] The critical analysis devoted by Bernard Dort to the themes in Godard's work leads him to denounce Godard as an "excessive romantic" (*Les Temps modernes,* No. 235, December 1965).

[10] See *Positif,* No. 56 (November 1963): "Franjudex"; Interview with Georges Franju and Jacques Champreux.

From Godard's first series of films to his second, in which the same basic themes seem to reappear, it is the very existence of the narrative that is questioned, and not simply its form. If, in *A bout de souffle, Une Femme mariée,* and *Alphaville,* a second film begins to slip in more and more profoundly behind the subject, the narrative nonetheless follows its course because of the distance that is always maintained between the search and the object of the search, between the apparent subject and the true theme; and the subjective presence of Godard, forming a kind of first-person style, does not indicate—as some seem to maintain—a "cinema of poetry," [11] since it is precisely this discernible presence of the camera, as it watches, gathers, hesitates, seeks, and captures, which gives the film its future and maintains its "collage" technique within a narrative perspective. *Pierrot le fou* marks a turning point to the degree that its composition wavers between two tendencies: the renewal of the narrative technique in the first part, in which the free editing style elicits a new form of adventure that is totally detached from events and reduced to its simplest discernible movement; and the destruction of the narrative in the second part, in which various distancing techniques (titles, subtitles, chapters, and commentaries) serve first and foremost to erase the future possibilities of the action by preceding them, thus leaving the field open to a poetic structure. The gap between the subject of the narrative and the theme of the search disappears more and more as the one gives way upon meeting the other: *Masculin-Féminin,* which is forced into immobility by the abandonment of any narrative, represents a series of investigations that necessarily remain external, since there is nothing there

[11] In a paper that was presented at the Pesaro festival in 1965, and which the *Cahiers du cinéma* reproduced in its entirety in its issue No. 171, Pasolini develops at great length his ideas on "this cinema of poetry," which would be particularly represented by the cinema of Godard, Bertolucci, or the Antonioni of *The Red Desert.* Characterized by a specifically poetic language, these works are supposed to have as their true heroes style itself, the description of a character's state of mind serving only as a narrative alibi beneath which a sub-film is supposed to take place. This idea seems debatable in that it presupposes the total assimilation of subjective language with poetic language. Actually, the first-person of Godard's style is more reminiscent of Joyce or the French "nouveau roman" than it is of the language of poets; furthermore, the reality of the pictures often superimposes an objective counterpoint over this subjective presence. It is the criterium of time, more than of character or even syntax, that allows us to make a clear distinction between poetry and the novel. And the constant presence of "narrativity" in Godard's best films offers us a cinema whose effect, rather than structure, should be poetic.

to give them an order or to orient them, and since the camera withdraws definitively from the situation, leaving it up to the various things filmed to take on their own meaning; thus the value of these behavior studies depends uniquely upon the powers of a kind of *cinéma-vérité,* whose insufficiency is brought out by Godard's artificial use of the technique. The lie-filled police inquiry that closes the film can only, therefore, be aimed at the film itself, which was limited to seizing necessarily insignificant appearances, and speeches whose stupidity, if it cannot be blamed on the characters (since the investigation is admittedly poorly oriented), must necessarily be turned against the investigator himself. *Masculin-Féminin* thus seems to have been shot completely in a vacuum, and it appears to serve uniquely as a self-denunciation by condemning its own uselessness. And this non-film is followed, in *Deux ou trois choses que je sais d'elle,* with the film of a film, in which the "how it is" becomes a "how to say how it is," in which fragments close to those of *Vivre sa vie* or *Une Femme mariée* are presented in their raw state, while Godard asks questions on their meaning while quoting Merleau-Ponty.

"I watch myself filming," Godard said about *Deux ou trois choses,* "and people can hear me thinking." [12] This poorly integrated heritage from the French "new novel" has had a deadly effect upon Godard. His cinematic style, which, up until this film, had been established within the destruction of thought, is now limited uniquely to the consciousness of this style and therefore uniquely to the manifestation of this thought, whether it be personal or quoted: spoken language, from which Godard more than anybody else had been able to make a sonorous mass in which only a few words had the right to emerge to the level of discernibility, is reborn in the heaviness of clarified meditation, in which the dynamic element of a narrative no longer blurs the literary composing elements.

It is in this manner that the search for a means permitting the expression of things is resolved at its limits through the simple recording of things expressing themselves or of Godard expressing things. It is not unimportant to note that this abandonment of the search coincides, in Godard, with a certain form of involvement within reality. If the problem of expression becomes bogged down in an impasse, the only solution—outside of silence—is to continue to speak without worrying any more about the language. But the triumph of the sociological ambitions of *Masculin-Féminin,* and the political orientation of the discourse of *Deux ou trois choses* suffer from the analytical deficiencies characteristic of a means of expression that always had global pretensions but that is rendered even more all-embracing through the abandonment of the narrative. If Godard has affirmed that the filmmaker, who has at his fingertips all the various means of expression must take in the totality of the world,[13] the organization of this totality into an organic unity is supposed to grow uniquely from the fragments that have been gathered. *Masculin-Féminin* would have no meaning until the other 121 similar films (of which this is supposed to be one of the three or four actually shot) were made. Of what Godard knows about "her," he proposes only "two or three things" which are presented in a primitive state, in an impossible state.

From the sociological point of view, as from the poetic point of view, it is the same temptation, either toward the immediate or toward the absolute, that causes the abandonment of the narrative. And it is quite indicative that in *Made in U.S.A.,* the assassination of poetry accompanies, and perhaps permits, the return to a narrative. It is a parodied return, to be sure, since, as in comic strips, each event and each color is reduced to its elementary form, and since, as already in *Pierrot le fou,* the characters neither say nor do, but rather say that they are saying, or that they have done, or that they will do . . . each time in an almost inaudible fashion. But this parody is necessary here not so that an untemporal world can be dreamed of, but so that a moment in the death of this dream world can be witnessed. Here it is only the breaks in the narrative that permit the recreation of an historic break: the reduction of politicians to police agents in the Ben Barka affair, which touched off Godard's protest in this film, makes up, in this one case, for Godard's inability to organize a political language, and it permits him, in this political parody of a detective thriller, to emphasize his scorn for a political action dragged down to the level of a police action. Far from being effaced, the narrative is only in the process of being destroyed. And this aggressive destruction, which shoves machine-gun shots, flayed faces, and corpses in the face of the audience, and

[13] See *Le Monde,* 27 January 1967; interview by Yvonne Baby.

which forces blood to flow from bodies not in a series of pictorial "reds," as in *Pierrot le fou,* but in veritable streams—this destruction accompanies the last convulsions of a liberty that has been shot and crushed beneath sounds and colors. But the power of this lacerating, electric montage, in which each shot is reduced to a violent jolt that throws a character against a wall to the sound of such strident tones as airplane motors, has no meaning without the contrast of the extremely long, immobile scenes in which a single face murmurs its nostalgia: "Adieu life, adieu love" (the title of the book being read); "Oh Richard, oh my king" (the spoken sentence); "If I speak of time, it is because it no longer is" (the second stanza of the Queneau poem quoted after the death of the poet, the first stanza having evoked "the contracted nostrils" of the police agent killed by the poet). *Made in U.S.A.* is just as much the story of a murdered poet as it is the story of a police-political affair; and the tremendous beauty of this film no doubt lies in a rediscovered union between Godard's personal journal and the journal of an era. *Made in U.S.A.* is a poetic film because in it Godard settles his accounts with poetry, because in it poetry never stops dying beneath the blows of history, because *poetry equals truth.* And if the film's convulsions are like the throes of death, were we not aware that beauty would henceforth be convulsive? Once again, poetry, in the cinema, is born from its loss and from the instants that are both snatched from and provoked by its death.

In this film, as in all those following *Pierrot le fou* (but to a lesser degree, since the narrative retains its dynamic force here), a wild thought appears, growing only out of the instants. It is a thought *about* history, next to history, a thought that cannot be integrated into a means of expression and remain in its shadow. One cannot be unaware of the simplicity of Godard's ideas on the right and the left after having seen the last ten minutes of the film; and the extremely long bar scene, in spite of its instants of grace, does nothing to hide Godard's thoughts about the meaning and nonmeaning of sentences. And while the narrative itself, in its broken violence, poetically creates a world that is near, different, and terrifying, a world that should be left to speak for itself so that it could be confronted, Godard's words reintroduce into this world a series of thoughts that run contrary to the proper understanding of this story, which tragically signifies the lack of thought. For, as is always the case with Godard, the object—the film—gives more food for thought than the subject—Godard himself thinking.

Thus, a dialectic that will never find a stopping point continues to follow its course. Godard seems to have attempted to resolve this dialectic by shooting two films simultaneously—a vain effort, since one finds the same opposition within *Made in U.S.A.* as one finds between this film and *Deux ou trois choses*. The expressive unity of a means of expression seeking its own definition and becoming authentic by inventing its own meaning is finally destroyed by this very meaning, once it has been attained. And this endless dichotomy between form and substance reveals a growing contradiction between Godard's revolutionary aesthetic and his tendency to moralize. While his works take their fullest form through a profound attention to the ephemeral, unformulated instant, his personal needs lead him to transform this instant into a formulated absolute. And if the absence of this absolute is the source, in Godard's most beautiful films, of a totally modern nostalgia, it is in the success of the search for this absolute that the significant power of his language disappears.

The problem can best be defined in terms of the role played by the narrative: the more and more pronounced destruction of the narrative is the sign of this need for an absolute which, by rejecting the past as well as the future, could lead, in its extreme application, to the negation of the film itself. But when this destruction is not fully accomplished, the very attempt permits, to the highest degree, the inveiglement of the present, and it is this element that always reveals the presence of Godard. More than any other filmmaker, he has been able to materialize what had been dormant in the cinema for over a half a century, namely the sense of the present second in its multiple components, an element that is diametrically opposed to that eternal, untemporal present that paralyzed the language of the cinema for so long.[14] Godard's best films—*Une Femme mariée,*

[14] André-S. Labarthe, in his article devoted to *Une Femme est une femme* (*Cahiers du cinéma*, No. 125, November 1961), has stressed this sense of the present in Godard, this time of attention as opposed to the historic past, the tense of knowledge. But in attributing this restoring of the present to a return to the true sources of the cinema, that is, the picture, he seems to underestimate the importance of the conquest of temporal expression that has taken place during the course of the history of the cinema. The whole field of duration, of

Alphaville, Made in U.S.A.—represent a gradually developed collection of these privileged instants in which both communication and the denial of immediate reality enter into play; furthermore, Godard's taste for the most exclusively feminine characters reflects the very nature of these instants, which are both the most sensitized to the current fashions and the most nostalgic of the being.

For the distance that Godard maintains, from his first film on, with respect to the narrative, a distance whose role quite often appears ambiguous,[15] must be seen as constituting the very core of his entire output, and not simply as the means of making his various works "talk." It is the distance between the instant and eternity, between narrative and poetry, between subject and theme. It is a distance that is always tending to disappear but that must be maintained as the very condition on which the work exists. If the narrative runs against itself, it is precisely in this race that it takes form. And it is in the acceptance of one's powerlessness, in the recognition of the impossibility to understand and speak that Godard says and makes us understand the most . . . and in the most direct way.

Wavering between sociology and poetry, Godard's language finds its home ground when it is fixed in neither the one nor the other but rather when it seeks out both extremes: this look at the present world remains imbued with the dream of another world, while the search for this other world tirelessly takes place through an inventory, which becomes more and more total, of the various moving signs of life.

---

memory, also explored by Antonioni and Resnais, opens up between Godard's instants and the immobile present of the first cinematic narratives. In order for the present to be perceived, filmmakers had to first learn to express the past.

[15] The opposite extremes of this debate can be seen in the points of view of Michel Mesnil ("Du péché d'indifférence," *Esprit*, No. 12, December 1962) and Jean Collet (*Jean-Luc Godard*, pp. 52–53) concerning *Vivre sa vie*. Mesnil reproaches Godard for an ironic use of this distancing technique, which would seem to empty things, and particularly social reality, of their truth or their content; Collet, on the other hand, sees in this a means for Godard's keeping his distance while looking within himself at the same time.

Jean-Luc Godard: Nihilism versus Aesthetic Distantiation

by ROYAL S. BROWN

> Her: *Words are written one after the other and not upon each other.*
> Him: *Pictures and sounds, on the other hand,* can *be put upon each other.*
> Her: *Yes, because a picture is never a picture but a contradiction of a picture, and idem for a sound.*
>
> (LE GAI SAVOIR)

One often has the impression of a deliberate tendency toward self-destruction in Godard's art. Because Godard, rather remarkably, creates stylization out of reality, and because he tends to examine all the elments of his films with an equal, documentary precision, even if it is Eddie Constantine playing Lemmy Caution playing Eddie Constantine, the possibility strongly exists that audiences will be left in a kind of neutral, Beckettian no man's land in which all roads lead to nihilism, to blowing one's self up with dynamite. Yet one can always feel, in Godard's pre-1968 films, the director leaning toward the moral radicalism that would later complement his cinematic revolution, and it was almost inevitable that Godard become politically involved; this did, in fact, occur, ostensibly after the events of May 1968 in France. It was as if the director's cinematic radicalism—and the radicalism of many of the characters he portrayed but deliberately avoided identifying with—had eventually permeated the director's moral consciousness. As Godard himself has remarked, "In my case, I owe my political formation to the cinema, which has rarely happened until recently, if I am not wrong." [1] In this way Godard was able to negate all the work he had done prior to his political involvement (see the "Film and Revolution" interview in this book) and make films, such as *British Sounds, Pravda, Vent d'est, Vladimir and Rosa,* and so forth, that were basically anti-movies representing only one small, and apparently minor, tool of revolutionary action. *Vent d'est,* for instance, offers an often muddled soundtrack whose verbal tirades represent not only a kind of "confession" on Godard's part, in which the director attacks everything from his former methods to Sergei Eisenstein, but also an autocriticism of the film itself, a technique suggested by but never made explicit in Godard's earlier films. All this remains deadly serious and decidedly one-sided, even if many of the film's visual images, such as the eating scene with Gian Maria Volonte and a young woman at the end of the film, manifest a Godardian flippancy that seems less than wholly revolutionary. And in *Vladimir and Rosa,* Godard's (or more accurately the Dziga-Vertov group's) most recent film as of this writing, much of the narration is done in a cartoon style that harks all the way back to Belmondo's monologue at the opening of *A bout de souffle*; and the stuttered, almost incoherent, and utterly hysterical political interview between Godard and his principal Dziga-Vertov collaborator, Jean-Pierre Gorin, as the two dodge flying tennis balls, seems to cast serious doubts on the seriousness of the director's polemic, if not his involvement. Even in the midst of his most politically active period, Godard does not seem to have lost that proclivity toward self-destruction or self-negation that rises from his total commitment to the present.

Indeed, if this negativistic, self-destructive tendency is strongly felt in many of Godard's pictures, it is often because, paradoxically enough, there seems to be a markedly autobiographical tone to many of them. For the very confessional quality of certain Godard films makes the director's various "distancing," or "distantiation" (to invent a word with more Brechtian overtones), techniques seem all the more contradictory. *Le Mépris* certainly offers the most obvious example of what seem to be direct allusions to the director's personal life. To begin with, there is the narrative itself, which revolves about a misunderstanding between a man working crea-

---

[1] "Lutter sur deux fronts" (conversation with Jean-Luc Godard by J. Bontemps, Jean-Louis Comolli, Michel Delahay, and Jean Narboni), *Cahiers du cinéma,* No. 194 (October 1967), p. 70.

tively in the cinema (as a scriptwriter) and his beautiful wife. But there are other things. The principal characters' desire to wear masks seems to parallel to an extent Godard's own attitude; in the latter case, the director is almost never seen without his tinted glasses; in the case of the characters in Le Mépris, Paul (Michel Piccoli) wears a hat and smokes a cigar in the bathtub because he wants to be like Dean Martin in Some Came Running (an allusion that further turns the film back in on itself and its director, at least cinematically). Likewise, Paul's wife Camille (Brigitte Bardot) at one point dons a black wig, and the effect is very much that of seeing Brigitte Bardot become Anna Karina. None of this was accidental. In an article by Jean Clay,[2] Piccoli is quoted as saying that Godard had him wear his shoes, tie, and hat, while Bardot had the impression that Godard was definitely having her deliver her lines and behave like Anna Karina, who was Godard's wife and favorite actress at that time. Perhaps, in fact, the sources of the kind of "contempt" portrayed in Le Mépris can be seen in Godard's quoting from Edgar Allen Poe's "The Oval Portrait" at the end of Vivre sa vie: the artist, in using his wife, in capturing and freezing, as it were, the beauty of the woman he loves, is in a sense murdering this same woman, creating an inevitable paradox between art and love. (The same paradox can be seen in different terms in Mallarmé's poem, "L'Après-midi d'un faune".) Interestingly enough, this is the one aspect of the picture to which Susan Sontag objects in an otherwise enthusiastic—and exceptional—article on Vivre sa vie;[3] Sontag sees this deliberate turning of the film upon its own director as an unforgivable mockery of the story itself. It is furthermore revealing to notice the evolution of Anna Karina's roles throughout the various films—in Pierrot le fou, which was filmed at the height of the couple's marital difficulties, Karina has suddenly lost almost all of the childlike, Giraudoux innocence (in spite of the stuffed animal she drags about with her) that characterized almost all her earlier Godard roles;[4] in Made in U.S.A., her last feature for Godard, she has been hardened to the point of being

[2] "Le Paradoxe de Jean-Luc Godard, nihiliste et créateur," Réalités, No. 212 (September 1963).

[3] See Against Interpretation (New York: Dell, 1969), pp. 199–211; reprinted in the Mussman anthology (see bibliography).

[4] See the line spoken by the hero of Le Petit soldat concerning Véronica (Karina): "The first time I met Veronica, she seemed to be stepping out of a play by Giraudoux."

the diametrical opposite of what she was in her early roles. And as far as the male heroes are concerned, the protagonist of *Masculin-Féminin* (Jean-Pierre Léaud), which followed *Pierrot le fou* and which marks the beginning of Godard's "second period," is perhaps the most solitary of all Godardian males, while the light in which Godard casts all the film's females is no doubt more incisively brutal than in any of his other works.[5]

But Godard is autobiographical in another way, a way that is infinitely more subtle and represents one of the most strikingly original elements of the cinema according to Jean-Luc. And it is here, as well, that what is perhaps the most strongly *positive* aspect of Godard's art comes into being. All of Godard's movies contain countless allusions, direct or otherwise, to any number of artistic and/or intellectual endeavors—poetry, philosophy, painting, political theory, music, and, of course, the cinema itself, to name the major areas from which Godard draws—whose choice seems to have been dictated solely on the basis of the director's own personal tastes and predilections. Every Godard film is a chapter in an amazingly broad intellectual and aesthetic autobiography. Indeed, it is doubtful that anybody will ever manage to discover all the scattered references that abound in Godard's cinema, so frequent is their use and so thoroughly are they integrated into the director's art. Thus, such films as *La Femme mariée, Le Mépris* and *Made in U.S.A.*, among others, feature shots of posters for movies by some of Godard's favorite directors (Cocteau, Hitchcock, Howard Hawks, and so forth). Actual movie directors also appear, either playing themselves (Fritz Lang in *Le Mépris*, Roger Leenhardt in *La Femme mariée*, Samuel Fuller in *Pierrot le fou*) or a quasi-fictitious character (Jean-Pierre Melville in *A bout de souffle*). *Une Femme est une femme* has the characters making allusions to works by Godard's friends and colleagues, such as Truffaut's *Tirez sur le pianiste*. Actual footage from other films, including his own, are even "quoted" on occasion. Fragments of plays are also quoted, either as plays (Shakespeare's *Romeo and Juliet* in *Bande à part*; Racine's *Bérénice* (*La Femme mariée*) and *Andromaque* (*La Chinoise*); Musset's *On ne badine pas avec l'amour* in *Une Femme est une*

[5] An article by Gabriel Vialle, "Deux ou trois choses que nous savons d'elles, elles, les femmes, depuis qu'il, Jean-Luc Godard, nous en a parlé . . . ," *Image et son*, No. 211 (December 1967), examines and basically denies the possibility of misogyny in Godard's films.

femme, and so forth) or are integrated into the actual dialogue of the film (LeRoi Jones' *Dutchman* in *Masculin-Féminin*). The same is true for novels (Céline and Queneau, for example) and poetry (Rimbaud, Aragon, Apollinaire, and Éluard). Even a history of art (by Elie Faure) opens *Pierrot le fou* as a moody narration that is accompanied by Antoine Duhamel's haunting music and a series of four different shots (including a tennis game, a kind of secret Godardian "leitmotif" that also shows up in *Weekend* and *Vladimir and Rosa*), only one of which (Ferdinand at the book store) has any logical relationship to the rest of the film; suddenly, however, Godard breaks the spell and reveals his "source" by showing Ferdinand sitting in a bathtub and reading the Faure book to his little girl, thus using the "quote" both *inside* the film (at the beginning) and *outside* it (once he has documentarized the source, although there is still the deliberately offbeat justification, within the film, of Ferdinand reading the book aloud). Paintings and other pictorial art, from Vermeer and Rembrandt to Renoir and Picasso, are likewise either incorporated into the settings (*A bout de souffle, Les Carabiniers, Weekend,* for example) or are shown "abstractly" (*Pierrot le fou*). Music, from Mozart to rock, is used both as a part of the soundtrack (such as the Beethoven Quartets in *La Femme mariée*) and as part of the "action" (pieces from radios, phonographs, and jukeboxes in numerous films; the Mozart Piano Sonata played in the barn in *Weekend*; the Rolling Stones rehearsal of "Sympathy for the Devil" in *One Plus One*). Philosophy, from Pascal to Lenin, is quoted, and actual philosophers (Brice Parain in *Vivre sa vie*, Francis Jeanson in *La Chinoise*) are brought in to play themselves and recreate their own ideas. Many of the characters' names also represent artistic and/or personal allusions—the hero's alias in *A bout de souffle* is that of a Hollywood cinematographer, Laszlo Kovacs; Ulysses, Venus, Cleopatra, Michelangelo are all characters in *Les Carabiniers*; the names of Lubitsch and Récamier appear in *Une Femme est une femme*; Camille (whose name could refer to several possible sources, including the heroine of Musset's *On ne badine pas avec l'amour*) is the main female character of *Le Mépris* (in the novel, her name is Emiglia, or Emilie); one finds Odile (the name of a Queneau heroine but also of Godard's mother) in *Bande à part*, and Ferdinand (the first-person character of Céline's novels) in *Pierrot le fou*).

This abundant use of allusions such as those mentioned above (in a far from exhaustive list) has been one of the principal points around which Godard's many critics have centered their attacks. In traditional cinema it would, in fact, be normal to expect that elements such as these be integrated logically into both the narrative of the film and into the psychologies of the various characters. In Godard's cinema, on the other hand, this represents one of the most hermetic aspects of an art that refuses to give reasons or explanations for its composing parts. Yet there are at least two very good fundamental reasons for this practice in Godard. To begin with, he is perhaps the first filmmaker to actually documentarize the diverse manifestations of intellectual and aesthetic undertakings.[6] By more often than not maintaining the external, objective identity of the allusions he uses rather than incorporating them subtly into some psychonarrative framework, Godard admits, as very few before him have done, to the importance of such elements as integral parts of natural reality. Thus the covers (with their attractive color abstractions) of books from Gallimard's *Idées* series take their place, in *Deux ou trois choses que je sais d'elle*, alongside the more traditional documentary elements of apartment buildings, cranes, and so forth.

But there is a second, and perhaps more profound justification for Godard's "allusionism," and this has to do with what one might call Godard's need for "aesthetic distantiation." And here we are at the heart of a fundamental contradiction that forms part of the core of the elusive Godard aesthetic. For, while the director manifests a documentarist's concern and even fascination for the *real*, he seems at the same time to harbor an almost neurotic abhorrence for the reality he deals with (an attitude strongly resembling, in its aesthetic implications, that of French poet Stéphane Mallarmé). One often has the impression that a certain ideal, a certain nonmaterialistic, or artistic, creation of a superior reality is offered as an ultimate possibility in many Godard shots. Thus, for instance, the courtship between Arthur and Odile, in *Bande à part*, is expressed not so much in the direct physical and/or emotional relationship between the two as it is in the passage from *Romeo and Juliet* read in French by Odile's English teacher during a class attended by Arthur shortly after he has met Odile. And in

---

[6] See the remarks by Ropars-Wuilleumier on this subject.

Weekend, Mireille Darc, a popular sex-film star, is shown, at one point, nude in a bathtub. Yet, almost as if in parody of Hollywood taboos, her nipples remain just barely covered by the water, while above her head Godard has hung a *painting* of a nude woman whose bare breasts are seen, nipples and all. The juxtaposition is not only doubly ironic (considering a normal French audience's knowledge of Mireille Darc's usual roles), but it also draws the attention of the spectator-voyeur away from the physical, sensual reality (Godard often gives the impression of being one of the most puritanical directors alive) toward a nonphysical, aesthetic creation. While Godard's films, then, often seem to create a nihilistic state arising from the mutual annihilation of two opposing extremes, as in *Alphaville,* the abstract beauty arising from the director's aesthetic distantiation often leaves the viewer with a positive orientation, or feeling, toward what appears to be an essentially negativistic art.

Furthermore, Godard's aesthetic distantiation is not based solely on the director's use of various allusions. In fact, it is here that one arrives at the foundation, the point of departure of Godard's cinematic technique. One of the principal aspects that the members of the "nouvelle vague" admired in, for instance, American cinema, is the relief taken on by pure cinematic virtuosity. This art-for-art's-sake attitude becomes even more marked in Godard due to the latter's methodical elimination of traditionalistic elements. Concentrating on Godard's use of camera movement, for instance, one becomes aware that the director often uses this for its own effect, often without any logical justification for it. In *Le Mépris,* a long conversation between the husband and wife is accompanied by a constant panoramic movement of the camera from the husband to the wife and back again. In a traditional film, the camera would alternately concentrate either on one face or the other during the conversation, thus stressing either the person talking or the reaction of the person listening. In this long shot in *Le Mépris,* on the other hand, the camera pans hypnotically back and forth in a totally arbitrary fashion that is obviously divorced from what is taking place within the narrative. By filming the entirety of a banal marital argument in a single shot, Godard seems to be daring the audience to be bored. He thus uses a balletlike camera rhythm where other directors would have edited together a logical series of shots. This arbitrariness is further stressed by the presence of a large table-lamp located at dead center between the husband and wife. Besides the fact that the white lampshade has the aesthetic function of a pure geometrical form, the lamp itself is turned on and off at regular intervals for no apparent reason. Furthermore, the composition of the shot, which takes full advantage of the wide-screen, is later repeated as a kind of plastic leitmotif—first, in the very next sequence, when a photographer steps between Piccoli and Bardot, who are seated across the aisle from one another in a theatre, and takes flash pictures at arbitrary intervals; then, as Bardot and Palance are seated on either side of a tiny rectangular window in the Capri villa; and, finally, at the end, when the car carrying Bardot and Palance is smashed between the two halves of a double tank truck. In *Weekend*, the whole incongruity of a piano salesman demonstrating his product (no less than a Beckstein grand!) by performing a Mozart sonata in a barn in the middle of the French provinces is complemented by slow, beautiful and hypnotic 360-degree pan shots (two to the right, one to the left, and the beginning of another to the right) that take in the court-yard around the barn and the various people who have stopped what they are doing to listen to the music.[7] This is further stylized by the fact that Jean Yanne, who plays the husband and incarnates bourgeois vulgarity, yawns on cue each time the camera passes him. *Weekend* is also punctuated by several arbitrary vertical pan shots upward, and features an extremely long tracking shot to the right during the sequence which, as it passes in review the almost surrealistically offbeat diversions of people waiting for a traffic jam to break, becomes, in the midst of this tragedy of modern civiliza-tion, one of the funniest scenes in any Godard film. Like *Weekend*, *One Plus One* also offers long sequences of music-for-its-own-sake (this time the rock song being rehearsed by the Rolling Stones) accompanied by a series of virtuoso camera movements—tracking shots, pan shots, and combinations of both—that create a stunning effect. The ultimate use of camera movement might very well have been in a film Godard never made of Beckett's play, *Ah, les beaux jours* (the producers wanted Godard to use Madeleine Renaud, while Godard wanted to use a young actress): here, Godard would have employed a long tracking shot, starting from far away so that

[7] The pianist here, Paul Gegauff, has also served as a scenarist for Claude Chabrol.

he could progress from a long-distance shot to an extreme close-up
during the hour and a half it takes the play to run.

And if Godard uses camera movement where most directors
would use editing, he likewise quite often uses editing to accomplish what others would do with different types of movement. As is
brought out in the Ropars-Wuilleumier article in this book, the
extraordinary rhythms growing out of Godard's films are created
at least partly by the clash between the animation of the editing
itself and the basically static nature of a large proportion of the
individual shots, each of whose striking, picturelike framing and
composition (often due at least partially to Godard's exceptional
cameraman, Raoul Coutard, who was director of photography for
most of the director's films through *Weekend*) represent a negation
of traditional cinematic time (reality is frozen) that is replaced by
the aesthetically (and artificially) produced time of the montage.
Ultimately, in fact, Godard has even incorporated the use of
totally black frames in various pictures, starting with *Le Gai
savoir*. Thus, Godard was able to state with a straight face that the
film that most resembles his *Made in U.S.A.* is Demy's *Les Para-
pluies de Cherbourg*, except that in Godard's work, "the people
aren't singing, but the film is." [8] And when Godard wrote, before
he had made a single film, of the "skillful and precise paraphrase
of reality" created by Otto Preminger's montage style,[9] he might
very well have been charting out his own aesthetic.

One might also note that the frequently abstract quality of a
single Godard shot is rendered possible—paradoxically, in a sense
—by the director's almost constant use of depth of field. By
carefully arranging and/or selecting the various physical elements
within a given field, and by using depth of field to bring them all
equally into focus, Godard is able to stress the abstract qualities
of the individual elements and bring out their geometrical relationships to one another, thus transforming reality into abstraction in
a manner that links him to such directors as Cocteau and Welles
and seems to contradict the depth-of-field theories of French cine-
philosopher André Bazin. Whether it is in the black-and-white
interrelationships of trees and surrounding terrain in such films as
Les Carabiniers and *Bande à part* or in the carefully set up paint-

[8] "Lutter sur deux fronts," p. 69.
[9] "Défense et illustration du découpage classique," in *Jean-Luc Goddard par
Jean-Luc Godard* (Paris: Pierre Belfond, 1968), p. 32.

cans and diverse elements in the apartment of *Le Mépris* or the garage of *Made in U.S.A.*, Godard chooses his frames with the consummate skill of a painter. Even the actors are often cast because of a particular or peculiar expressivity of their faces—such as the soul-revealing face of Karina, the almost grotesque, angular face of Jack Palance, or the "American Gothic" (although the actors are French) collection of faces of the jurors in *Vladimir and Rosa*.[10] Ultimately, Godard seems to have been the first to make systematic use of cinematic "still life" (in which movement is allowed) through such devices as the extreme close-ups of a cup of coffee and the burning tip of a cigarette in *Deux ou trois choses que je sais d'elle*, and the shots of white leader tape, followed by regular brown magnetic tape, snaking its way through the exposed heads of a tape recorder in *Vladimir and Rosa*. Even the human body is subjected to this kind of treatment, as in *La Femme mariée* and *Le Mépris*. The late film historian and critics Georges Sadoul emphasized the relationship between "God-art" and "pop-art" in his review of *La Femme mariée*;[11] certainly, the transforming of everyday, modern artifacts into works of art in which the aesthetic beauty of these elements speaks for itself represents, in principle at least, one of the goals of pop art.

Several excellent articles, including the ones by Aragon, Wuilleumier, and Jacob in this book, stress Godard's Fauvist taste for striking color abstractions in which, once again, an aesthetic element—here colors, frequently primary—is almost forcibly detached from the physical or functional object with which it is associated and allowed to exist for its own sake, on its own terms.[12] Godard's use of music, on the other hand, is in many ways just as revolutionary as his use of the other basic elements of the cinema, and yet this is one area that has perhaps not received sufficient atten-

---

[10] Among others, Jean Collet (in his monograph on Godard; see bibliography) and James Blue's interview in the Mussman anthology (see bibliography) offer excellent insights into Godard's "faces."

[11] See *Les Lettres françaises*, 10 December 1964.

[12] See also René Richetin, "Notes sur la couleur au cinéma," *Cahiers du cinéma*, No. 182 (September 1966), pp. 60–67, dealing with the aesthetics of color in the cinema in general, and with Godard's *Pierrot le fou* (positively) and Louis Malle's *Viva Maria* (negatively); and Paul J. Sharits, "Red, Blue, Godard," *Film Quarterly*, Vol. XIX, No. 4 (Summer 1966), an excellent general analysis of Godard's use of color, particularly revealing for *Le Mépris*.

tion in studies of the director's art.[18] *Pierrot le fou,* for instance, is complemented by what is perhaps one of the most extraordinarily beautiful film scores ever written. Yet like most Godard scores, it was composed in a manner totally opposed to the traditional methods of sound-track composing. For *Pierrot,* for instance, Godard simply told composer Antoine Duhamel that he wanted several different themes in a more or less romantic vein à la Schumann. Nothing was divided up into minutes and seconds, and nothing in the music had to correspond precisely to anything in the film; what Godard sought was an aesthetic, an atmospheric correspondence, and he was able to obtain this to perfection by giving the composer full creative liberty—indeed, M. Duhamel has said that, for this reason, he values his two collaborations with Godard above all others. For *Alphaville,* in fact, Godard apparently took great pains to keep composer Paul Misraki as much in the dark as possible concerning the nature of the film while the score was being composed. Consequently, what Godard usually obtains from composers rises above the category of film-score music and becomes more or less another pure aesthetic element, like the classical scores he frequently uses, that is juxtaposed on the broad artistic canvas of the film.

Once Godard has a score, whether composed especially for the film or already existing, he edits it very much in the manner in which he edits his films, often cutting off a phrase in the middle, picking it up again later, stopping it again, but rarely allowing it to reach any kind of cadence or musical stopping point. The melancholy, bittersweet theme composed by Michel Legrand for *Vivre sa vie,* for instance, scarcely lasts, as a whole, longer than two or three minutes; yet, besides the two jukebox numbers, it represents the film's entire musical support, because Godard simply used, more often than not, brief cuts from the music that repeat and overlap in an absorbing, hypnotic fashion. Godard even manages, in yet another intracinematic point of reference, to throw in musical comedy in totally unexpected contexts. In *Pierrot le fou,* for instance, Godard presages the tragic conclusion of the film by

---

[18] There is, however, an extremely revealing interview-montage on the subject of music and sound by Abraham Segal in *Image et son,* No. 215 (March 1968), pp. 72–82. The issue, which deals entirely with "Le Son au cinéma," also contains an interview, by Claude Cobast, with Antoine Duhamel, pp. 105–7.

having Karina and Belmondo do a song-and-dance number (in the middle of a forest) in which Karina worries about the luck line of her palm, while Belmondo is more interested in the line of her hips. And, just before he jumps on a boat to go and murder Karina-Marianne and her lover, Belmondo-Pierrot-Ferdinand runs across nightclub entertainer Raymond Devos, whose hilarious three-note "Est-ce que vous m'aimez?" (Do You Love Me?) routine represents a bitterly ironic echo of the hero's torment.[14] Another striking example is Jean-Pierre Léaud's "Allô, allô, tu m'entends?" (Hello, Hello, Do You Hear Me?) routine in a telephone booth in *Weekend*. And an entire study could be done of *Une Femme est une femme* as an anti-musical-comedy.

Godard's revolutionary use of the various composing elements of the cinematographic medium might be considered, as it has been, as pure revolt for the sake of revolt. Yet for many, the upheaval Godard has brought about in the seventh art has culminated in the creation of a new language, the invention of a new means of communication whose elements are more genuine because, instead of depending upon the arbitrary abstractness of words and their purely relativistic meanings, these elements become their own meaning by being rooted in the immediate sensorial attributes of concrete reality . . . but a concrete reality transformed through the artistic means at the disposal of the filmmaker and through their juxtaposition with a superior (according to Godard) aesthetic reality. That Godard himself is acutely aware of this is borne out by the enormously important role given to the problems of communication, particularly through verbal language, in all his pictures. From Patricia in *A bout de souffle*, who asks the police the meaning of a vulgar French word that Michel uses to describe her betrayal before he dies ("Qu'est-ce que c'est: dégueulasse?"), to the women's lib girl (Anne Wiazemsky) in *Vladimir and Rosa*, who has her uncomprehending boyfriend stand directly behind her and try to "think with her voice," many of Godard's protagonists are consciously aware of the problems of language and the meaning of words. Godard even engages the heroine of *Vivre sa vie* in a lengthy conversation on the meaning of language with a real-life linguistic philosopher, Brice Parain, author of *Petite métaphysique*

---

[14] The original French version of this routine can be found in *Image et son*, No. 211 (December 1967), p. 86.

de la parole. It is not surprising, then, that Godard occasionally stretches language to the breaking point and uses it in much the same way as do, for instance, the authors of the so-called theatre of the absurd. At the beginning of *Made in U.S.A.,* for example, the conversation between Paula Nelson and the poet David Goodis concerning the latter's fiancée could fit beautifully into Ionesco's *Bald Soprano,* while the absurdly false logic of the same author's *Rhinocéros* (in Act I) turns up in the mouth of Emile Brontë in *Weekend.* Godard also offers his own version of Babel in several films: at one point in *Le Mépris,* there are no fewer than four different languages being spoken (English, German, French, and Italian); and in the remarkable short, whose original double-language title, *L'Aller et retour des enfants prodigues andate e ritorno dei figli prodighi,* itself indicated the linguistic confusion involved, Godard presents two simultaneous dialogues (once again reminiscent of Ionesco) in which the heroine of one couple speaks French and her partner speaks Italian, while the other couple comments on and translates—again, one in French, one in Italian—the first couple's dialogue and offers as well various observations on the cinema. It is likewise within this same aesthetic that Godard deliberately renders inaudible certain spoken passages in his films, from the whisper of many of his own commentaries to the painfully loud playback from the tape recorder (Godard's own voice again) in *Made in U.S.A.* Furthermore, he often has his camera show a close-up of a single word, which occasionally turns out to be a part of a larger word with a totally different meaning. Indeed, the forms and colors of words often become more important than their alleged meanings.

Within the sometimes oppressive negativism of most of his films, then, Godard seems to offer something resembling a "positive" solution. To be sure, the solution proposed is not, perhaps, very practical (at least until the advent of his Dziga-Vertov films), for what he accomplishes through his cine-aesthetic is the replacing of one, negative reality with a *created,* positive one—the vulgarity of physical love is replaced by bodies beneath sheets, paintings, and sculptural nude shots; the impossibility of communication through language is replaced by linguistic abstractions in which juxtaposed sounds and word-forms offer a new type of language; even the cacophony of modern life is transformed (as in *Deux ou trois choses*) into a kind of *musique concrète;* the temporality-laden emotivity of dramatic progression is eliminated through distantiation and replaced by reactions dependent almost wholly upon aesthetic realities that are both juxtaposed upon and created through the film. These realities belong to a universe that is all the more autonomous for the director's fascination with the creative process, as opposed to a final, immutable creation. Like Mallarmé, each of whose poems is not only an attempt at pure poetry but a description of the creative process, each of Godard's films represents a self-created meditation on the very formation of each of the cinema's composing elements. And as with Mallarmé, who in many ways seems to be the aesthetic forerunner of Godard, the artist is able to achieve a victory over the nihilism of the real world by taking the physical objects that compose it and poetically transforming them, through a hermetic artistic language, into an extratemporal ideal. Slightly modifying Mallarmé's famous axiom from *Un Coup de dés jamais n'abolira le hasard,* "Nothing will have taken place but the place itself . . . except, perhaps, the cinema."

Jean-Luc Godard, ou La Raison Ardente

by TOM MILNE

Godard has always been two or three years ahead of his time. All the same, one wasn't quite prepared for the way everything else (from *The Red Desert* downwards) began to look rather old-fashioned and strained as soon as *Une Femme Mariée* appeared on the scene. Comparisons are impossible, of course: *The Red Desert* is in its own way just as remarkable a film. It is simply that Godard has realized—and found a technique for dealing with his realization—that modern life is so complex, and human relationships so intangibly tangled, that fully rounded and polished artistic statements with all the ends tucked neatly out of sight are no longer possible. The *ne plus ultra* of shifting moral values which we have come to through nuclear anxiety, failure to communicate and all the rest of it, ends up in the old problem which Godard didn't quite solve in *Une Femme est une Femme*: ". . . juxtaposing things which didn't necessarily go together, a film which was gay and sad at the same time." That film, even more than *Bande à Part*, is *Une Femme Mariée*.

There is a story (true) which has always horrified me. A DTs patient is stamping frantically in a corner, trying to kill a horde of imaginary rats, and when the male nurse tells him that there are no rats there, he says, "I know . . . but I can *see* them." How does one express that knowing and that seeing, complementary and contradictory, on the screen?

A film like *Fail Safe* deals with the most nerve-edged subject in

From Sight and Sound *34, no. 3 (Summer 1965): 106–11. Reprinted by permission of the publisher.*

123

the world—nuclear destruction by accident. But as a letter in
The Observer recently pointed out sanely and cogently, such accidents could under no circumstances happen. So, logically, one
knows they couldn't happen, but one still *sees* (feals) that they
could: and Lumet's film tells only half the story. Following a
parallel line of reasoning, Antonioni tells only half the story in
The Red Desert. Giuliana, convincingly enough, is wracked by
modern life, by the machines which are taking over from man, the
poisonous gas exuding from the factories, and the increasing in-
stability and incommunicability between humans. But as seen by
Antonioni and portrayed by Monica Vitti as stammering incom-
prehensibly, cowering against walls, crouching inexplicably in a
field to devour a workman's half-eaten sandwich, Giuliana is fit
only for the madhouse.

Admittedly it may be argued that she has cracked under the
strain, but Antonioni is not documenting a case history. He is trying to document a state of mind, and modern Ravenna, I am sure,
is not populated by berserk beings like Giuliana: they almost certainly go about their business normally, even though they may,
deep down inside, be just as unalterably affected by the alienation
of living in the technological society which Antonioni delineates
so subtly in his vision of Ravenna's landscape of terrible splendors.
Giuliana doesn't live with us in our world, she is off in a world of
her own. One senses that Antonioni is straining so hard to communicate Giuliana's alienation that a strand has snapped between
her and normal life: he has tucked away most of her loose ends
too neatly. She behaves almost as though she had become a mind-
less automaton, and as such, she loses a dimension. Charlotte (in
Une Femme Mariée) is in her own way just as much of an automaton, without ever losing that dimension. She lives, loves, walks,
talks, enjoys, and she communicates; and when she comes to the
end of her brief cord and communication stops, she turns to the
camera to say "I don't know." In the same way, Godard himself
can turn to the camera, or metaphorically turn the camera to us,
and say "I don't know." There are so many contradictions and
inexplicable factors in modern living which the artist can't tuck
away in the corner of his canvas, disguised with a few bold strokes
of the brush: at some point, almost inevitably, he must in all
honesty resort to the "I don't know."

"Fragments of a film made in *1964*"—
Subtitle of *Une Femme Mariée*

This *Red Desert-Femme Mariée* comparison is not entirely fortuitous or malicious. Gérard Guégan has suggested interestingly (*Cahiers du Cinéma* 163) that the little boy's curious monologue in *Une Femme Mariée,* captioned "L'Enfance," might be a description of the making of a rocket; in which case there is a direct parallel with the strange science fiction aura which surrounds Giuliana's little son in *The Red Desert.* I don't see the monologue this way myself, but the similarities abound anyway with Giuliana's attempts to "reintegrate herself with reality." For *Une Femme Mariée* one might turn the phrase, and say that Charlotte's problem is "disintegration from reality." Godard's subtitle quoted above refers to the collage effect of the film, which moves freely between fragments—scenes, bits of scenes, bits of bits of scenes, a printed page, a word, half a word. But at the same time (one must never expect single strands from Godard), it is a film about fragmentation. The film opens with a disembodied hand sliding slowly forward across a white sheet; and it ends with the same hand (Charlotte's) slowly withdrawing, leaving blankness, nothing.

The scenes of love-making which open and close the film are composed entirely of human fragments—a hand, a leg, a head, a trunk. The effect is extraordinary, as though the world had split into separate pieces, separating people from one another. This feeling of dislocation is carried through the whole film: three people having an after-dinner chat in a comfortable living-room are suddenly transported separately, a head in close-up against a neutral background, to have their thoughts bared; conversations and actions are punctuated by cut-in signs and placards; printed words are broken down to form new, minatory meanings; a photographic session projected in negative strips away the flesh from girls frisking in a swimming pool; even a simple taxi-ride necessitates three taxis instead of one.

The anguish which runs through the film, implicitly in Charlotte's behavior, explicitly in Godard's direction, comes from this separateness: Charlotte senses her solitude, senses the ultimate impossibility of human relations. Unlike Giuliana, it doesn't make her behave insanely, it just governs her life like an invisible hand pushing her relentlessly along. When she and Robert (her lover) part at the end, full of hopes and promises to return to each other and get married, Charlotte knows that it is all over, not so much because there is any reason for the affair to end, as because there seems to be no reason for it not to. It would be wrong to suggest that this feeling of almost cosmic disintegration dominates the film in any explicit sense. *Il faut vivre sa vie*—and in addition to their more anatomical aspect, the love scenes have a deep tenderness, underlined by their accompanying leitmotif from a Beethoven Quartet. Almost clinically un-erotic, these scenes are at the same time infused with passion, as though love were being subjected to an amazed and wondering eye through a microscope. Charlotte is living her life happily and unthinkingly in the present tense, with the menace no more than a background which one has got so used to that one no longer notices it: a radio blaring its grotesquely inflated list of road casualties to an empty room, a voice mentioning Auschwitz and evoking only puzzlement ("Auschwitz? . . . oh yes . . . thalidomide . . ."). There are more pressing things to attend to, urging themselves on Charlotte's attention from all sides.

"IF ONE TAKES AWAY THE OUTSIDE, THERE IS THE
INSIDE . . . AND WHEN ONE TAKES AWAY THE
INSIDE, THERE IS THE SOUL"—*Vivre sa vie*

Une Femme Mariée operates on various levels, and works on all of them. At bottom, it is the eternal triangle, almost classically exposed. Charlotte has a lover, Robert; she has a husband, Pierre, with whom she still enjoys physical passion; she is pregnant, but doesn't know which of them is the father, and is afraid. But unlike Truffaut's *La Peau Douce*, which was a case history, Godard's hymn to *la peau douce* is a sociological document. Charlotte is not a woman, but Woman. What Godard is after in his portrait is that mysterious, anonymous being assailed on all sides by the shrill voices of advertisements, advising her to dress, paint and otherwise distort herself towards some nebulous ideal of sameness and sinfulness. "Triumph," says the girl in a brassière poster, proudly snapping her shoulder-straps. "Crescendo . . . My Sin . . . Scandal . . ." urges a perfume ad. "Just how far can a woman go in love?" asks a newspaper poster, helpfully offering instruction "of total frankness." Charlotte follows all the rules towards the goal of tasting both married love and illicit love, and finds that they are exactly the same.

It has been suggested that Godard made a mistake in using Macha Méril instead of Anna Karina to portray Charlotte, on the grounds that with Karina there would have been more "soul." This seems to me to be beside the point. *Vivre sa vie* was a portrait of a woman which stripped off layer after layer until the soul was bared; it was a film of the inside, by way of moral philosophy. *Une Femme Mariée* is a film of the outside, totally unconcerned with ethics or morals, and consequently calls for a totally different heroine. Karina is almost magically personal: those wide, startled eyes, that grave, total absorption, the sudden liberating irruption into dance, would have destroyed the smooth surface texture of *Une Femme Mariée*. No woman's magazine would be able to reduce the Nana of *Vivre sa vie* to a set of statistics, or categorise her spontaneously joyous dance round the billiard-table so as to be able to produce a marketable recipe. Instead, we have Macha Méril/Charlotte putting on a record, which bears its label "Erotica" in large and clear letters, and listening to a woman laughing endlessly, idiotically and presumably erotically, with the same sort of robot attention with which she follows instructions to see whether or not she measures up to "an ideal bust." In other words, she conforms, as Macha Méril's deliciously cool and witty performance makes amply clear.

This is not to suggest that Godard suggests that Charlotte is soulless; it is simply that in her life, and the routine which surrounds her, the outlets are blocked. Godard, in fact, makes it quite clear that, ultimately, Nana, Odile (in *Bande à Part*) and Charlotte are of the same species, though their particular contexts in life draw the soul from Nana, the emotion from Odile, and the body from Charlotte. But they converge at a point: "on est coupable." Suddenly, out of nothing, Charlotte reveals her concern: "All the people in the streets . . . I want to know . . . I want to know them all. Him . . . him . . . him . . . that one is perhaps going to die tomorrow. He waits for a phone call before committing suicide . . . And then no one calls. So he kills himself." Then, on a beautiful close-up of her sadly bowed head, comes the all-embracing "on est coupable"—we are guilty. The link is direct with the close-up revealing Nana's startled comprehension of guilt during the police interrogation of her supposed theft, and of Odile in the Métro suddenly discovering her kinship with those who dwell in misery.

"EVEN A QUIET COUNTRYSIDE . . . EVEN A ROAD
WHERE CARS, PEOPLE, COUPLES, PASS . . .
MAY LEAD TO A CONCENTRATION CAMP"
Nuit et Brouillard

Charlotte's sudden cry of kinship with the person waiting in
despair for the sound of another voice has obvious reference to her
own situation. In the following sequence, her lover telephones to
say that he is leaving for Marseilles to act in *Bérénice*; she immediately calls her doctor for the result of her pregnancy tests, puts down
the phone, buries her head in the bedclothes like a child afraid of
the dark, and mutters the end of a phrase, ". . . Not to Be . . ."
This fear in the dark is echoed, vaguely at first, in the commentary
(Charlotte's interior monologue) which intermittently accompanies
the action, and from which one can pick phrases like "Jealousy . . .
When does he return? . . . It's dangerous." Later it grows more
specific: "When one is dead . . . With lassitude." But for the most
part Charlotte lives in the daylight, burying these thoughts inside
her and clinging desperately to the blithe unconcern of the present:
"That's . . . why I like the present. Because . . . I don't know
what's happening to me . . . It prevents me from going mad." Even
so, the danger signals are omnipresent. As she goes to meet her lover
at Orly airport, Godard cuts in close-ups of the street signs and warnings which surround her—DANGER—ARRÊT D'URGENCE—a poster of
Hitchcock glaring threateningly. But her mind is elsewhere, and she
doesn't see these warnings: warnings not so much of a jealous husband as of the end of love, of an empty world waiting like a cage
to imprison her. Sitting in the airport cinema, Charlotte and her
lover look at each other; the slow, even commentary of Resnais' *Nuit
et Brouillard* quietly begins, "Même un paysage tranquille . . .";
and they walk out unheeding, heading for the hotel bedroom and
the parting of their ways.

"I'M VERY COMFORTABLE LIKE THIS. AND
ANYWAY, IT'S THE IDEAL POSITION FOR THE
SPECTATOR IN THE CINEMA"—CHARLOTTE IN
Une Femme Mariée

To describe the film in terms of concentration camps and dis-
located, fragmented worlds, may make it sound portentous, which is
the last thing of which *Une Femme Mariée* can be accused. In the

first place, it is too sure-footedly relaxed to allow portentousness. In
the second, it is consistently and caustically funny. There is, for
instance, Godard's teasing insolence: Charlotte fires point-blank
questions about contraception and whether sexual pleasure constitutes proof of paternity at a doctor who stammers helplessly in his
embarrassed efforts to circumnavigate dangerous reefs. There is his
love of the outrageous: the maid regaling her mistress with a sca-
brous, joyous and graphic description of her love life (drawn from
Céline's novel *Mort à Crédit*). Or the flippant: a conversation about
life, love and boys (WHAT EVERY WOMAN SHOULD KNOW) between two
schoolgirls, one nonchalant (SHE KNOWS), one wide-eyed (SHE DOESN'T).

Charlotte's crack about spectators in the cinema, delivered while
hunched down comfortably in the front seat of Robert's car, almost
disappearing from sight, is the metaphorical equivalent of Godard's
easy, informal approach to filmmaking. A film is enjoyable to make,
and made to be enjoyed. The surface texture of the film, already
broken up by interviews, digressions, cut-ins of street signs, book
titles and so forth, is also studded with puns and gags, both visual
and verbal:—

—a portrait of Molière is accompanied by a quotation from
Bossuet's commentary on the theatre ("I think it has been
sufficiently demonstrated that the representation of the natural
passions leads to sin"), which wryly evokes the queues of rain-
coated men who will walk out of the cinema, sadly deceived by
the erotic promise of *Une Femme Mariée*; but Molière himself
is then cited in defence of the theatre's power "to anticipate sin
by purifying love."
—Charlotte's panic about her pregnancy while visiting the doctor
("J'ai peur"), is abruptly followed by a shot of her slipping
and falling headlong while running across the street; a cut-in of
part of a word, "ÈVE" (The Fall); then the complete word,
"RÊVES" (her fantasy of fear).
—when Robert and Charlotte drive along the quais after making
love, the camera follows behind their open car; but after grey
and misty cut-in shots of Maillol's Tuileries statues of naked
women, the camera proceeds *in front* of the car, with the couple
now seen through the windscreen as mistily as the statues. The
uncomplicated happiness of their love-making is already reced-
ing as Charlotte slips away from Robert back to her husband.
"Paris pleure après qu'il a plu/Mais plaira-t-il encore autant
qu'il a plu?" asks the commentary untranslatably. (Paris weeps

after the rain/But will it please as it did before? or: Paris weeps
after it has pleased, etc.)

None of these apparent digressions really digress, nor are the puns
as simple or extraneous as they may seem. As in Joyce's linguistic
dislocations, they throw out hooks in all directions, forming a mesh
of meaning: and it is this which prevents the film from falling apart,
giving it its superbly firm, ordered texture.

With Godard an image can be, at one and the same time, a private
joke, a public gag, a clue, an imaginative link, or a serious statement.
When he uses the Hitchcock poster, for instance, it is a) a *hommage*
to one of his favourite directors; b) a wry comment on the fact that
Hitchcock is one of the few directors grand enough in France to
warrant having his face on cinema posters; c) a legitimate means of
underlining the minatory aspect of the film; and d) it serves as
quotation marks to the thriller parody which runs through the film.
Whenever Charlotte leaves her lover or goes to meet him, she plays
an absurd game of hide-and-seek, glancing round huntedly, crouching in doorways, and dodging from taxi to taxi as though hounded
by a mysterious pursuer. The game reaches an extremely funny cli-
max at the entrance to the Orly airport hotel, with Charlotte and
Robert slinking about in dark glasses and resorting to elaborate
subterfuges about dropped keys which loudly signal their guilt.
Their behavior is ridiculous, pushed to the edge of parody; yet at
the same time there is a recoil action hinging on the Hitchcock-
thriller quotation. Charlotte's husband has in actual fact set a private detective on her tail once before: so maybe her clumsy evasions
are not merely absurd, but true. How *does* one behave, assuming one
doesn't belong to the world of Philip Marlowe and Lemmy Caution,
if one suddenly discovers one is being tailed by a private eye? One is
reminded of the cheap-thriller scene in *Le Petit Soldat*—ridiculed as
being impossible—in which an assassin walks the street with his gun
in full view. Godard commented simply that it *was* possible because
it happened that way when the scene was shot on location: none of
the bystanders showed alarm, jumped on Michel Subor, or even
noticed. Fascination with the *vérité* of *cinéma* and the *cinéma* of
vérité is one of the constants of Godard's work, and determines the
rigorous yet tangential attitude of his camera, at one moment probing for the truth behind the façade, at the next leaping away to show
that it is all façade anyway.

Charlotte: Qu'est-ce que ça veut dire exactement, "regarder"?
Pierre: "Re-garder" * . . . J'sais pas . . . Ça veut dire garder
deux fois . . .
Charlotte: Si c'est deux fois . . . alors, c'est precieux.

Godard has already defined what he means by the infinite value
of the probing "re-gard," in a review of Franju's *Tête contre les
murs:* "to direct, to make a film, write a script, is to let the camera
look long enough on faces and objects to mark them deeply . . ."
Une Femme Mariée is focused steadily on three faces: the husband,
grave and puzzled, haunted by memories of what Charlotte once was
to him; the lover, serene and untroubled, content with her presence;
and Charlotte, presenting the same candid, troubled gaze to both,
uncertain as to the difference, if any, in her feelings for them. Godard
fixes these images on the screen and invites us to see what lies behind
them; at the same time, by inviting his characters to step out of character (in the interviews, for instance), he invites us to take another
look at the façade. We are reminded not only that this is "truth
twenty-four times a second," but that it is perhaps as true a truth as
any.

When Charlotte questions Robert, *cinéma vérité* style, about his
profession as an actor, for instance, we are aware that she is afraid
he may be acting a part, simulating his love for her; and, captivated
as we are by her, we share her concern. Robert, in his reply, gets
tangled up in his definition that in the theatre he is speaking a given
text, whereas in real life his words are his own; while we in turn
get tangled up in the realization that Bernard Noël, the actor playing Robert and simulating Robert's love with a given text, is here
speaking his own words as a real-life actor and casting doubt on his
own sincerity in the role of Robert. And in the last sequence of the
film, Godard makes brilliantly imaginative use of this paradoxical
confrontation between fact and fiction. Robert and Charlotte are
moving inevitably towards a separation, yet they themselves are
only obscurely aware of the fact, and cannot put even their half-
knowledge into words. While they live out the fiction that they will
meet again, marry and be happy, the play *Bérénice* presents the
truth of their situation through a theatrical fiction. As they lie in

* Based on a pun: "What does it mean, regard?—Reguard, to keep twice—
Then it must be very precious."

bed waiting for the departure of Robert's plane, Charlotte cues him in rehearsing the part he will be playing in Marseilles. Hesitantly and stumblingly read, Racine's poetry describes, not the parting of Bérénice and Titus (the lines are selected and rearranged), but of Robert and Charlotte. A trick? Perhaps, but perfectly legitimate in an art where all is, after all, illusion.

Parenthetically: this is Godard's most subtle ending to date. His love of flamboyantly theatrical dénouements is satisfied, but this time it happens at double remove: by proxy, as it were, and also off-stage.

D'UNE INFINIE TRISTESSE L'AMOUR, C'EST
COMME UN JOUR. ÇA S'EN VA . . . ÇA S'EN VA—
Une Femme Mariée

The subtlety of the ending is matched by a new clarity and assurance throughout. The whole film is organized with astounding precision, so that its patchwork elements are like the spokes of a wheel, leading outwards from the hub and also providing support for the frame. The hub, of course, is Charlotte, while the frame is her circular voyage between husband and lover; and the whole superstructure of the film dovetails into an analysis of the cul-de-sac of her existence.

Charlotte is haunted by doubts as to whether her chance of true happiness lies with husband or lover: in his ruthless analysis, Godard demonstrates that there is no difference in kind, only in procedure. "Love," says the song which Charlotte sings, "is of infinite sadness. It vanishes like the day." The film opens with the tender, fragmented scenes of Robert and Charlotte making love, and almost identical imagery is used later for Pierre and Charlotte. The only real difference is between the old and the new, between husband and lover. Robert looks at Charlotte's body with adoration and utter contentment; Pierre looks with the same adoration, but instead of content, an uneasy bewilderment. Robert accuses Charlotte of using his razor, and when she protests, drops the matter; Pierre makes the same charge, and it ends in an ugly domestic scene. Godard further underlines this distinction by indicating the priorities of husband and lover: Robert and Charlotte make love, then get dressed, chat, and leave; Pierre and Charlotte get dressed for dinner, put their son to bed, entertain their guest, talk, listen to a record, then make love. And in the final sequence in the hotel room at the airport, a subtle change has occurred: the behaviour of Robert and Charlotte is turning into that of Pierre and Charlotte. A shot from the Pierre-Charlotte sequence, of four hands washing together in a hand-basin, is repeated, and an aura of domesticity has crept in: they talk, turn on the radio, walk in and out of the room, fetch a glass of water, remake the single beds, light a cigarette, and only then do they make love. The point is clinched by a repetition of the shot in which Pierre kisses Charlotte's temple, inaudibly saying "Je t'aime, je t'aime" over and over again; only this time Charlotte is in the role of suppliant, kissing Robert and muttering "Je t'aime, je t'aime."

Even if love is transient, however, it is of infinite tenderness, as the second verse of Charlotte's song affirms: "Like the day, it returns." The corollary to the lover who grows like the husband, is the husband who becomes like the lover and so closes the vicious circle. As remarkable as anything else in the film is the way in which Godard moves his actors and his camera in choreographing the re-establishment of their relationship by Charlotte and Pierre through several lengthy sequences. The first nervous flurry of their meeting at the airport, where they are unable to talk privately, resolves itself into a wonderfully easy lateral tracking shot as Pierre talks casually to Charlotte, their little son runs happily in circles round them, and Leenhardt and his secretary amble along a few paces behind.

Once in their own apartment, however, left alone for the first time, the constriction returns as they dress for dinner; the camera remains virtually fixed on Charlotte, while Pierre moves nervously in and out of frame, trying to reassert his relationship with his sulkily withdrawn wife. Their uneasy politeness towards each other is emphasized and carried through to the wonderfully funny scene in which they edgily entertain Roger Leenhardt to after-dinner coffee and liqueurs, feverishly darting about the room attending to their duties as model hosts, while delivering an enthusiastic house-agent's eulogy on the delights of their ultra-modern home. Then, left alone again in their bedroom, a dispirited sullenness sets in; Pierre sits gloomily hunched against the wall, while Charlotte insists with maddening obstinacy on listening to the "Erotica" record which doesn't belong to them. Gradually, movement begins again: Charlotte goes to fetch a drink, leans desultorily against the wall, drags her feet along the carpet, lounges past Pierre; from there on it is only a step to a quarrel, a fight, and a run for bed. If anyone still harbours doubts as to Godard's technical competence, a study of his brilliant manipulation of this complex succession of linking moods and movements should be sufficient to dispel them once and for all.

"SOLEIL, VOICI LE TEMPS DE LA RAISON ARDENTE"—
GUILLAUME APOLLINAIRE, QUOTED BY
ROGER LEENHARDT IN *Une Femme Mariée*

Godard is the most open-ended of artists. He doesn't make problem pictures of the sort which deal with a controversial subject and come up with an answer. He assumes that the controversy is embedded in life, and maybe isn't even controversial. *Le Petit Soldat* refused to tackle the Algerian "problem," and yet, as Godard says, the film now stands as "witness to an epoch" and its complex moral repercussions. In *Une Femme Mariée*, Charlotte's questions to the doctor about contraception and sexual pleasure, and Robert's casual assertion of police corruption—both delivered as though the subjects were unexceptional and needed no apology or introduction—reveal far more about defensive attitudes, and also hurt more, than any amount of reasoned, documented attacks.

Nor does he start with an answer and work backwards in order to find the given data (perhaps one of the troubles with *The Red Desert*). "Intelligence," in Roger Leenhardt's definition, "is to understand before asserting"; and what we are left with at the end of *Une Femme Mariée* is simply a closely and passionately documented question-mark. Charlotte may yet meet with Robert again and marry him; she might go back to Pierre; she might kill herself; or she might just conceivably escape from the web, meet her Franz, and set sail like Odile to discover the wonders of the world. But we have the evidence, and whatever the outcome may be, as soon as we discover what it is, we will know why: because we understand Charlotte, and we understand the world which has shaped her.

What Is Art, Jean-Luc Godard?
by ARAGON

What is art? I have been asking myself this question ever since I saw Jean-Luc Godard's *Pierrot le fou,* in which Belmondo-the-Sphinx asks an American director the question, "What is the cinema?" There is one thing of which I am sure; and thus I can begin all this, in spite of my trepidations, by an assertion which, at least, stands like a solid beam driven into the middle of a swamp: art, today, is Jean-Luc Godard. It is perhaps for this reason that his films, and in particular this film, have provoked insult and scorn; people say things about Godard's films that they would never say about a current commercial production—they allow themselves to go to extremes having nothing to do with criticism: they attack the man.

The American, in *Pierrot le fou,* says about the cinema what one could say about the Vietnam war, or any war, for that matter. And the statements have a strange ring to them when they are considered in the context of that extraordinary scene in which Belmondo and Karina, in order to earn some money, improvise a little play before an American couple and their sailors somewhere on the Riviera. He plays Uncle Sam, she plays the niece of Uncle Ho. "But it's damn good, damn good!" exclaims (in English) the delighted sailor with the red beard . . . because the film is in color, of all things. But I'm not going to tell you what happens in the film, like everybody else. This is not a review. Furthermore, this film defies review. You might as well go count the small change in a million dollars! What would I have said if Belmondo, or Godard, had asked me, "What is the cinema?" I would have answered in a different way, by talking about certain people. The cinema, for me, was at first

From Les Lettres françaises, *no. 1096 (September 9–15, 1965): 1, 8. Reprinted by permission of the publisher. Translated by Royal S. Brown.*

Charlie Chaplin, then Renoir, Buñuel, and now Godard. That's all; it's quite simple. Somebody is going to say I'm forgetting Eisenstein and Antonioni. You're wrong, I'm not forgetting them. Or several others, for that matter. But I'm not talking about the cinema, I'm talking about art. Therefore, the question must be discussed in this context, in the context of another art, of one art with another one, a long history, in order to resume what art has become for us—I mean contemporary art, a modern art—painting, for example. In order to characterize it through its personalities.

Painting, in the modern sense of the word, begins with Géricault, Delacroix, Courbet, Manet. And then the multitude follows. Finding its raison d'être because of these painters, or in using them as a starting point, or in opposing them, or in going beyond them. A flourishing such as has not been seen since the Italian Renaissance. In order to be entirely summed up in a man named Picasso. What interests me, for the moment, is this period of pioneers in which one can still compare the young cinema to painting. The game of saying who Renoir is, or who Buñuel is, doesn't amuse me. But Godard is Delacroix.

First of all because of the way his work has been received. At Venice, it would appear. I wasn't at Venice, and I didn't belong to the juries that handed out the prizes and the Oscars. I saw, I found myself seeing *Pierrot le fou*, that's all. I won't talk about the critics. They're good enough at dishonoring themselves! Nor am I going to contradict them. There were some, of course, who were taken by the film's grandeur—Yvonne Baby, Chazal, Chapier, Cournot. . . . All the same, I can't pass up this chance to mention Michel Cournot's extraordinary article—not so much because of what he says, which manifests an almost exclusive obsession with the reflections of personal life in the film (for Cournot, like so many others, is intoxicated by cinema-truth, whereas I much prefer cinema-lie). But all right! at least we have here a man who lets himself go when he likes something. Furthermore, he knows how to write, if you'll pardon the expression—even if there is only one left—to me, that's important. I love language, marvelous language, delirious language: nothing is rarer than the language of passion in this world, where we live with the fear of being caught unawares, a fear that goes back, you'd better believe it, to the flight from Eden, to that moment when Adam and Eve notice they are naked, before the invention of the fig leaf.

What was I talking about? Ah! yes;[1] I love language, and it's for that reason that I love Godard. Who is completely language.

No, that's not what I was talking about; I was saying that Godard's work has been received like Delacroix'. At the Salon of 1827, which is just as good as Venice, Eugène had hung up his *La Mort de Sardanapale,* which he called his *Massacre no. 2,* because he too was a painter of massacres and not a painter of battles. He had had, he says, a number of difficulties with "the jackass members of the jury." When he saw his painting on the wall ("My little daub is perfectly placed") next to the paintings of the other artists, it gave him the impression, he said, "of a premiere where everybody boos." This, before the booing ever started. (. . .)

It happens that I went to look at *La Mort de Sardanapale* a little while ago. What a painting this "massacre" is! Personally, I greatly prefer it to *La Liberté sur les barricades,* which I'm sick and tired of hearing about. But that isn't really the question here. The problem is just how the *art* of Delacroix resembles, in this case, the *art* of Godard in *Pierrot le fou.* Doesn't the relationship strike you immediately? I'm speaking for those who have seen the film. Apparently the relationship has not struck *them* immediately.

While I was watching *Pierrot,* I had forgotten everything one is apparently supposed to say and think about Godard. That he has tics, that he quotes all over the place, that he is preaching to us, that he believes in this or in that . . . in short, that he is unbearable, talky, and a moralist (or an immoralist); all I could see was one single thing, and that was that the film is beautiful. Superhumanly beautiful. All you see for two hours is that kind of beauty which the word "beauty" defines quite poorly: what has to be said about this procession of pictures is that it is, that they are quite simply sublime. Today's readers are not very fond of the superlative. Too bad. I find this film shot through with a sublime beauty. The word is ordinarily reserved for actresses and for the special vocabulary of theater people. Too bad. Constantly, sublimely beautiful. You'll notice that I hate adjectives.

Pierrot is, therefore (like *Sardanapale*), a color film. Using a wide screen. Which stands apart from all other color films because the use of a *means* in Godard always has an *end,* and because this means

---

[1] For tic collectors: this is, in my writing, a tic. This note turns it into an *auto-collage.*

almost constantly involves its own self-examination. It is not simply because the film is well photographed and because the colors are beautiful. . . . It *is* well photographed, and the colors *are* beautiful. But there is something else involved. The colors are those of the world such as it is . . . how is it said? You have to have remembered: "How horrible life is! but it is always beautiful." [2] If it is said in other words in the film, it amounts to the same thing. But Godard does not stop with the world such as it is: for instance, suddenly the screen becomes monochrome, all red, or all blue, as during the sophisticated cocktail party at the beginning, a sequence that probably provoked the initial irritation of a certain number of critics (which reminds me of a certain evening at the Champs-Elysées, during the premiere of a ballet for which Elsa [Triolet] had done the scenario, Jean Rivier the music, Boris Kochno the choreography, and Brassaï the settings; the name of the work was *Le Réparateur de radios*, and the audience went wild booing and hissing, because the ballet showed people dancing in a nightclub, and, after all, what would you expect? all the members of Parisian high society found themselves to be the target!). During the party sequence, the abandonment of polychromaticism without returning to black and white *means* J.-L. Godard's reflection on both the world, into which he introduces Jean-Paul Belmondo, and on the technical means of expression at his disposal. This is further borne out when this scene is almost immediately followed by a color effect which is in turn followed by a shot of fireworks and then, slightly later, by bursts of light that follow one another without any possible justification in a nocturnal Paris in which the passion of the hero for Anna Karina suddenly becomes a reality; this latter effect takes the arbitrary form of discs, of colored moons sweeping across the windshield like rain, coloring their faces and their lives with an arbitrariness that seems to deny the world while marking the entrance of a deliberate arbitrariness into their lives. For J.-L. G., color does not exist simply to show us that a girl has blue eyes or that a certain gentleman is a member of the Legion of Honor. By necessity, a film by Godard that offers the possibility of color is going to show us something that could not be shown in black and white, a kind of *voice* that cannot resound when colors are *mute*.

In Delacroix' pallet, the reds—vermilion, Venice red, the red

<hr>

[2] This is not a quotation; all the sentences I may quote are the dreams of a deaf man.

lacquer of Rome, or madder, mingling with white, cobalt, and cadmium (does this represent a particular kind of Daltonism on my part?)—eclipse for me all the other hues, as if the latter were only put there to serve as a background for the reds. One might quote the words of Philarète Chasles concerning Musset: "He is a poet who has no color . . . ," and so forth. "Personally, I prefer gaping wounds and the vivid color of blood. . . ." This sentence, which has always remained in my mind, came back to me quite naturally when I saw *Pierrot le fou.* Not only because of the blood. Red sings in the film like an obsession. As in Renoir, where a Provençal house with its terraces reminds one here of the *Terrasses à Cagnes.* Like a dominant color of the modern world. So insistently does Godard use the color that when I came out of the film, I saw nothing else in Paris but the reds: signs indicating one-way streets; the multiple eyes of the red stoplights; girls in cochineal-colored slacks; madder-colored shops, scarlet-colored cars, red lead paint on the balconies of run-down buildings, the tender carthamus of lips; and from the words of the film, only the following sentence, which Godard has Pierrot say, remained in my mind: "I can't stand the sight of blood," which, according to Godard, comes from Federico Garcia Lorca. From which work? What does it matter . . . from the *Lament on the Death of Ignacio Sanchez Mejias,*[3] I can't stand the sight of blood, I can't see, I can't, I . . . The entire film is nothing but this immense sob caused because the hero is unable to, because the hero cannot stand to see blood, or to shed it, or to be obliged to shed it. A madder, a scarlet, a vermilion, a carmine-colored blood perhaps . . . the blood of the *Massacres de Scio,* the blood of *La Mort de Sardanapale,* the blood of July 1830, their children's blood that will be shed in the three *Médée furieuse* paintings (the one from 1838 and the ones from 1859 and 1862), all the blood that covers the lions and tigers in their battles with horses. . . . Never has so much blood flowed on the screen, red blood, from the first cadaver in Anna-Marianne's apartment until her own blood; never has blood on the screen been so conspicuous as it is in the automobile accident, in the dwarf killed with a pair of scissors, and I don't know what else,

---

[3] In the *Llanto por Ignacio Sanchez Mejias* (1935), the sentence is not formulated in the same manner. It is in the second part of this poem, entitled *La sangre derramada* ("wasted blood"), that you find the refrain "Que no quiero verla!" ("How I don't want to see it!"). Godard told me: "It's Lorca, but it could just as well not be Lorca!"

"I can't stand the sight of blood; *Que no quiero verla!*" And it isn't Lorca but the car radio that coldly announces the death of 115 Viet Cong soldiers. . . . Here, it is Marianne who speaks up: "It's terrible, isn't it, how anonymous it is. . . . They say 115 Viet Cong, and it doesn't really mean anything. And yet they were all men, and you don't know who they are, whether they loved a woman, whether they had children, whether they'd rather go to the movies or the theater. You don't know anything about them. All they say is that 115 were killed. It's just like photography, which has always fascinated me. . . ." Here, you don't see the blood, or its color. But everything seems to revolve around this color, in an extraordinary way.

For nobody knows better than Godard how to show the order of disorder. Always. In *Les Carabiniers, Vivre sa vie, Bande à part*, this film. The disorder of this world is its basic matter, arising from the modern cities, shining with neon and formica; in the suburban areas or in interior courtyards, which nobody ever sees with an artist's eyes; the twisted girders, the rusty machines, the trash, the tin cans: this whole shantytown of our lives; we couldn't live without it, but we conveniently put it out of our minds. And from this, as well as from automobile accidents and murders, Godard creates beauty. The order of what by definition cannot have any order. And when the two lovers, who have been thrown into a muddled and tragic adventure, cover up their tracks by blowing up their car next to a wrecked car, they cross France from the north to the south, and it seems that, in order to continue covering up their tracks, they once again, they still have to walk through water, in order to cross that river that could be the Loire . . . and later on in that lost area near the Mediterranean where, while Belmondo is beginning to write, Anna Karina walks (in the water) in a kind of hopeless rage from one end of the screen to the other while repeating the following sentences like a song for the dead: "What's there to do? Don't know what to do. . . . What's there to do? Don't know what to do. . . ." All this concerning the Loire.

As I watched this river, with its islets and its sand, I thought that at least it is the one you see in the background in the *Nature morte aux homards* (which is in the Louvre), which Delacroix is supposed to have painted at Beffes, in the Cher River near the Charité-sur-Loire. This strange arrangement (or disorder) of a hare and a pheasant with two lobsters (cooked vermilion red) on the net of a hunting bag and a rifle, all in front of the vast landscape with the river and its islands may very well have been painted for a general living in the Berri province; it nonetheless remains an extraordinary slaughter, this *Massacre no. 2-bis*, which was done around the same time as *La Mort de Sardanapale* and which appeared next to the latter painting in the Salon of 1827.[4] It represents the trying out of a new technique in which the color was mixed with a copal varnish. All the nature scenes in *Pierrot le fou* are similarly varnished with some kind of 1965 copal, which makes it seem as if we are seeing these sights for the first time. What is certain is that there was no predecessor for the *Nature morte aux homards*, that meeting of an umbrella and a sewing machine on a dissection table in a landscape, just as there is no other predecessor than Lautréamont to Godard. And I no longer know what disorder is, and what order is. Perhaps Pierrot's madness is that he is there to put into the disorder of our era the stupefying order of passion. Perhaps. The desperate order of passion (one sees despair in Pierrot from the very beginning, the despair of his own marriage, on the one hand, and the passion, the lyricism that represent his only hope of escaping from it).

The year that Eugène Delacroix, suddenly, left for Morocco, crossing France through "snow and bitter, freezing cold . . . a gust of wind and rain," 1832, there was no Salon at the Louvre because of an outbreak of cholera in Paris. But in May a charity exposition replaced the Salon, and here five small paintings lent by a friend represented the absent Delacroix. Three of them seem to have been done in rapid succession, probably during the period 1826–1827: the *Étude de femme couchée* (or *Femme aux bas blancs*), which is in the Louvre; the *Jeune femme caressant un perroquet,* which is in the Lyons museum; and *Le Duc de Bourgogne montrant le corps de sa maîtresse au Duc d'Orléans* (I have no idea where this one is located).[5]

---

[4] And why, in the foreground, is there a blue Wyvern, a heraldic animal found in various legends of the Berri region? And what about the hunter who had cooked his lobsters!

[5] The person in question here is Louis I of Bourgogne, the lover of the Queen of France Isabeau de Bavière, and of her uncle from Orléans, Philippe le Hardi. It is not hard to understand why these paintings were not shown with the *Sardanapale* in 1827 and that the absence of Delacroix was necessary in order for the "friend" who owned them (probably Robert Soulier) to send them to the exposition of 1832. It is not hard to imagine the scandal they provoked in the midst of a cholera epidemic.

These paintings were done in the midst of Delacroix' relationship with Mme Dalton, but it is impossible to know who the three nude women of these works actually were, or even whether it was the same woman. No doubt the *Jeune femme au perroquet* has the same heavy eyelids one sees in the *Dormeuse,* whicn is apparently Mme Dalton. But neither one resembles the portrait of this lady done by Bonington. In Delacroix' *Journal,* a number of young women who came to pose for him make a brief appearance, and the artist made notes about each one of them in a very particular kind of code. Whatever the case may be, *Le Duc de B. etc.* is held to be the sequel to the first two *Études,* and nobody doubts that there was a striptease coincidence between this painting and life, Eugène no doubt being the Duc de Bourgogne and his friend Robert Soulier the Duc d'Orléans. And everyone knows how Mme Dalton went from one to the other. But the perversity of the painter is not really the point here—in *Pierrot le fou,* it is Belmondo who plays with a parrot. And I'm not saying all this to show how, if I wanted, I too could indulge in the delirium of interpretation. Furthermore, isn't this the answer to the question I started off with? Art is the delirium of the interpretation of life.

If I wanted to, furthermore, I would approach J.-L. G. from the painters' side to show the origin of one of the characteristics of his art for which he is the most often reproached. Quotations, as the critics call them; collages, as I propose they should be called (and it seems to me that Godard, in his interviews, has used the same term). Painters were the first to use collages, in the sense that Godard and I mean here, even before 1910 and their systematic utilization by Braque and Picasso; there is, for instance, Watteau, whose *L'Enseigne de Gersaint* represents an immense collage, in which all the paintings on the wall of the shop and the portrait (that is being packed) of Louis XIV by Hyacinthe Rigaut are *quoted,* as everybody likes to say. In Delacroix, all you need is a painting from 1823, *Milton et ses filles,* to find a "quotation" used as a means of expression. There was certainly some stimulus that made Delacroix use, as the subject of a painting, a man who cannot see, in order to show us his thought: the pale blind man is sitting in an easy chair with his hand on an embroidered tapestry covering a table; his fingers seem to be feeling the colors of the tapestry, while there is a pot of flowers that escapes him. But below his two daughters seated on low chairs, one taking down the words of *Paradise Lost,* the other holding a musical instrument that has become silent, one sees an un-framed painting on the wall showing Adam and Eve fleeing the Garden of Paradise and the Angel who is banishing them—defense-less, naked, and ashamed. This is a collage intended to show us the invisible; that is, the thought of the man with the empty eyes. This technique has not been lost since that time. There is the painting by Seurat, for instance, *Les Poseuses,* in which, in the painter's studio, three undressed women, the one at the right taking off some black stockings, are next to the huge painting of *La Grande Jatte,* which is quite appropriately "quoted" here so that the whole thing will be something else than what we call a striptease. And how about Courbet when he makes a collage of Baudelaire in a corner of his *Atelier?* In the same way Godard, in *Pierrot,* stamps the letter with Raymond Devos before sending it, as he had done with the philosopher Brice Parain in *Vivre sa vie.* These are not characters from a novel; they are signs to show us how Adam and Eve were banished from Paradise.

Furthermore, if there is, in this area, a difference between *Pierrot le fou* and Godard's other films, it lies in a certain overall impres-sion that people will not fail to see as Godard simply trying to outdo himself. People have already been reproaching the director of *Le Mépris* and *Le Petit soldat* for this technique for years now. They find it to be a mania they hope he will get rid of. The critics hope to discourage him, and they stand ready to applaud a Godard who would simply stop being Godard and make films the way everybody else does. They obviously have not succeeded, if this film is any indication. If anyone should be discouraged, it is the critics. The growth of this *system* of collages in *Pierrot le fou* is such that there are entire sections (*chapters,* Godard calls them) that are nothing *but* collages. The entire cocktail party at the beginning. Or even before that. The collages simply continue; everybody recognizes (because Belmondo holds the paperback edition of Elie Faure's history of art in his hand) that the text on Velasquez that begins the whole story is by Elie Faure. On the other hand, they're not sure why, later on, Pierrot is reading the most recent printing of the *Pieds-Nickelés* comic strip. This in a story in which Belmondo waves a *Série noire* novel about, as if to say, "Here is what a novel is really all about!" That gives me quite a laugh: when I was young, nobody said anything if I was found reading Pierre Louys or Charles-Henry Hirsch; but my mother forbade me to read the *Pieds-Nickelés.* I hate to think of what would have happened to me if she had ever caught me with a copy of *L'Épatant*, in which the comic strip appeared. I don't know what the black-leather-jacket generation must think of the *Pieds-Nickelés*; but for people of my generation whose memories are not entirely grisly, the resemblance between the *Pieds-Nickelés* and the characters of the "organization" in the complicated game in which Pierrot has become involved is immediately evident—so much so, in fact, that this whole affair, when Belmondo reads *Les Pieds-Nickelés*, takes on a slightly more complex meaning than it seems to have at first glance.

That is not the essential point—but when everything is said and done, you have to accept the idea that the collages are not illustrations of the film, but that they are the film itself. That they are the very matter of paintings, and that painting would not exist outside of them. Thus, all those who persist in taking the matter for a gimmick would be better off, in the future, changing records. You may hate Godard, but you cannot ask him to practice any other art than his own . . . the flute or water-painting. You must see that Pierrot who is not named Pierrot and who screams at Marianne, "My name is Ferdinand!" finds himself next to a Picasso which shows the artist's son (Paulo, as a child) dressed up as a Pierrot-type clown. And certainly the large number of Picassos[6] on the wall does not manifest any desire on Godard's part to show off his talents as a connoisseur, certainly not when Picassos can be bought at your local neighborhood department store. One of the first portraits of Jacqueline, in profile, shows up, somewhat later, with the head pointed downward because in the world and in Pierrot's brain, everything *is* upside down. Not to mention the resemblance between the hair painted on the canvas and the long, soft locks of Anna Karina. Or Godard's obsession for Renoir (Marianne is named Marianne Renoir). Or the collages involving advertising ("There was the Greek civilization, the Roman civilization, and now we have the ass-hole civilization . . ."), beauty products, underwear.

What Godard is particularly reproached for are his spoken collages

[6] Picassos . . . the industrialization of the work of art has become a new socio-logical phenomenon. And you can have on your walls (in a smaller version than the original) the *Guernica*, for instance, as a permanent explanation of Algeria, of Vietnam, of Santo Domingo, of the Indo-Pakistani conflict (an "up-to-date" remark). . . . Snobbery is out of date. A Picasso means something and is taken by the everyday spectator for what it has to tell: once again, we are right in the middle of the era of the *Massacres de Scio*, of the *Sardanapale* era.

—too bad for those who did not react, in *Alphaville* (which is not my favorite Godard), to the humor of Pascal being quoted by Eddie Constantine as he is being questioned by the robot-computer. Godard is also reproached, along with everything else, for quoting Céline. In *Pierrot*, it happens to be *Guignol's Band*—but if I were to start talking about Céline, this could go on forever. I prefer Pascal, no doubt, and I certainly cannot forget what the author of *Voyage au bout de la nuit* became. But this does not prevent the fact that *Voyage*, when it appeared, was a damn beautiful book, and that subsequent generations, who lose themselves in the novel, find us unjust, stupid, and partisan. And we are just that. These are misunderstandings between a father and son. But you can't solve them by commandments: "My young Godard, thou shalt not quote Céline!" And so he quotes him, fancy that.

As for me, I am quite proud to have been quoted (or "collaged") by the creator of *Pierrot* with a regularity that is none the less remarkable than the determination Godard shows as he shoves Céline in your face. None the less remarkable, but much less remarked upon by the critics, either because they haven't read my works or because I annoy them just as much as Céline, but offer them fewer areas to attack than Céline, so that only their irritation remains and they use the weapon of silence, an irritation that becomes worse because it remains mute. In *Pierrot le fou*, a large extract, spoken by Belmondo, of *La Mise à mort* . . . —a good two paragraphs; I don't know all my works by heart, but I can certainly recognize them when I hear them—shows me once again the kind of secret understanding that exists between this young man and me on certain essential things—let him find his tailor-made expression either in my works or elsewhere, where I have my dreams (the cover of *L'Ame* at the beginning of *La Femme mariée*; the French translation, *Admirables fables*, done by Elsa of Mayakovsky's work, on the lips of the partisan girl about to be shot in *Les Carabiniers*). When Baudelaire, in his poem "*Les Phares*," had used Delacroix ("*Lac de sang, hanté des mauvais anges* . . .") in a "collage," the aged painter wrote to him, "A thousand thank-you's for your good opinion—I owe you a great many just for *Les Fleurs du mal*; I've already talked to you about your volume in passing, but it deserves a great deal more. . . ." And when, at the Salon of 1859, the critics tore Delacroix apart, it was Baudelaire who took his side and answered for him, and the painter wrote to the poet, "Since I've had the good fortune to please you, I can console myself over the reprimands I received. You treat me in a manner that is usually reserved for *great people who have died.* You make me blush while making me very happy at the same time. That is the way we're made."

I'm not quite sure why I'm quoting this, why I'm making a *collage* of this in my article—everything is backwards here, except that, actually, when, in that intimate little theater, where only Elsa sat with me, I heard these words that I knew but did not immediately recognize, I blushed in the darkness. But I'm not the person who resembles Delacroix. It's the other one. That child of genius.

Here I am back at the beginning. What is new, what is great, what is sublime always provokes insults, scorn, and outrage. And this is always more unbearable for an older man. At the age of sixty-one, Delacroix met with the worst affront given by those who hand out glory. How old is Godard? And even if the game had been lost, the game is won, he can believe me on that. (. . .)

How many films has Godard already shot? Every one of us is a Pierrot le fou in one way or another, Pierrots who sit down on the railroad tracks, who wait for the train to come and run over them, and who dash out of the way at the last minute, who continue to live. Whatever the ups and downs of our lives may be, and whether or not they resemble Pierrot's. Pierrot blows himself up, but at the last second he decided he didn't want to. Nothing is over, particularly since others will follow the same path; only the date will change. How alike it all is. . . .

I set off to talk about art. And I've only talked about life.

Atonal Cinema for Zombies

by GILLES JACOB

> *"Why did Hamlet worry about visions*
> *after death? isn't life haunted by much*
> *more frightening visions?"*
>
> CHEKHOV, *Notebooks*

Recently, French director Jean-Pierre Melville took it upon himself to shoot a "Godard" film between eight o'clock in the morning
and six o'clock in the evening, using an outline invented the same
day by some twenty journalists invited for this purpose. Conclusion: it takes Godard a week (or two, or three) to do the same
thing. . . . He's being lazy!

Thus, each time a new Godard comes out—around two times a
year—the quarrels start up all over again and misunderstandings
run rampant. For some, who are becoming more and more rare
but who are all the more virulent because they are beginning to
stand out, Godard represents nothing more than a booby trap, a
practical joker expert in the art of making fun of everybody, an
impostor who has read all the articles published on him and who,
like a parasite on his own reflection, tries his best to pass himself
off as Jean-Luc Godard. For others, he is a boring filmmaker with
muddled ideas who makes more duds than good films ("and has he
ever made a completely good film?"); the members of this group,
heaping neither unctuous praise nor bitter scorn upon the director,
would rather talk about something else. Others are irritated by
Godard's cavalier attitude toward his audiences: it isn't hard to
skim through a book that bores you some of the time and fascinates
you the rest of the time; but in the movies, it isn't as easy. How can
you show the same detachment toward a film that appears im-

From Cinema 67, *no. 113 (February 1967): 68–86. Reprinted by permission of the publisher and the author. Translated by Royal S. Brown.*

provised and effortless and seems to be an uncontrolled source of automatic writing? How can you see the film without looking at it, whether discretely or distractedly?

Yet another, somewhat more subtle group, claims that there is an inherent contradiction between the unfinished impression given by Godard's films and the constant use of the same words and themes that occupy his entire work, as if the director considered each of his films as only approximations of his thought or as a point of departure for a new search. Perfection, says this group, can be approached only through work, reflection, and revision. There's no such thing as improvisation in art. A film must be presented as a finished piece, and not as the rough draft of a sketch, using the fallacious pretext that the work exists and is all that is necessary. No doubt a work of genius can be created in a sudden spurt, right on the sound stage; but against this, consider how many vain attempts result in a second-best expedient that is not replaced, for lack of anything better. The appearance of improvisation that gives this effort some character is but a supplementary fragment of the effort. And, once the preplanned take is ready to shoot, how much easier it is to upset everything when one has the possible excuse of improvisation. Thus the opinion of this group is that even the impromptu must be organized and worked out.

Finally, there are people, of which I am one, who prefer to see a Godard film as a partial, biased, and impassioned vision resembling its single creator; as a series of digressions broken up by the hesitations of the analysis as well as by the diverse directions taken by a manner of thinking which is itself hesitant and, it must be said, often muddled, but which occasionally touches on *two or three things* that are among the most profound of our times. These people feel that that inquisitive and apparently insensitive individual behind the dark glasses refuses to limit himself to attracting attention to the cues of a preestablished, and therefore frozen, shot, when he would rather be filming the pulse of life. They feel that Godard's art grows from a mysterious florescence of the imagination, from an immediate outburst of the conscious mind; that a Godard film simply *is*, as opposed to a film that is *made*; and that in seeing a Godard film, which seems to be being made before their eyes, without their knowing at first what direction the work will take, they are seeing contemporary art speaking, as an expression of what people are, in its most natural form.

This is why, to come back to Melville's little joke I mentioned at the beginning (other people have tried the same thing; all you have to do is see the results, for example in Lelouch's early films), I am sure that this kind of bet can be won, but also that the result would be a Godard film without Godard—in other words a shadow. For Godard—and neither Aragon nor the young people all over the world who have shown great interest in Godard have failed to notice the fact—is one of the last of today's poets, and he is a poet who is in perfect tune with a generation that has grown up on the movies. And the fact that this profession of faith has been occasioned by the appearance of a new and important work, even if it is not the one I like the best, takes nothing away from this conviction. For the problem appears to me to be less one of judging whether *Made in U.S.A.* is better than *Bande à part* (at present, I would give first place to *Pierrot le fou*) than of accepting Godard and putting him in his proper perspective.

And if, in fifty or a hundred years, Godard comes to be considered, as a few of us predict, as one of the most important creators of our era, it is precisely because he will have given the least superficial chronicle of it by using the most superficial of its elements— pictures, posters, comic strips, newspaper clippings, book titles, graffiti . . . everything which, for a sociologist storing up the present for the future, constitutes the word filled with its true meaning before misunderstanding has transformed it into lie. Because Godard will have filmed, as has nobody else, the Champs-Elysées of *A bout de souffle*, the Geneva of *Le Petit soldat*, the Porte Saint-Martin of *Une Femme est une femme*, the cafés and the streets of *Vivre sa vie*, the shantytowns and abandoned property of *Les Carabiniers*, the Capri of *Le Mépris*, the dreary suburban villa of *Bande à part*, the Orly Airport of *Une Femme mariée*, the bypass highway of *Alphaville*, the cross-country tableau of France of *Pierrot le fou*, the elevated *métro* line of *Masculin-Féminin*, the Atlantic-City-les-Moulineaux of *Made in U.S.A.*, and the huge construction projects in present-day Paris of *Deux ou trois choses que je sais d'elle*, a film that was shot almost simultaneously with *Made in U.S.A.*, the second part of a diptych the director intended to have projected simultaneously—first one reel from one, then a reel from the other, and so forth; an ideal approach to these two most recent "Godards," in fact, would by necessity be to study them simultaneously. Because Godard will have contributed to the dismembering of the narrative, to the total disarticulation of the conventional cinematographic syntax; because, with his incoherent, deliberately discontinuous and yet obvious style, Godard will have helped set free an art ensnared in the rapidity of its momentum, somewhat in the manner of the dodecaphonic composers. Whether he is serious or not, Godard is, at any rate, the first serial film-maker.

Because, finally, with his vocation for provocation and his global interests, Godard will have left a personal stamp even on the most stupid puns and the most farcical alliterations, admirably illus-trating Valéry's idea that "stupid people feel that joking is not being serious and that a play on words is not an answer."

For the moment, however, I am quite afraid that these misunder-standings will not subside with the appearance of *Made in U.S.A.*, even though Godard's mood here is one of anger and not of joking.

I don't know exactly during what period Godard's twelfth film is supposed to take place; but this time it is not *"Figaro-Pravda"* that is being read in a world that is both close and far away, but *Ouest-France, Le Monde, La Quinzaine littéraire, L'Express, News-week,* and *Le Nouvel observateur*; and the journalist who appears for an instant and obtains only the classic "no comment" from the policemen she is questioning probably works for one of these papers and not for the "Atlantic City Magazine."

Nor does the audience hear that scratchy and inhuman voice of Alpha 60, the electronic computer of *Alphaville*; instead, it is Godard's voice, whose monotonous and by now familiar timbres offer extracts from authors who have recently come on the scene.

Are we only in Atlantic City, where Anna Karina is supposed to have come to avenge her former lover, who has been murdered under mysterious circumstances? In Atlantic City, does one find a café with a French name, "A la descente de la gare"; a street named "Rue Jean-Jaurès"; an advertising ashtray recognized by every Frenchman; a book published by Gallimard; an air-pressure guide, posted on a garage wall, for Michelin tires; a film-poster studio for the "Lux Film" company; a tollbooth on the West highway where a car from the Europe 1 radio station stops? Of course not. Once again, we find ourselves in one of those typically Godard settings that we are beginning to easily recognize. And it is the meeting places (bars, cafés, swimming pools), the places you pass through (garages, airport waiting-rooms), the deserted places (movie thea-ters, streets), the antechambers of anguish (doctor's offices) and the temporary shelters (hotel rooms, unfurnished apartments) of these settings that emerge in a lacerating fashion. We are especially in the France of 1967, an assuredly Americanized France overwhelmed by gadgets, modern comforts, and "Made in U.S.A." products; the coy and satiated France of de Gaulle, a country less worried about the up-and-coming legislative elections than about getting instant relief from two gluttonous meals with the help of Alka-Seltzer.

Under the Fifth Republic, the bourgeoisie no longer represents a simple question of class: it has become an entire mentality. A search for a "better way of life" has bit by bit numbed the life of the man in the street who, within the concrete verticality of soulless metropolises, rarely gets excited about anything beyond the love affairs of a princess, gastronomic pleasures, and the amount of horsepower for a certain car. Listen to the speech by Michel-Ange that Godard wanted to use (but later cut) to end *Les Carabiniers*: "You haven't understood anything, you haven't seen anything, or heard anything; go home in your compact cars, swallow your tranquilizers and sleep well." And what indeed can the artist do when he is faced with this resigned torpor, if not to try to instigate the hope of a violent reaction? If not to react against the proliferation of the symbols of this civilization, from free key rings advertising a product to the latest hair style, all studied by specialists in the mechanism of mass psychology (the badge saying "Kiss Me, I'm Italian" worn by Jean-Pierre Léaud). As Godard himself has said, "It is always easy to manipulate a crowd: you begin like Audiard and it all ends up in the Nuremberg speeches."

With *Made in U.S.A.*, Godard, whose evolution has much the same character as Bresson's, has arrived at his nonfigurative stage. Any vestiges of realism or narrative disappear. No more plot, even a very loose one—an attempt, furtive notations manifesting no qualms about contradiction, the journal of a "journey to the end of night," with its blank spaces and its crossed-out words. Until this film, you could always see Godard's protagonists telling one story or several . . . when they weren't giving speeches—all that is left in *Made in U.S.A.* is interrogations. And the police force (but which police force?) remains silent—as does the sound track much of the time. In this film, there is only a young woman about whom we know nothing, save that she seems related to Godard's earlier heroines, and that she is more an Anna Karina imbued with the mythical past of her former meetings with the creator of *Une*

Femme est une femme than she is a Paula Nelson who, as the director is quick to point out, is not sure that she is fulfilling her role as a Humphrey Bogart type avenger through love, but rather through duty, through the memory of a dead love. Love itself has disappeared. According to Goddard, who is not indulging in paradox, "To be sure of living, you have to be sure of loving. You have to be sure of dying."

As for the other characters: they are not even silhouettes but rather automatons we can recognize because we have met them before; what we have here are the puppets of *Alphaville*. In *Made in U.S.A.*, you can no longer take the tranquilizers recommended by Michel-Ange and copiously taken by the creatures of *Le Nouveau monde* (in ROGOPAG) and Alphaville—do debrained robots need tranquilizers?

At the beginning of the film, we see Karina feeling one of these robots to make sure he is unarmed. But isn't she also touching him to see whether he really exists in flesh and blood rather than as disincarnated ectoplasm, such as those feelingless characters in *The Red Desert*, in which only objects and "things" rise to the surface, as in the beautiful finale of *The Eclipse*? (Here Godard seconds Antonioni, as later on he seconds Resnais.) Humanism is no longer on the run, as I wrote about *Pierrot le fou*; it is dead in a cultureless world in which dictionaries are no longer used for anything but carrying firearms.

Godard's technique is transformed, becomes even more abstract and fragmented, in this vision of a world plunged into pain, cruelty, sex, and death. He uses any excuse to denounce something or someone new—"The moment the audience sees Subor with a gun in his hand. . . . Everybody laughs. . . . What I would have wanted would have been for all the people who were in the street while I was shooting that scene to scream, stop and jump on him. His mission was to escape from them. . . . Well, it was just the opposite; nothing hapepned at all." This scene from *Le Petit soldat*, as Godard recalled it during the Journées d'Annecy (see *Cinéma 65*, No. 94), is an excellent example of the extent to which Godard reacts to people's indifference, to their refusal to "become involved." Today, it seems that he can stand even less the apathy and nonreactionism of the zombies that we are—the lukewarm and calm inurement to assassinations, murders, torture, kidnapping, intimidation, power abuses, flouting of the law, the growing ascendency of a police state.

Whether it is a question of the Algerian War *(Le Petit soldat)*, the Vietnam war *(Pierrot le fou)*, the assassination of Kennedy *(Masculin-Féminin)*, the Ben Barka affair or the Charonne subway catastrophe *(Made in U.S.A.)*, Godard strips these events of their familiarity and presents them in the form of schematic elements such as submachine guns, revolvers, handcuffs, tape recordings, cars, money, swastikas, all of which are considered as essential material in their functions. More than ever, Godard, in *Made in U.S.A.*, has managed to disincarnate the object (such as a scream or an emotion-laden color) in order to attain the heights of an explosive and striking lyricism, which becomes even more evocative through its very abstraction, although this does not prevent the director from occasionally taking refuge in the moments of calm and tenderness represented by the instants when the camera concentrates on the pure face of Anna Karina in front of the greenery.

Thus, I know of no more unbearable image than the one, which seems innocuous and perhaps precisely because it seems innocuous, in which a cop quite calmly uses the end of his shoe to push down the head of his handcuffed prisoner, who is lying on the ground and trying to raise his head. The atrocity of this gesture is reinforced by the tranquillity with which it is executed—it is as if the policeman barely stopped what he was doing for a moment to wipe off his shoe.

Everywhere, right at the surface of the film, death is present, that hideous death that represents one of the constants of Godard's work. In a sequence that is just as striking as the swimming-pool scene in *Alphaville*, we even witness the sudden awareness of death: at the same moment as Jean-Pierre Léaud in the film, we feel the extraordinary sensation that he is going to die when Anna Karina suddenly asks him, "If you had to die, would you rather be warned, or would you rather have death come all at once?" "All at once," answers Léaud without thinking, with naive conviction. Immediately, he realizes that he has signed his death warrant, and the shot is fired before he even has the time to make a move. He calls out "Mama" several times; and this death, which appears ridiculous on paper, moves us; for even when his hour of death has arrived, he acts and mimes his death and falls the way some second or third gangster would fall in that American cinema with which he is so imbued, imitating some Ted de Corsia or Elisha Cook Jr., just as Paul in *Le Mépris* imitates the Dean Martin of *Some Came Running*. Cocteau comes to mind here. Or more particularly, Thomas, the impostor, who says to himself, " 'A bullet; I'm lost if I don't pretend to be dead.' But in him, fiction and reality were one and the same thing. Guillaume Thomas was dead."

"Aren't you fed up with these murders?" somebody in the film asks a man named Robert McNamara; the latter answers, "It's my job, it represents my happiness." And the Richard Nixon, who is sitting next to him, adds, "I'm with him." And what can you say about the individual, played by the amazing Laszlo Szabo, who uses the murder of other people for ideas for a novel he does not have the time to write—his own death (at the hands of Paula-Karina's accomplice, David Goodis) interrupts this sinister undertaking.

Unlike Fuller or Ray, to whom he dedicated his film, and unlike other American filmmakers he paradoxically admires, Godard never shows actual violence taking place but rather, uniquely, its consequences. Already, in *Pierrot le fou*, violence was avoided by a puritanical camera that turned such scenes into modern paintings. In *Made in U.S.A.*, it is the screen itself that takes its place. This is because the director does not want to give the spectator the pleasure (the enjoyment?) of this violence that he condemns; nor does he want to fall into mawkishness; instead, he tries to find equivalents for the newsreel extracts, which are transposed to the level of his art and seen from the angle of his experimentation with pictures and sounds. Which explains his use of ellipsis and his turning to abstraction. Which also explains his choice of anonymous silhouettes and his use of allegorical elements. The violent scenes are either evoked in fixed and therefore devitalized shots (already seen in *Pierrot le fou*) or skimmed over (Paula is kidnapped and knocked out in a fraction of a second). And the brief, two-chord bursts from Beethoven's Fifth, alternating with a limpid and melancholic theme by Schumann, which keeps returning as a leitmotif, give this symphony in blood-red a definitive and implacable quality. Blood, pools of blood, gaping wounds all leave their indelible impression on the projection of *Made in U.S.A.* And the horrible, bloody vision of that skeleton—victim, conscience, remorse, or all three at the same time?—of that skull with its ocular globes intact, staring fixedly into nothingness, covered with bandages like the invisible man.

Now, in this era of creeping Gaullism, the invisible man in France is the man of the left, who is both sentimental and impotent; or at least that elegant and acceptable left that has greeted

Godard's latest film with sarcasm and boredom, incapable as this group is of going beyond its own conflicts and seeing that it is being betrayed from the inside.

For to the themes that are already dear to him—the Americanization of contemporary life (the film's title); communication: language and words ("a bar cannot be two things at once," "you accumulate words by the ton, but that isn't all, you have to make something out of them . . . ," "If you really want me to, I'll try to make some sentences, but I don't like to do it. . . . The barman is not in the pencil's pocket") (see also *Vivre sa vie, Une Femme mariée,* and Godard's work, passim); war (*Les Carabiniers*); torture (*Le Petit soldat, Pierrot le fou*); advertising ("advertising is a form of fascism"); the police state ("words fail me to tell you how much I hate the police"); homages to the cinema he loves: Doris Mizogushi, rue Preminger, inspector Aldrich, Widmark, a certain Mark Dixon, detective—to all these themes that are dear to him, and to others that cross the screen, punctuated by the deafening roar of jet planes, with a vengeful freedom—this same freedom painted in blue letters that are shot up several times but that are always reborn—to these themes, Godard adds still another one, a supreme one: politics.

One thus better understands that the "rue Jean-Jaurès" is not put into the film by accident, but that it glorifies a man who, in his time, sacrificed his life for the unification of the diverse tendencies of the socialist left; one also sees that the theme of mutation, of transformation that has permeated each Godard film enters in here only in the form of the hypothetical desire to see the left change somehow.

Until *Made in U.S.A.,* Godard was a fascist for some, a communist for others (but didn't people say the same thing about *Citizen Kane?*); and for still others, he simply stood outside the fight. At present, one can now measure Godard's evolution since an ambiguous *Petit soldat* and a universal *Les Carabiniers.* It is no longer simply a question of the cloak-and-dagger dealings of secret agents; of spies who consort and agree amongst themselves, taking on double and even triple roles; nor is it simply a question of police forces (official or secret) that remain silent (a silence materially concretized in the film by the occasional elimination of the sound track). The Ben Barka affair raised the corner of a veil (which was quickly relowered) on certain intolerable actions which, undercover or otherwise (see also Sakkiet, the kidnapping of Argoud), make the most lugubrious inventions of modern crime novels seem like fairy tales. *Made in U.S.A.* is a deliberately, consciously made political film. Not a film on politics such as, for example, *Mr. Smith Goes to Washington, All the King's Men, Advise and Consent,* or *Le Combat dans l'île,* but a political *act* that is just as serious as putting a ballot in the ballot box, a critical analysis of our society, a warning speech in which, this time, the filmmaker has become so unequivocably involved that he felt he had to record it himself. He seems to be telling us, "I, Jean-Luc Godard, an artist and therefore a seeker, denounce the violence that is taking place in all its forms, and the liberal, impotent ethics of a scattered left. . . ." And in constructing, in using the Ben Barka affair as a point of departure, a theory based on his own views (which are occasionally a bit nebulous) on economy, politics, and ethics, Jean-Luc Godard runs into a certain bitterness, as is borne out by the long, final dialogue between Karina and Philippe Labro on the highway.

A political film, says Godard, is Walt Disney plus blood. Which is to say characters from cartoons or comic strips embroiled in the drama. Which is also to say the Manicheism of the good guys and the bad guys, the simplification of the notions of left and right, the separation of the nice people from the mean people, the wise men from the lunatics. On one hand, the wicked witch; on the other, the benevolent dwarfs; but in the middle, there is the cadaver of Snow White with, as with Rimbaud's *"Dormeur du val,"* a big, red hole in her right side.

Godard's crystallization becomes singularly clarified by a thought that Richard Brooks places in the mouth of one of his *Professionals*: "Perhaps since the beginning there has only been one revolution, the good guys against the bad guys. It's all a question of knowing who the good guys are and who the bad guys are." At least we now know what side of the barricades Godard and Brooks stand on. And if it is true, as Michel Flacon has pertinently noted, that there is only one true subject in art—the revolution—one might say that, in *Made in U.S.A.,* Godard takes on, in his own way, the role of the *Exterminating Angel.* Gone is the bated foil. Godard shoots red, blue, or yellow bullets, but never does he shoot blanks; and after this rather spectacular veering toward the left, I would not be surprised to see Godard turning toward Mao in

one of his upcoming films. But it is also with forms that Godard
makes revolution.

The whole affair had begun as early as *Pierrot le fou* and the
arrival of the most intense, pure hues and their inseparable juxtaposition on the canvas of the screen. One need only remember the
luminous, colored rapture and the luxurious shimmering of the
Mediterranean in *Pierrot*. Those tubes of color that Derain com-
pared to sticks of dynamite (the ending of Pierrot) gleam red once
again in *Made in U.S.A.* Whether he is a painter or not, Godard
is a colorist. His film is based on a contrast: on the one hand, there
is blood ("not blood, red!"), politics, money, fear; on the other
hand, there is color, which escapes from Godard's pallet like
multicolored scarves of an absolute purity, banishing any inter-
vention of color values in order to obtain impassioned reactions;
these colors are sometimes used as a vehement indictment; at other
times, they seem to say, "and yet how beautiful life (and love) could
be" (*Adieu Life, Adieu Love*).

Color represents the very superstructure of the film; it is color
which, taking precedence over the settings (which are generally neutral places one passes through and are hidden or camouflaged by
color—hotel, bar, garage, an exercise room, a warehouse), offers a
dynamic interplay of colored splashes in which the reds, the ochres,
the light violets, the yellows, and the oranges of a dress with multicolored squares that reminds one of Klee are not limited to appearing in the form of an absolute abstraction; rather, they create
rhythms, and they express ideas and feelings. Seen by Godard, a
red car-jack or a red telephone are like an apple seen by Cézanne.
The vibration of colors creates movement in a quasi-musical structure. A young woman passes by: yellow against a grey background,
red against a blue background, blue stripes against emerald foliage.
There is a girl with a Veronese blouse and a black dog; another girl
in an orange mini-skirt against an ochre wall, another in a yellow
knitted dress against cobalt blue shutters or a green shack. On a
wall, a red and white towel, and in the foreground, a girl in a
yellow sweater. In the physical-improvement exercise room, women
in carmine gym suits are pedaling, with blue hues and woodwork
in the background. One finds all these poetic transmutations in
those axes, more often than not vertical, which betray Godard's
physical passion for color. There is nothing less subdued, less re-
fined, less discrete. It is the reign of color for its own sake, color

unanimated by any light-plays or any reflections, and unaltered by any shadows. Immersing himself in pure color and relying uniquely on his visual sensitivity, Godard melodically juxtaposes his various unified surfaces, delights in unforeseen consonances and sudden dissonances, brings out the intensity of his hues through appropriate contrasts and thus succeeds in transforming his colors into a vibrant and fluid matter, into a sonorous explosion, a warm, vital stream that bursts forth like a Byzantine mosaic.

Made in U.S.A. is perhaps the third or fourth film in color. It arrives in its turn after *Muriel, The Red Desert,* and *Pierrot le fou.* Following Antonioni's cold dominant colors and the deliberately banal and ugly gamut of hues used by Resnais, Godard's fanfare sounds the fall-in. For this color has a function, the function of waking up the spectator just as the brutal interruptions of sound do. In *Muriel,* Resnais had already used, as an alarm to make the audience lucid, bright daylight shots interspersed with night shots. And Godard himself, at the risk of irritating, shone spotlights in his audiences' eyes in *Alphaville* and, in his very next film used windshield wipers against a blinding light (*Pierrot le fou*).

Gauche année zéro, gauche année zéro. Watch out! This book title (*The Lowest Point of the Left*) becomes a repeated outcry, the most serious Godard has made to this point—an outcry of anger, but also of despair. It is the tireless and anguished appeal of an artist who is keenly aware of the endangered freedom of expression, of the increasing presence of violence in daily life and of the pressure of the fingers of censorship tightening around his neck. In order to translate the emotions that assail him, Godard splashes the screen with consonant and dissonant colors whose beauty radiates with the lyrical frenzy of all the hues of the prism; but this should not distract us from the essential: it would be insane for this outcry not to be heard.

Seeing the rather unappetizing spectacle of the hesitant waltzes of an unfindable left, Godard suggests that it wash its dirty linen in private and, in order to do this, that it add a bit of sunflower to its dirty clothes. Not like "Crio" ("advertising is a form of fascism"). Like Van Gogh.

COMMENTARIES

An Audacious Experiment: The Sound Track of Vivre sa vie

JEAN COLLET

◆◇◆

Those who have seen Jean-Luc Godard's *Vivre sa vie*—and particularly all those who have heard it—will perhaps be amazed to find an article on this film appearing in *La Revue du son*. One's first impression is that the sound quality of this film does not seem particularly remarkable; in fact, the dialogues are not even always audible. In the first scene, for instance, certain lines are lost in the din of the typical noises one hears in a café. The spectator who does not want to lose a word of what is being said has to really strain his ears. And even this does not always work.

One has to realize, however, that the sound track of *Vivre sa vie* represents the result of an extremely audacious experiment, a kind of challenge Godard kept in mind throughout the entire film. For not only was this film shot in natural settings, the sound track (both dialogues and noises) was also recorded directly. On a single track. This is no doubt the first sound film shot outside a studio and involving no sound editing. Almost the only mixing that was done was the addition of the music to a sound track recorded live during the shooting of the film.

This experiment is nothing less than revolutionary. For years now, shooting techniques have been becoming less and less restricted, thus allowing the visual part of the cinema to get rid of

From La Revue du son, *no. 116 (December 1962): 513. Reprinted by permission of the publisher and the author. Translated by Royal S. Brown. When submitting this article, M. Collet wrote the editor that "these remarks on* Vivre sa vie *are only of historical interest; today, all of the cinema and television utilize these techniques." It is precisely because of the historical interest that this article is included here, as it shows one of the many ways in which Godard was technically ahead of his times.*

the various artifices that had long weighed it down. The proof of this lies in the greater and greater utilization of natural settings. But paradoxically, this greater fidelity in the realm of pictures seems to have brought about a much less authentic use of sound. In order for a film to be shot in natural settings, the dialogues had to be post-synchronized—all of the synchronous noises had to be fabricated after the fact, as did the various appropriate "atmosphere" sounds. There were thus three or four sound tracks that had to be edited and mixed in addition to the dialogue track. In this manner, it was quite easy to obtain an irreproachable sound quality. But there was no question of authenticity. And it is only because most directors have manifested great scorn for the "sound" end of their work that they have been able to permit such an incoherent aesthetic: pictures shot live and sound conscientiously pieced together with the help of a thousand or so gimmicks.

Jean-Luc Godard's idea was simple: apply to sound the same demands as for the pictures. Capture life in what it offers to be seen—and to be heard—*directly*. To obtain this result with the pictures, Raoul Coutard had to break with the tradition of "beautiful photography" that made the heyday of French cinema (permit me not to mention any names here . . .) through 1958. Now, nobody would think of reproaching Coutard for his overexposed shots. In order to obtain the same result with sound, the same types of prejudices had to be swept away. Here, it was the engineer *Guy Villette* who had the courage to assume the responsibility of this undertaking. (It is to this same sound engineer that we owe the soundtrack of *l'Année dernière à Marienbad* and of Orson Welles' *The Trial*.)

The material used was a portable, synchronous tape recorder of the "Perfectone" variety; the initial recording was made on 6.35 mm, which was eventually transferred onto a perforated, 35 mm strip. The need to record both words and surrounding noises in particularly reverberant places (cafés, streets, and so forth) should have necessitated the use of extremely directional microphones, each one intended for a specific function. American studios have a number of such microphones at their disposal (RCA for instance), but these were not to be found in the French studios at the time. Therefore, either AKG–D.25 or Neumann-type microphones, both of which are less directional than the American varieties, were employed.

In the best conditions, the sound recording was done with several microphones, and the mixing was more or less done during the shooting; during Nana's conversation with Brice Parain, for instance, each person speaking had a microphone. In other cases, however, the recording had to be made with a single microphone (such as the first café scene), and the level of the surrounding noises was thus relatively high.[1]

Godard refused to cheat with the rules he had set up for himself, even in the scenes where this kind of cheating would have seemed indispensable, such as in the café sequence when Nana plays the jukebox. Normally, the record in question would simply be recorded directly onto the sound track. If one wants to be "true to life," one usually settles, during the recording, for distorting the fidelity of a jukebox record by boosting the bass. Here, however, the sound was actually recorded in a café, with a great amount of care. And it is thus the jukebox we are really hearing. The same goes for the twist, during which we continue to hear the noises of the billiard game.

The interest offered by this method is obvious—the director opts for the real, rather than for the realistic. Being "realistic" always implies having a point of view on what is real, an interpretation of the facts. Here, an attempt has been made, thanks to the special machines used, to establish a material point of view, rather than a human judgment. The microphone is capturing what it hears, just as the camera is, and the artist avoids intervening at this level of the creation. And reality has its surprises, such as the noise of a heavy truck that fills the room and rises like a dramatic crescendo the first time Nana goes through the act of prostituting herself. Another example is in the very last sequence when, at the moment of Nana's death, a hospital bell is heard chiming in the silence of the deserted street. Such details cannot be invented. And the normal criterion of sound quality becomes worthless next to these moments of unexpected beauty that spring up out of everyday life.

---

[1] Critic Claude Mauriac, in an otherwise extremely praiseworthy review of *Vivre sa vie* (*Figaro littéraire*, 22 September 1962, p. 18), found this to be a flaw, feeling that Godard's café ended up being "less like a real café than the ones to be found in traditional films, in which the noises of the city and the various sounds of life have been erased and then reintroduced into the film" (editor's note).

Two or Three Things about an Apartment Complex

GEORGES SADOUL

❖❖

How can *Deux ou trois choses que je sais d'elle* be characterized? As "Pieces of a broken mirror." But I've already said that about *Made in U.S.A.* But this new film, which is more difficult than its predecessor, carries even further the breaking up of the mirror.

In 1923, Eisenstein spoke of "shock attractions," and this term does not seem out of place in talking about *Deux ou trois choses.* For if this film is basically a portrayal of a day in the life of a woman living in a high-rise apartment complex, her actions and the people she meets bring about no small number of shocks, striking images that shatter the unities of space, time, and action into tiny fragments.

But the film does not stop there. There is also the muffled commentary given to us by Jean-Luc Godard himself, who explains to us his deepest intentions and who makes various remarks that are no doubt riddled with literary quotations. And Godard is not the only one to speak in the first person. His characters also explain themselves on occasion, with their eyes fixed almost directly on the eyes of the audience, contrary to all the "rules."

But let's forget about the *broken mirror* and the *shocks,* since there is no blood in this film, as there is in *Strike, Potemkin, Pierrot le fou,* or *Made in U.S.A.* It is more appropriate here to talk in terms of a series of flashes, or even better, of a series of rapid visions mingled with soliloquies and reflections about two or three things.

Elle (Her) is a well defined and precisely described woman: Marina Vlady. But it is also a city (Paris) and its periphery, a city in

From **Les Lettres** françaises, *no. 1175 (March 23–29, 1967): 20, 22. Reprinted by permission of the publisher and Mme Sadoul. Translated by Royal S. Brown.*

the midst of transformation, a city completely overwhelmed by huge buildings and speculations as it hasn't been for over a hundred years, since the heyday of Baron Haussmann. (. . .) But whereas the Paris of Napoleon III could be considered, as in certain novels by Zola, as a self-contained city isolated from the rest of the world, the Paris of the "Gaullist Power" (to use Godard's own language) cannot, in this era of jets, television, satellites, radio, and so forth, be separated from the rest of the planet.

The opening of *Deux ou trois choses* . . . , which is its most brilliant and striking part, reminding one of the tone of an Aragon or a Mayakovsky, takes to task the Delouvrier plan for dividing up the Parisian region. But also, and even more violently, it attacks the Vietnam war, the Americans, and President Johnson. (It should thus have come as no surprise when the radio announced the other day that, along with Agnès Varda, Jacques Demy, and Alain Resnais, Jean-Luc Godard was going to leave for Hanoi to shoot a film on the war in Vietnam.)[1]

An American appears in a sequence in which the heroine and another woman are selling themselves to him. At one point, the American says, "Well, one dead Vietcong costs the American treasury a million dollars. With that kind of money, President Johnson could buy himself twenty million chicks like these." After which the American goes on to praise the "civilization" that has given us the jeep and napalm.

The idea for *Deux ou trois choses* came to Godard via an investigation entitled "Prostitution in the High Rises," which appeared in the *Nouvel observateur* in March and May of 1966. Is it the filmmaker or is it the investigator who gives us the social causes for this prostitution? A woman, in order to live and pay the rent, becomes a whore. She ends up marrying one of her lovers. They settle in a high rise, with all their household items having been bought on the installment plan. After a year or two of these "roses on credit," it's the husband himself who asks his wife to prostitute herself so that the monthly payments can be met.

In *Deux ou trois choses*, a perfectly honorable mother, who perhaps does some acting when she feels like it, does a bit of "hustling"

---

[1] Godard and Resnais were eventually unable to go to North Vietnam to shoot their sequences, which they instead shot in Paris, for *Loin du Viet-nam*. (editor's note)

in Paris, either with or without the knowledge of her husband, who waits for her patiently in a Paris café, where he always manages to strike up a conversation.

Before becoming a filmmaker, Jean-Luc Godard took courses in ethnography at the Musée de l'homme. One can still see traces of Jean Rouch in Godard, if one considers that, instead of studying the customs of the Blacks in Africa, he studies the lives of Parisian men and women of today.

In *Deux ou trois choses*, there is none of the lyrical violence of *Pierrot le fou* or *Made in U.S.A.* Growing out of the "cinema eye" technique, the film's successive and deliberately fragmented glimpses form a social statement that follows in the footsteps of *Une Femme mariée* or *Masculin-Féminin*, except that in *Deux ou trois choses* there are even fewer elements relating to anything resembling a storyline.

The relationship between *Une Femme mariée* and "pop art" seemed all the more evident to me in Venice in 1963, when the showing of Godard's film in the Festival coincided with an exposition devoted to the "pop" tendency in American art. In *Deux ou trois choses*, the leitmotiv of an interchange under construction on the North highway outside of Paris reminds me of Fernand Léger and the words that Aragon spoke at the tomb of his friend. Aragon spoke of what Léger had particularly liked in modern life: the bright red gasoline pumps and the high-tension-line pylons.

I often pass near the Gif-sur-Yvette cemetery, where Fernand Léger is buried. The view of the Chevreuse valley is being completely transformed. What used to be a country cemetery now has not only pylons and gas pumps for neighbors, but also a supermarket, two completed high-rises and another that is under construction, around which are swarming, as they would around a highway interchange, the bright yellow cranes, the blue dump trucks carrying away tons of earth, the scarlet steam shovels, the bulldozers, the giant cement mixers. And this *"ballet mécanique,"* to use Léger's language, is not limited to the periphery of Paris. It is taking place in the heart of the city. The tallest monument at the Place de la Concorde is no longer, at present, the Obelisk, but a gigantic crane whose jib is itself longer than the monolith imported by Louqsor.

Zola defined *La Curée* (. . .) in the following manner: "It is an unhealthy plant growing in the midst of the imperial dung heap."

One can apply Zola's remarks to *Deux ou trois choses* by eliminating the adjective "unhealthy" (which can also apply to incestuous loves) and by replacing "imperial dung heap" with "Gaullist power." (. . .) In a recent interview, Michel Butor stressed the relevance and importance of Zola, who for a long time remained "relegated to a kind of purgatory" by critics who found that it was not "stylish to be interested" in Zola's work. Butor was quite right in pointing out that "Zola and Hugo had to be gotten rid of because they were always in the way." It was, in fact, a group of conservatives who, around 1920, refused the Pantheon to these two authors and consigned them to a morgue labeled "Nineteenth-Century Stupidity." But this did not dampen the enthusiasm of the masses for these two authors whose works, today, have been published in record numbers in pocket editions.

Let me repeat that, if Renoir's films of the 1930s can be considered, à la Zola, as a "natural and social history of France at the end of the Third Republic," it appears more and more evident that, as that *grand ensemble*[2] which is Godard's work takes form, this important body of films can be called a "social investigation of France during the times of Gaullist power," an investigation in which one finds more than one "J'accuse."

Zola, as Butor has remarked, was "born in the confluence of Balzac and Hugo." His *Rougon-Macquart* is closely related to Balzac's *Comédie humaine* and Hugo's *Les Misérables*. Before the war, Renoir's films were closely tied to the novel, even though the surrealists and the futurists had condemned the novel (at least in its nineteenth-century form) as an outdated genre. But even these avantgarde minds were far from denying the basic facts, the various pieces of evidence suitably chosen and juxtaposed through some "collage."

The more Godard advances in his work, the less place the novel has in his films. *A bout de souffle* was still tied to the novel, but the novel accepted as a kind of obligation in order to convince a producer to risk thousands of dollars in the affair. *Pierrot le fou*, which continues along the path established in this first film, is not in the least a "cine-novel" (or even a "cine-new-novel," à la Robbe-Grillet). Rather it is a lyric poem, a kind of untamed epic. If there is a story-

---

[2] Besides its literal meaning of "important body" (of works, etc.), *grand ensemble* is also the French expression for a high-rise apartment complex. It is on the double meaning of this expression, unrenderable in English, that Sadoul bases the main thought of this article. (editor's note)

line that one can refer to in *Pierrot*, it is to be found in the plot of the *Pieds-Nickelés* comic strip that is one of the film's leitmotivs.

Even more so than *Made in U.S.A.*, *Deux ou trois choses* is related, particularly through Godard's commentary, to the comic strips. But there is no point in looking for a plot that is even as coherent as in *Mandrake the Magician*. In this extremely modern film, we are no longer in the era of black suits, capes, top hats, and Georges Méliès.

The title of the film defines its content. It is not a question of saying everything about a woman or a city, or of defining and explaining them in some kind of logical diagram. Instead, only "two or three things" are said about "them," and it is up to the audience to complete the puzzle by imagining a past and a future for them, whereas only a few fragmentary aspects of their present are given, as seen from four different angles. "1) Objective description; 2) subjective description; 3) an attempt at research on the structure; 4) life." Having thus stated his position in the film, Godard, who previously defined his work as "an essay on colors and sounds," concludes: "In a film of this nature, it is as if I were trying to write a sociological essay in the form of a novel and could only use musical notes to express myself."

When I was in the midst of studying Eisenstein the other week, I was able to find certain points in common between the Russian director and Robert Bresson. Having now come back to Dziga Vertov, a genius whose work is certainly not well enough known, I find myself comparing *Deux ou trois choses* with *Symphony of the Donbas*, a film that even Godard, with his exemplary cinematic erudition, has probably not seen.

There is a fundamental difference, however. Whereas Vertov showed a world being constructed, *Deux ou trois choses* witnesses a regime that is decomposing. But cannot one still apply to Godard's film the goal Vertov set for himself; that is, to "capture live a feverish moment of the present and restore it in its atmosphere of noises, hammers, whistles, and locomotives"? Chaplin was so enthused over *The Symphony of the Donbas* that he referred to it as "one of the most beautiful symphonies I have ever heard." Let us hope that this unique symphony of noises and colors created by Godard will arouse similar enthusiasm, and particularly that it will be understood by the general public, which is all too often confused by novelty, by these two or three things which make up a part of a *grand ensemble* that is both contemporary France and the work of Godard.

La Chinoise: Child's Play?
ROYAL S. BROWN

In an interview made shortly after *La Chinoise* was released, Godard was asked the following question: "You had told us, two or three years ago, how difficult making political films seemed to you, since this type of work would require as many points of view as there were characters, not to mention that of Sirius, which would take in all of them. Do you still feel this way?" [1] Godard's answer was negative; this statement was made, he felt, at a period when he thought it was necessary to be objective. *La Chinoise,* then, would be something less than a documentary, or even the "adventure-documentary" that would seem to have been Godard's earlier ideal. A number of critics seem to agree: one article on Godard's recent radical political evolution, for instance, stated that "Among Godard's earlier films, *La Chinoise* (1967) is closest to his new interests." [2] Furthermore, the violent reactions of the Moscow-oriented French Communists to the anti-Russian frenzy shown by most of the students in *La Chinoise* would seem to bear witness to the film's effect as a political polemic.

Ostensibly, of course, *La Chinoise* does appear to be much more politically oriented than Godard's earlier films, and even more so than the work that followed it, *Weekend.* To begin with, the subject itself is politics, or, to be more accurate, *the* politics of the characters portrayed in the film. This represents a first for Godard. And Godard does stack the cards in favor of polemic by creating a certain amount of unity in the political opinions of most of the characters.

[1] "Lutter sur deux fronts," conversation with Jean-Luc Godard by J. Bontemps, J.-L. Comolli, M. Delahaye, and J. Narboni, *Cahiers du cinéma,* No. 194 (October 1967), p. 15.

[2] Colin L. Westerbeck, Jr., "A Terrible Duty Is Born," *Sight and Sound,* Spring 1971, p. 82.

Yet there is immediately at least one element that not only reveals
Godard's constant desire for objectivity-through-dialect, but also
harks back to some of the director's earliest films. This element is
the appearance in the film of philosopher Francis Jeanson (with
whom Anne Wiazemsky, who plays Véronique, had in fact studied)
who, toward the end of the film, becomes involved in a conversation
with Véronique on a train. As in certain films before *La Chinoise*
(notably Brice Parain's appearance in *Vivre sa vie*; Godard had
wanted to get Roland Barthes for *Alphaville*, but Barthes refused),
Godard brings in a philosopher from real life for the purpose of
having him expose his own "real" ideas within a "fictitious" context
—("Fiction is fiction, reality is reality, and all movies are fiction,"
says Godard). But Jeanson's role in *La Chinoise* is not only to objectively present ideas, it is also to methodically contradict the
whole revolutionary raison d'être of the students shown in *La
Chinoise*. Godard has said that, *in his opinion,* he favored Véronique's point of view over Jeanson's in the way the sequence was
handled, but that audiences would take the side they wanted. The
chances are, in fact, that the character sided with by each member
of the audience will be the one whose opinions are closest to his
own. For there is nothing in this sequence that really makes a fool
out of either character: for some, Jeanson is made out to be a "kill-
joy, philosophizing ancestor," [3] while for others, Anne Wiazemsky
says "just about anything she wants, which obviously leads Jeanson
into developing long reasonings to refute her points of view. . . ." [4]
Indeed, according to the latter critic and many others, Véronique's
arguments are ". . . absolutely not those of the Marxist-Leninists,
except by accident," which gives Jeanson's points of view an apparent additional strength. Certainly, Jeanson is not the caricatured
cavalry officer of *Vent d'est* or the comic-strip Judge "Himmler"
(Hoffman) of *Vladimir et Rosa*; Godard, intentionally or not, gives
him "equal time," and for many, Jeanson wins the debate. For
others, Véronique wins. From the strict point of view of the film
itself, however, the whole thing remains at the level of unresolved
dialectic, thus definitely putting *La Chinoise* into the same aesthetic
lines that dominate all of Godard's earlier films.

And there is another character, that of Henri (Michel Semeni-

[3] Paul-Louis Thirard, in *Positif*, No. 89 (November 1967).
[4] Guy Gauthier, *La Saison cinématographique*, No. 219 (September 1968).

ako), whose presence further broadens the perhaps unintentional objectivity of Godard's film. Having been kicked out of the "Aden-Arabie" cell for "revisionism" and for desiring peaceful coexistence, Henri, like Jeanson later on, is given his "equal time" and is allowed to present, as he eats breakfast in a kitchen, a convincing case against the terrorist, unidirectional tactics desired by the other students. Indeed, both the arguments and the very character itself took on, for many, a strength that Godard had apparently not foreseen. When asked to explain this phenomenon, Godard said that he felt that the four-against-one situation to which Henri was exposed caused people to favor the underdog. Yet once again, Godard could have made Henri into a ludicrously unlikable person, which he has shown no small talent for doing (as with the character played by Jean Yanne in his next film, *Weekend*). Instinctively, Godard seems to have been unable to dispense with the ideological balance that both Henri and Jeanson give to *La Chinoise*.

The settings for both the scene with Henri in the kitchen and Jeanson and Véronique in the train also stand in sharp contrast to the settings for most of the rest of the film. The apartment where the students have set up their isolated "cell" is filled with artificiality: the primary colors (plus more greens than usual) Godard always uses are arbitrarily splashed around (he takes great advantage of the fact that Mao's book is red . . . bright red); the various props (blackboards, books, radios, tape recorders, toys); the writing on the walls; the carefully arranged shapes and forms—in general, the whole atmosphere is not unlike that of a children's playroom (this is not meant derogatorily). Furthermore, the various sequences shot in the apartment are frequently interrupted in the editing by certain graphic intercalations such as book titles, "pop-art" drawings, and so forth. On the other hand, the scenes with Henri, once he has been kicked out of the group, take place in a banal kitchen, and Henri goes about prosaically fixing and eating his breakfast as he discusses the essence of his "revisionism." The sequence with Francis Jeanson breaks even more strongly with the general style of the rest of the picture. Here, Godard uses one of his favorite techniques of filming a long sequence (this one lasts just over eleven minutes) in which two or three people do nothing but talk about "ideas" (see also *Vivre sa vie*, *La Femme mariée*, *Le Mépris*, and so forth); the shots are seldom varied, the people rarely move, and there is generally nothing cinematic to distract from the intellectuality of the scene. (In the *La Chinoise* sequence, there are a few very brief intercalated shots of signs, and at one point, Godard fades in some Vivaldi for a minute or so; otherwise, the editing remains relatively static, and the only sounds are natural ones.) The basic technique used in this scene, plus the setting itself—a train compartment filmed in soft colors with the landscape moving by the window—set it strongly against the earlier scenes. One is reminded of the heroine of Fellini's *Juliet of the Spirits*, who, at the end of the film, finally walks out into a "real" world whose muted, dull colors seem to invite Juliet out of the bright-hued phantasmagoria in which she has been living throughout most of the film. This is the first time Véronique is seen outside of the "cell"; the next time (she remains unconvinced by Jeanson's logic) is when she performs her act of terrorism (which is only suggested by a "pop-art" interpolation of a man being shot with a revolver); but this time, the "exterior" becomes merely an extension of the "interior," since Véronique—almost comically, almost childishly—kills the wrong person the first time, and since the getaway car drives right up across the courtyard to the front door of the apartment building.

Thus, Godard very clearly delineates between the calm, adult and rather natural world of the liberals (Yvonne's peasant background is also evoked in one or two country shots that l'*Humanité* accused of being "postcards") and the frenetic, active, theatrical, and childlike world of the radicals. Godard makes it clear that the five students are more or less playing games in a bourgeois apartment that has been left by the parents of a friend of Véronique's for the summer. From the very outset of the film, Godard stresses the theatrical aspects of what is going on: the film itself is called "a film in the process of being made"; throughout much of the movie, the characters are interviewed by an offscreen voice that can usually not be understood. Early in the film, Guillaume (Jean-Pierre Léaud), the actor, tells and illustrates the anecdote of a Chinese student who stood before a group of reporters in Moscow and, as he told of Russian brutalities against the Chinese, removed bandages from his face. When his face was revealed, there were no scars, and the reporters became angry. "They hadn't understood," Guillaume says, "that it was theater." And this seems to have been exactly the misunderstanding that caused a large number of people, both pro-Russian and pro-Chinese, to react violently against the movie. The members of the Chinese embassy in Paris actually re-proached Godard for not showing scars on Léaud's face as he re-moved his anecdotal bandages (and Godard's reaction to this—"There, it is obvious that they didn't understand"—echoes the very lines he gave to Léaud in the film). As in his earlier films, Godard leads the audience away from emotional identification with the characters through theatrical distantiation, as is brought out when Guillaume erases from a blackboard all the names of a number of writers, playwrights, and philosophers (starting with Sartre; this is one way in which Godard *does* seem to break strongly with his own past) except for that of Brecht (it should be remembered that Godard divided such an early film as *Vivre sa vie* into a series of tableaux in order to stress the Brechtian, theatrical elements of the picture).

Furthermore, Godard here, as in *Alphaville*, seems to be showing us that action, no matter how important it may be, belongs to the domain of role-playing. The five students in *La Chinoise* literally act out in all possible ways the many facets of their revolutionary commitment, from street theater to suicide, from playing with toy tanks and planes to political assassination. Never is anything they do believable in the ordinary sense of the word, nor do they seem to accomplish anything outside the role-playing itself, any more than children really accomplish anything with their games. Yet to take this role-playing perspective as derogation on Godard's part is to not understand that, for Godard, acting equals action. For the young people of *La Chinoise*, as for the characters in many of Godard's earlier films, words—the words of a Francis Jeanson, the words of a society in general—mean nothing, words do not communicate, as is illustrated in the sequence in which Véronique communicates her love to Guillaume by playing romantic music (the opening of Schubert's Piano Sonata in A, Op. 120) on a record player while verbally telling him she can't stand him; as Godard has said, "I use music in that way in my films; it's to make people understand better." [5] Yet, in the midst of a materialistic society, in the midst of a directionless existence, the acts have only them-selves with which to be justified, and the distinction, then, between

---

[5] Interview-montage by Abraham Segal, *Image et son*, No. 215 (March 1968), p. 80. Earlier, Godard had stated, "I try to use music like another picture which isn't a picture, like another element. Like another sound, but in a different form" (p. 79).

acting and action becomes meaningless. For the people who act, role-playing becomes a way of bringing them closer to an undefined reality; as Véronique says at the end of the film, "Yes, O.K., it's fiction, but it has brought me closer to what is real." For people who watch this action (that is, the film), it is likewise a manner of being brought closer to what is real; indeed, Véronique's line might stand as a motto for all of Godard's films.

The meeting between Véronique and Francis Jeanson sums up the entire film. Many people reproached this sequence as a phony blend of reality and fiction that inevitably favored Jeanson's point of view. Godard's answer to this was that Jeanson, by dint of being in a movie, is a "fictitious" (whatever the word means) character. One can also see the scene, however, as a meeting between two basic social forces: those that act (in all senses of the word) and those that talk. Both characters are fictional because they are in a movie; Véronique is doubly fictional because she believes in, and acts out, action. But if Godard seems to manifest a kind of nostalgia for the childlike innocence that leads to the play-acting of the "Aden-Arabie" students in *La Chinoise*, he is also careful to show not only the other side but also the foibles of the characters he ostensibly favors. And he deliberately chose the strongest opposition; had he pitted his five students against the depraved bourgeois couple of *Weekend*, or had he shown the opposition strictly in terms of the puppet-Uncle Sams and toy planes of street theater and of his "Dziga-Vertov" films, then *La Chinoise* could be separated from such films as *Masculin-Féminin* and even *Alphaville*, which preceded it. *La Chinoise* is more political only inasmuch as the action-acting it documents is politically oriented; but it is no more involved in a specific, unambiguous direction than are any of Godard's earlier films. And in recent interviews, the "Dziga-Vertov" Godard has denounced *La Chinoise*, along with almost all his other earlier films, as totally bourgeois.

Filmography[1]

FILMS MADE BY JEAN-LUC GODARD

1954

Opération béton. 20 minutes. *Production Co.:* Actua Film (Geneva). *Photography:* Adrien Porchet. *Editor:* Godard. *Music:* Handel, Bach.

1955

Une Femme coquette. 10 minutes. 16 mm. *Production Co.:* Jean-Luc Godard (Geneva). *Script:* Hans Lucas (J.-L. G.), based on Maupassant's story *Le Signe. Photography:* Hans Lucas. *Editing:* Hans Lucas. *Music:* Bach. *Cast:* Maria Lysandre (*The Woman*); Roland Tolma (*The Man*); Jean-Luc Godard (*The Client*).

1957

Tous les garçons s'appellent Patrick ou *Charlotte et Véronique* (*All Boys Are Called Patrick*). 21 minutes. *Production Co.:* Les Films de la Pléïade (Pierre Braunberger). *Script:* Eric Rohmer. *Photography:* Michel Latouche. *Editing:* Cécile Decugis. *Music:* Pierre Monsigny, Beethoven. *Cast:* Jean-Claude Brialy (*Patrick*); Anne Colette (*Charlotte*); Nicole Berger (*Véronique*).

1958

Charlotte et son Jules. 20 minutes. *Production Co.:* Les Films de la Pléïade (Pierre Braunberger). *Photography:* Michel Latouche. *Editing:* Cécile Decugis. *Music:* Pierre Monsigny. *Cast:* Jean-Paul Belmondo (*Jean;* voice dubbed by Godard); Anne Colette (*Charlotte*); Gérard Blain (*The New Boyfriend*).

Une Histoire d'eau. 18 minutes. *Production Co.:* Les Films de la Pléïade (Braunberger). *Co-Director:* François Truffaut. *Script:* Truffaut. *Photography:* Michel Latouche. *Editing:* Godard. *Cast:* Jean-Claude Brialy (*The Man*); Caroline Dim (*The Girl*); Jean-Luc Godard (*Narrator*).

---

[1] For complete details, consult the filmographies in the book by Richard Roud and the pamphlet by Abraham Segal (see bibliography). All scripts are by Godard unless otherwise indicated. When two English-language titles are indicated, the first is American, the second the British version.

1959

A bout de souffle (Breathless). 89 minutes. *Production Co.:* Georges de Beauregard, Société Nouvelle de Cinéma. *Script:* Godard, based on an idea by François Truffaut. *Photography:* Raoul Coutard. *Editing:* Cécile Decugis, assisted by Lila Herman. *Music:* Martial Solal, Mozart (Clarinet Concerto). *Cast:* Jean-Paul Belmondo *(Michel Poiccard,* alias *Laszlo Kovacs);* Jean Seberg *(Patricia Franchini);* many minor roles. *Awards:* Prix Jean Vigo 1960; Best Director, Berlin Festival 1960; Best Photography (Raoul Coutard), German Critics 1960.

1960

Le Petit soldat (The Little Soldier). 87 minutes. *Production Co.:* Georges de Beauregard, S.N.C. *Photography:* Raoul Coutard, assisted by Michel Latouche. *Editing:* Agnès Guillemot, Nadine Marquand, Lila Herman. *Music:* Maurice Leroux. *Cast:* Anna Karina *(Véronica Dreyer);* Michel Subor *(Bruno Forestier);* Henri-Jacques Huet, Paul Beauvais, Laszlo Szabo, Georges de Beauregard.

1961

Une Femme est une femme (A Woman Is a Woman). 84 minutes. *Production Co.:* Rome-Paris Films (Beauregard, Carlo Ponti). *Script:* Godard, based on an idea by Geneviève Cluny. *Photography:* Raoul Coutard (Eastmancolor, Franscope). *Editing:* Agnès Guillemot, Lila Herman. *Music:* Michel Legrand. *Song, "Chanson d'Angéla"* by Michel Legrand, J.-L. G. *Sound:* Guy Villette. *Cast:* Anna Karina *(Angéla Récamier);* Jean-Paul Belmondo *(Alfred Lubitsch);* Jean-Claude Brialy *(Emile Récamier);* Marie Dubois, Nicole Paquin, Marion Sarraut, Jeanne Moreau, Catherine Demongeot. *Award:* Jury's Special Prize; Best Actress (Anna Karina), Berlin Festival 1961.

La Paresse (sketch in *Les Sept Péchés Capitaux). Production Co.:* Films Gibé, Franco-London Films (Paris), Titanus (Rome). *Photography:* Henri Decaë (Dyaliscope). *Editing:* Jacques Gaillard. *Music:* Michel Legrand. *Cast:* Eddie Constantine *(Himself);* Nicole Mirel *(The Starlet). Other Episodes Directed by:* Claude Chabrol, Edouard Molinaro, Jacques Demy, Roger Vadim, Philippe de Broca, Sylvain Dhomme.

1962

Vivre sa vie (My Life to Live; It's My Life). 85 minutes. *Production Co.:* Les Films de la Pléiade (Braunberger). *Documentation: Où en est la prostitution?,* by Judge Marcel Sacotte (Paris: Editions Buchet-Chastel). *Photography:* Raoul Coutard, assisted by Claude Beausoleil. *Editing:* Agnès Guillemot, assisted by Lila Lakshmanan. *Music:* Michel Legrand; Song, *"Ma môme, elle joue pas les starlettes,"* by Jean Ferrat, Pierre Frachet. *Sound:* Guy Villette, Jacques Maumont. *Cast:* Anna Karina *(Nana Kleinfrankenheim);* Sady Rebbot *(Raoul);* André-S. Labarthe *(Paul);* Brice Parain *(The Philosopher);* many minor roles. *Awards:* Jury's Special Prize and

Italian Critics' Prize, Venice Festival 1962; German Critics' Prize for Best Foreign Film, 1962–63.

Le Nouveau monde (sketch in *RoGoPaG*). 20 minutes. *Production Co.:* Lyre cinématographique (Paris), Arco Film (Rome). *Photography:* Jean Rabier. *Editing:* Agnès Guillemot, assisted by Lila Lakshmanan. *Music:* Beethoven (Quartets 7, 9, 10, 14, 15). *Cast:* Alexandra Stewart *(Alexandra)*; Jean-Marc Bory *(The Narrator)*; Jean-André Fieschi, Michel Delahaye, Alexandre Alexandre, and the voice of André-S. Labarthe. *Other Episodes Directed by:* Roberto Rossellini, Pier Paolo Pasolini, Ugo Gregoretti. *RoGoPaG* was banned shortly after its release and later rereleased, with cuts in the Pasolini film, under the title of *Laviamoci il Cervello.*

1962–63

Les Carabiniers (The Riflemen; The Soldiers). 80 minutes. *Production Co.:* Rome-Paris Films (Paris), Laetitia (Rome) (Beauregard, Ponti). *Script:* Jean-Luc Godard, Jean Gruault, Roberto Rossellini, from Jacques Audiberti's French adaptation of Benjamino Joppolo's play, *I Carabinieri*. *Photography:* Raoul Coutard, assisted by Claude Beausoleil. *Editing:* Agnès Guillemot, Lila Lakshmanan. *Music:* Philippe Arthys. *Cast:* Marino Masè *(Ulysse)*; Albert Juross *(Michel-Ange)*; Geneviève Galéa *(Vénus)*; Catherine Ribeiro *(Cléopâtre)*; many minor roles.

1963

Le Grand escroc (sketch in *Les Plus belles escroqueries du monde*). 25 minutes. *Production Co.:* Ulysse Productions (Paris), Primex Films (Marseille), Vides (Rome), Toho (Tokyo), Caesar Film (Amsterdam). *Photography:* Raoul Coutard (Franscope). *Editing:* Agnès Guillemot, Lila Lakshmanan. *Music:* Michel Legrand. *Cast:* Jean Seberg *(Patricia Leacock)*; Charles Denner *(The Swindler)*; Laszlo Szabo *(The Inspector)*. *Other Episodes Directed by:* Hiromishi Horikawa, Roman Polanski, Ugo Gregoretti, Claude Chabrol. Godard's sketch cut from film.

Le Mépris (Contempt). 105 minutes (84 in Italian version). *Production Co.:* Rome-Paris Films, Films Concordia, Compagnia Cinematografica Champion (Beauregard, Ponti, Joseph E. Levine). *Script:* Godard, based on Alberto Moravia's novel, *Il Disprezzo*. *Photography:* Raoul Coutard (Franscope, Technicolor). *Editing:* Agnès Guillemot, Lila Lakshmanan. *Music:* Georges Delerue. *Cast:* Brigitte Bardot *(Camille Javal)*; Michel Piccoli *(Paul Javal)*; Jack Palance *(Jeremy Prokosch)*; Fritz Lang *(Himself)*; Giorgia Moll *(Francesca Vanini)*.

Montparnasse-Levallois (sketch in *Paris vu par . . .*). 18 minutes. 16 mm., later blown up to 35 mm. *Production Co.:* Les Films du Losange (Barbet Schroeder). *Script:* Godard, based on an anecdote from Giraudoux told by Belmondo in *Une Femme est une femme*. *Photography:* Albert Maysles (Eastmancolor). *Editing:* Jacqueline Raynal. *Cast:* Johanna Shimkus *(Monika)*; Philippe Hiquilly *(Ivan)*; Serge Davri *(Roger)*. *Other Episodes Directed by:* Claude Chabrol, Jean Douchet, Jean-Daniel Pollet, Eric Rohmer, Jean Rouch.

1964

Bande à part (Band of Outsiders; The Outsiders). 95 minutes. *Production Co.:* Anouchka Films, Orsay Films. *Script:* Godard, based on the novel *Fool's Gold (Pigeon Vole)* by D. and B. Hitchens. *Photography:* Raoul Coutard, assisted by Georges Liron. *Editing:* Agnès Guillemot, Françoise Collin. *Music:* Michel Legrand. *Cast:* Anna Karina *(Odile)*; Claude Brasseur *(Arthur)*; Sami Frey *(Franz)*; Jean-Luc Godard *(Narrator)*.

La (Une) Femme mariée (The Married Woman; A Married Woman). 95 (originally 98) minutes. *Production Co.:* Anouchka Films, Orsay Films (Philippe Dussart). *Photography:* Raoul Coutard. *Editing:* Agnès Guillemot, Françoise Collin. *Music:* Beethoven (Quartets 7, 9, 10, 14, 15); "Java" by Claude Nougaro, Song, *"Quand le film est triste"* by J. D. Loudermilk, G. Aber, L. Morisse, sung by Sylvie Vartan. *Cast:* Macha Méril *(Charlotte Giraud)*; Bernard Noël *(Robert, the Lover)*; Philippe Leroy *(Pierre, the Husband)*; Roger Leenhardt *(Himself)*; Jean-Luc Godard *(Narrator)*.

1965

Alphaville ou Une étrange aventure de Lemmy Caution. 98 minutes. *Production Co.:* Chaumiane Production (André Michelin), Filmstudio (Rome). *Photography:* Raoul Coutard. *Editing:* Agnès Guillemot. *Music:* Paul Misraki. *Cast:* Eddie Constantine *(Lemmy Caution)*; Anna Karina *(Natacha von Braun)*; Akim Tamiroff *(Henri Dickson)*; Howard Vernon *(Professor Léonard Nosfératu,* alias *von Braun)*.

Pierrot le fou. 112 minutes. *Production Co.:* Rome-Paris Films (Beauregard, Paris, Dino de Laurentis, Rome). *Script:* Godard, based on Lionel White's novel *Obsession. Photography:* Raoul Coutard (Techniscope, Eastmancolor). *Editing:* Françoise Collin. *Music:* Antoine Duhamel; Vivaldi (Flute Concerto). Songs. "Jamais je ne t'ai dit que je t'aimerai toujours," "Ma ligne de chance," by Bassiak. *Sound:* René Levert. *Mixing:* Antoine Bonfanti. *Cast:* Jean-Paul Belmondo *(Ferdinand)*; Anna Karina *(Marianne)*; Dirk Sanders, Raymond Devos, Graziella Galvani, Roger Dutoit, Hans Meyer, Jimmy Karoubi, Christa Nell, Pascal Aubier, Pierre Hanin, Laszlo Szabo, Jean-Pierre Léaud, Samuel Fuller, Alexis Poliakoff, Princess Aicha Abidir.

1966

Masculin-Féminin (Masculine Feminine). 110 minutes. *Production Co.:* Anouchka Films, Argos Films, Svensk Filmindustri, Sandrews. *Script:* Godard, loosely based on two stories by Guy de Maupassant, *La Femme de Paul* and *Le Signe. Photography:* Willy Kurant. *Editing:* Agnès Guillemot. *Music:* Francis Lai, Mozart (Clarinet Concerto). *Cast:* Jean-Pierre Léaud *(Paul)*; Chantal Goya *(Madeleine)*; Marlène Jobert *(Elisabeth)*; Michel Debord *(Robert)*; Catherine-Isabelle Duport; Eva Britt Strandberg; Birger Malmsten; Elsa Leroy; Françoise Hardy; Brigitte Bardot; Antoine Bourseiller.

Made in U.S.A. 90 minutes. *Production Co.:* Rome-Paris Films (Beauregard), Anouchka Films, Sepic. *Script:* Godard, based on Richard Stark's novel, *Rien dans le coffre*. *Photography:* Raoul Coutard (Techniscope, Eastmancolor). *Editing:* Agnès Guillemot. *Music:* Beethoven (Symphony no. 5), Schumann (Symphony no. 3); Song, "As Tears Go By," by Mick Jagger, Keith Richard. *Cast:* Anna Karina (*Paula Nelson*); Laszlo Szabo (*Richard Widmark*); Yves Alfonso (*David Goodis*); Jean-Pierre Léaud (*Donald Siegel*); Marianne Faithful; Ernest Menzer; Jean-Claude Bouillon; Kyoko Kosaka; Rémo Forlani; Jean-Pierre Biesse; Sylvain Godet; Roger Scipion; Rita Maiden; Philippe Labro; Jean-Luc Godard (*Voice of Richard Politzer*); etc.

Deux ou trois choses que je sais d'elle. 90 minutes. *Production Co.:* Anouchka Films, Argos Films, Les Films du Carosse, Parc Film. *Documentation:* Catherine Vimenet, "La Prostitution dans les grands ensembles," *Le Nouvel observateur,* 29 March and 10 May 1966. *Photography:* Raoul Coutard (Techniscope, Eastmancolor). *Editing:* Françoise Collin. *Music:* Beethoven (*Quartet no. 16*). *Cast:* Marina Vlady (*Juliette Janson*); Roger Montsoret (*Robert Janson*); Anny Duperey (*Marianne*); Jean Narboni (*Roger*); Jean-Luc Godard (*The Narrator*); Raoul Lévy (*John Bogus, The American*); Christophe Bourseiller; Marie Bourseiller; Joseph Gehrard; Helena Bielicic; Robert Chevassu; Yves Beneyton; Jean-Pierre Laverne; Blandine Jeanson; Claude Miler; Jean-Patrick Lebel; Juliet Berto; Anna Manga; Benjamin Rosette; Helen Scott.

Anticipation, ou L'Amour en l'an 2000 (sketch in *Le Plus vieux métier du monde*). *Production Co.:* Francoriz Films, Films Gibé, Rialto Films, Rizzoli Films. *Photography:* Pierre Lhomme and Service de recherches du laboratoire L.T.C. (Eastmancolor, both positive and negative). *Editing:* Agnès Guillemot. *Music:* Michel Legrand. *Cast:* Anna Karina (*Natacha*); Jacques Charrier (*Dick*); Marilu Tolo (*Marlène*); Jean-Pierre Léaud (*Bellboy*); Daniel Bart; Jean-Patrick Lebel. *Other Episodes Directed by:* Franco Indovina, Mauro Bolognini, Philippe de Broca, Michael Pfleghar, Claude Autant-Lara.

1967

La Chinoise, ou plutôt à la chinoise. 90 minutes. *Production Co.:* Anouchka Films, Les Productions de la Guéville, Athos Films, Parc Films, Simar Films. *Photography:* Raoul Coutard (Eastmancolor). *Editing:* Agnès Guillemot. *Music:* Karl-Heinz Stockhausen, Schubert (Piano Sonata, Op. 120), Vivaldi. *Cast:* Anne Wiazemsky (*Véronique*); Jean-Pierre Léaud (*Guillaume*); Juliet Berto (*Yvonne*); Michel Semeniako (*Henri*); Lex de Bruïjn (*Kirilov*); Omar Diop (*Comrade X, Omar*); Francis Jeanson (*Himself*); Blandine Jeanson. *Award:* Jury's Special Prize, Venice Festival 1967.

Caméra-Oeil (episode in *Loin du Viêt-nam*). 115 minutes (entire film). *Production Co.:* S.L.O.N. (Chris Marker, etc.). Eastmancolor. *Other Episodes Directed by:* Alain Resnais, William Klein, Joris Ivens, Agnès Varda (episode not included), Claude Lelouch.

L'Amour (original title: *L'Aller et retour des enfants prodigues andate e ritorno dei figli prodighi*) (sketch in *La Contestation*; Italian title: *Amore e Rabbia*; original title: *Vangelo 70*). 26 minutes. *Production Co.:* Castoro

Films (Rome), Anouchka Films (Paris). *Photography:* Alain Levent (Techniscope, Eastmancolor). *Editing:* Agnès Guillemot. *Music:* Giovanni Fusco. *Cast:* Christine Guého (*Her*); Catherine Jourdan (*Female Witness*); Nino Castelnuovo (*Him*); Paolo Pozzesi (*Male Witness*). *Other Episodes Filmed by:* Bernardo Bertolucci, Pier Paolo Pasolini, Carlo Lizzani, Marco Bellochio/Elda Tattoli (the latter episode replacing the sketch by Valerio Zurlini, which was later released separately as *Seduto alla sua Destra*).

Week-End. 95 minutes. *Production Co.:* Films Copernic (France), Ascot Cineraïd (Rome), Comacico, Lira Films. *Photography:* Raoul Coutard (Eastmancolor). *Editing:* Agnès Guillemot. *Music:* Antoine Duhamel, Mozart (Piano Sonata, K. 576); Song, "Allô, allô, tu m'entends," by Guy Béart. *Cast:* Mireille Darc (*Corinne*); Jean Yanne (*Roland*); Jean-Pierre Léaud; Yves Alfonso; Daniel Pommereulle; Jean-Pierre Kalfon; Blandine Jeanson; Virginie Mignon; Ernest Menzer; Lsazlo Szabo; Paul Gegauff; Juliet Berto; Valérie Lagrange; J. C. Guilbert; Anne Wiazemsky; Michel Cournot.

1968

Le Gai savoir (Merry Wisdom; Happy Knowledge; etc.). 95 minutes. *Production Co.:* Originally O.R.T.F. (French Radio and Television); later Anouchka Films (Paris), Bavaria Atelier (Munich). *Photography:* Georges Leclerc (Eastmancolor). *Editing:* Germaine Cohen. *Music:* Cuban Revolutionary Hymn. *Cast:* Juliet Berto (*Patricia Lumumba*); Jean-Pierre Léaud (*Emile Rousseau*).

Un Film comme les autres (A Movie Like the Others). Time estimates run from 100 to 120 minutes. 16 mm. Ektachrome. Filmed by the "Dziga-Vertov" Group, with shots by the "Etats Généraux du Cinéma" interspersed. *Distributor:* Leacock-Pennebaker Films (U.S.A.).

One Plus One (producer's title: *Sympathy for the Devil*). 99 minutes. *Production Co.:* Cupid Productions, Inc. (Iain Quarrier, Michael Pearson). *Photography:* Anthony Richard (Eastmancolor). *Editing:* Ken Rowless, Agnès Guillemot. *Music:* Mick Jagger, Keith Richard, "Sympathy for the Devil." *Cast:* "The Rolling Stones" (Mick Jagger, Keith Richard, Brian Jones, Charlie Watts, Bill Wyman); Anne Wiazemsky (*Eve Democracy*); Iain Quarrier; many minor roles.

1968-69

One American Movie/1 A.M. Definitively abandoned by Godard in March 1970. 16 mm. Ektachrome. Footage from this film, plus footage on the film being made, were put together by the producer, D. A. Pennebaker, and entitled *One P.M.* 1971. 90 minutes. *Production Co.:* Leacock-Pennebaker, Inc. *Script:* Pennebaker, Godard. *Photography:* Richard Leacock, D. A. Pennebaker. *Editing:* Pennebaker. *Cast:* Richard Leacock, Jean-Luc Godard, Anne Wiazemsky, Eldridge Cleaver, Tom Hayden, Jefferson Airplane, LeRoi Jones, Tom Luddy, Paula Madder, Rip Torn.

FILMS MADE BY THE DZIGA-VERTOV GROUP

1969

British Sounds (See You at Mao). 52 minutes. 16 mm. *Production Co.:* Kestrel Productions (for London Weekend Television). *Photography:* Charles Stewart (Eastmancolor). *Editing:* Elizabeth Koziman. *Research:* Mo Teitelbaum.

Pravda. 76 minutes. 16 mm. Agfa-Gevaert color. *Production Co.:* Centre Européen Cinéma Radio Télévision (Claude Nedjar). *Collaboration:* Jean-Henri Roger, Paul Burron.

Vento dell'est (Vent d'est; East Wind). 100 minutes. 16 mm. (also 35 mm. blow-up). *Production Co.:* CCC (Berlin); *Poli Film* (Rome); Anouchka Films (Paris). Script: Daniel Cohn-Bendit. Photography: Mario Vlupiano (Eastmancolor 7254). *Cast:* Gian Maria Volonte *(Cavalry Officer)*; Anne Wiazemsky; Glauber Rocha; George Götz; Christian Tullio; Marco Ferreri.

Lotte in Italia (Luttes en Italie; Struggle in Italy). 76 minutes. 16 mm. Eastmancolor 7254. *Production Company:* Cosmoseion (Rome), for the RAI (Italian Radio & Television). This film apparently represents mostly the work of Jean-Pierre Gorin.

1970

Jusqu'à la victoire (Till Victory). 16 mm. Eastmancolor 7254. This film, representing "methods of thought and work in the Palestinian revolution," remained unfinished and was being reedited (as was *Vent d'est*) at the time of Godard's accident in June 1971.

1971

Vladimir (or Wladimir) et Rosa (Vladimir and Rosa). 106 minutes. 16 mm. Color. *Production Co.:* Grove Press Evergreen Films (U.S.A.), German Television. *Cast:* Jean-Luc Godard; Jean-Pierre Gorin; Anne Wiazemsky; Yves Alfonso; Juliet Berto; Claude Nedjar; etc.

1972

Tout va bien. 95 minutes. Color. *Producer:* Alain Coiffier. *Script:* Godard and Gorin. *Photography:* Armand Marco. *Editing:* Kenout Peltier. *Sets:* Jacques Dugied. *Cast:* Yves Montand, Jane Fonda, Vittorio Caprioli, Pierre Oudry, Jean Pignol, Elisabeth Chauvin, Anne Wiazemsky. This film, which opened 28 April in a number of Paris theaters, was the joint effort of Godard and Gorin, who seem to have dropped the "Dziga-Vertov" title.

UNFINISHED FILM:

Communication(s?). Begun in Canada in 1969.

Besides the works mentioned in the Chronology (Giraudoux' *Pour Lucrèce*, etc.), Godard had also, at one time or another, considered making films of *Le Lys dans la vallée* (after Balzac) and of *La Bande à Bonnot* (after Bernard Thomas' turn-of-the-century novel).

Selected Bibliography

1. FILM SCRIPTS [1]

Charlotte et son Jules: L'Avant-Scène du cinéma, no. 5 (June 1961).

Une Histoire d'eau: L'Avant-Scène du cinéma, no. 7 (September 1961).

A bout de souffle: L'Avant-Scène du cinéma, no. 79 (March 1968). Novel based on film by C. Francolin (Paris: Seghers, 1960).

Le Petit soldat: Cahiers du cinéma, nos. 119, 120 (May, June 1961). In English: New York: Simon and Schuster; London: Lorrimer, 1967 (introduction by Nicholas Garnham). Novel based on film by Claude Saint Benoit (Paris: Julliard).

Une Femme est une femme: Extracts in Collet book (see "Books on Godard"). "Scenario" and extracts as recorded on disc (with commentary by Godard) in *Jean-Luc Godard par Jean-Luc Godard* (see "Works by Godard").

Vivre sa vie: L'Avant-Scène du cinéma, no. 19 (October 1962).

Les Carabiniers: Hamburg, Germany: "Cinemathek" Collection (in German). Extract (in Italian) in *Filmcritica,* no. 150 (October 1964).

Le Grand escroc: L'Avant-Scène du cinéma, no. 46 (March 1965), with *Une Femme mariée.*

Le Mépris: Filmcritica, no. 139–40 (November–December 1963), reconstruction (in French) by Godard.

Bande à part: Film (West Germany), no. 2 (February 1965). Extract (in Italian) in *Filmcritica,* no. 150.

Une Femme mariée: L'Avant-Scène du cinéma, no. 46 (March 1965), with *Le Grand escroc.* In English (based on subtitles): *The Married Woman* (California: Berkley Publishing Co., "Medallion" Series, 1965). Deluxe edition (entitled *Journal d'une Femme Mariée*) with numerous photographs, extracts from dialogue: Paris; Denoël, 1965.

Alphaville: New York: Simon and Schuster, 1966; London: Lorrimer, 1966 (in English; translation and introduction by Peter Whitehead).

Pierrot le fou: New York: Simon and Schuster, 1969; London: Lorrimer, 1969 (in English; translated by Peter Whitehead; preceded by translation by Tom Milne of the interview with Godard, "Let's Talk About Pierrot," from *Cahiers du cinéma,* no. 171 (October 1965). Extracts (in French) in *Image et son,* no. 211 (December 1967).

[1] Scripts in languages other than French or English are not listed unless they are the only version available.

Masculin-Féminin: New York: Grove Press, 1969 (in English; numerous stills; followed by English translations of the two Maupassant stories, documents, and reviews).

Made in U.S.A.: London: Lorrimer, 1967 (in English; translation and introduction by Michael Kustow; preceded by "Synopsis" and "The Left and *Made in U.S.A.?*" by Godard, and by two articles on the Ben Barka affair). Extract (in French) in *Image et son,* no. 211.

Deux ou trois choses que je sais d'elle: Paris: Seuil, "Collection Points/ Films," 1971 (originally in *L'Avant-Scène du cinéma,* no. 70 (May 1967); followed by reviews, commentaries, and a bio-filmography). "Scenario" and working notes published in Marie Cardinal, *Cet été-là* (Paris: Julliard, 1967); also contains descriptions (not particularly interesting) of Mme Cardinal's work with Godard and Bresson.

La Chinoise: L'Avant-Scène du cinéma, no. 114 (May 1971).

Caméra-Oeil (in *Loin du Viêt-Nam*): *Peace News,* 5 January 1968.

Le Gai savoir: Paris: Union des écrivains (no. 2), 1969.

2. SELECTED STILLS FROM FILMS

Jean-Luc Godard: Films 1957–1969 (Paris: *L'Avant-Scène du cinéma,* "Album-Diapositives No. 4," 1970). 120 slides (frame enlargements) from most of Godard's features and shorts from *Tous les garçons . . .* through *One Plus One.* Also contains booklet "Jean-Luc Godard: Filmographie complète de 1957 à 1969 et légendes des 120 diapositives," by Abraham Segal.

3. WORKS BY GODARD

Jean-Luc Godard par Jean-Luc Godard. Paris: Editions Pierre Belfond, Collection "Cahiers du cinéma," 1968. English translation by Tom Milne to be published by Viking Press (U.S.A.) and Secker and Warburg (England). Selections of Godard's critical writings, plus interviews, from *Cahiers du cinéma, Arts,* etc. See Collet book for a complete list of articles by Godard.

Interviews

Besides the interviews contained in the *Jean-Luc Godard par Jean-Luc Godard* book, other interviews can be found in the following publications:
1) *L'Express* (28 December 1959; Michèle Manceaux); 2) *Le Monde* (21 September 1962; "A propos de *Vivre sa vie,*" Nicole Zand); 3) *Télérama* (No. 663, 1962; Jean Collet, on *Vivre sa vie*); 4) *Arts* (No. 892, 15 August 1962 (?); Michel Polac); 5) *Cinéma 63* (No. 77, May 1963; presentation of *Le Mépris,* by Godard); 6) *Cinéma 65* (No. 94, March 1965; "Le Dossier du mois: Godard par Godard"); 7) *Cahiers du cinéma* (No. 177, April 1966);

8) *Le Nouvel observateur* (12 December 1966; "Le Monde moderne"); 9) *Les Lettres françaises* (26 December 1963; 14 May 1964; 19 November 1964); 10) *La Revue d'esthétique* (no. 2–3, April–September 1967); 11) *Cahiers du cinéma* (no. 194, October 1967; "Lutter sur deux fronts," Bontemps, Comolli, Delahaye, and Narboni; translation appears in *Film Quarterly*, vol. XXII, no. 2, Winter 1968–69); 12) *Image et son* (no. 211, December 1967; Philippe Pilard); 13) *New York Film Bulletin* (no. 46, 1964; Andrew Sarris; reprinted in *Interviews With Film Directors* (New York: Bobbs-Merrill, 1967); 14) *Cinéthique* (no. 1, January 1969; "Un Cinéaste comme les autres," J.-P. C., Gérard Leblanc); 15) *Rolling Stone* (no. 35, 14 June 1969; Jonathan Cott); 16) Interviews in (15) and translation of (10) and (14), as well as translations of several other interviews, can be found in *Kinopraxis* (no. 0, 1970; published by Jack Flash, 2533 Telegraph Avenue, Berkeley, California); 17) *Cinéma 70* (no. 151, December 1970; "Le Groupe 'Dziga-Vertov,'" Marcel Martin); 18) *La Revue du cinéma (Image et son)* (no. 245, December 1970; "Une Réapparition de Jean-Luc Godard," report on R.T.L. interview by Guy Gauthier, pp. 136–37).

4. Books on Godard

Cameron, Ian, ed., *The Films of Jean-Luc Godard*. New York: Praeger, 1969. An excellent collection of essays and articles (through *One Plus One*) by an international group of critics.

Collet, Jean, *Jean-Luc Godard*. Paris: Seghers, Collection "Cinéma d'aujourd'hui," 1963; 3 subsequent editions; 5th edition planned for 1972; in U.S.A.: New York: Grove Press, 1970. Pioneer work, still one of the best.

Estève, Michel, ed., *Jean-Luc Godard au-delà du récit*. Paris: Lettres Modernes, Collection "Études cinématographiques," 1967. Collection of articles, many with a strong literary orientation, by Italian and French critics.

Mussman, Toby, ed., *Jean-Luc Godard*. New York: E. P. Dutton & Co., 1968. Articles by renowned critics (Sontag, Kael, Sarris, Milne, Roud, etc.) plus many translations of important interviews and articles by Godard.

Roud, Richard, *Godard*. New York: originally Doubleday & Co., Collection "Cinema World," 1968; updated version: Bloomington, Indiana: Indiana University Press, and London: Secker and Warburg, Collection "Cinema 1," 1970. A thorough, intelligent, and extremely informative study on Godard's films.

Vianey, Michel, *En attendant Godard*. Paris: Grasset, 1966. An unsuccessful and highly pretentious attempt to "recreate" Godard in a writing style that tries its best to be Godardesque.

In preparation: James Roy MacBean. Comprehensive, in-depth analysis of all Godard's films (California: University of California Press).

5. REVIEWS AND ARTICLES [2]

General Articles

Bory, Jean-Louis, "Jean-Luc Godard," in *Dossiers du cinéma: Cinéastes 1,* ed. Jean-Louis Bory and Claude Michel Cluny. Paris: Casterman, 1971.

Cournot, Michel, "Jean-Luc ex-Godard," *Le Nouvel observateur,* no. 292 (15 June 1970). One of the most revealing articles on Godard's "Dziga-Vertov" period.

Dadoun, Roger, "Un Cinéma 'sauvage' et 'ingénu,' " *Image et son,* no. 211 (December 1967).

Dort, Bernard, "Godard ou le Romantique abusif," *Les Temps modernes,* no. 235 (December 1965). An essentially negative statement in which the author expresses himself brilliantly.

Flatley, Guy, "Godard Says Bye-Bye to Bardot and All That," *New York Times* (17 May 1970), p. D–11.

Giammanco, Roberto, "Impotenza e estraniazione in Godard." *Giovane Critica* (Catania), no. 14 (Winter 1967).

Goldmann, Annie, "Jean-Luc Godard," *La Nouvelle revue française,* no. 165 (September 1966).

Lefèvre, Raymond, "Godard sans sous-titres," *Image et son,* no. 211 (December 1967).

Lebesque, Morvan, "Les Bouffons," *Le Canard enchaîné,* no. 2415 (1 February 1967).

Pilard, Philippe, "Jean-Luc Godard: Thèmes et variations," *Image et son,* no. 211 (December 1967).

Pollak-Lederer, Jacques, "Jean-Luc Godard dans la modernité," *Les Temps modernes,* no. 262 (March 1968). Like the Bernard Dort article, Pollak-Lederer's long essay is negativistic but nonetheless offers interesting insights.

Price, James, "A Film Is a Film: Some Notes on Jean-Luc Godard," *Evergreen Review,* no. 38 (November 1965).

Silverstein, Norman, "Godard and Revolution," *Films and Filming* (June 1970).

Simon, John, "Godard and the Godardians: A Study in the New Sensibility," in *Private Screenings.* New York: Macmillan, 1967; and Berkley "Medallion" series, 1971. A scathing, largely irrelevant but eloquent attack on Godard and his cultists.

Simsolo, Noël, "La Révolution par le film selon Jean-Luc Godard ou comment contester le cinéma de consommation," *Cinéma pratique,* no. 97.

Sontag, Susan, "Godard," in *Styles of Radical Will.* New York: Farrar, Straus and Giroux, 1969; also New York: Dell, "Delta" series, 1970. Essential reading.

[2] Extremely selective; for more exhaustive lists, see the Collet book, the Estève anthology, and Claude Gauteur, "Godard et ses critiques," *Image et son,* no. 213 (February 1968). Articles mentioned in footnotes within this book are generally omitted from this bibliography.

Villelaur, Anne, "Jean-Luc Godard," *Dossiers du cinéma: Cinéastes 1,* ed. Jean-Louis Bory and Claude Michel Cluny. Paris: Casterman, 1971. Essentially negative.

Articles and Reviews of Specific Films

Breathless:

Cortarde, René, *"A bout de souffle:* Naissance du cinéma vaudois," *Arts* (24 March 1960).

Croce, Arlene, review in *Film Quarterly* 14, no. 3 (Spring 1961).

Kael, Pauline, *"Breathless* and the Daisy Miller Doll," in *I Lost It at the Movies.* Boston: Atlantic Monthly Press–Little, Brown, Inc., 1968.

Sadoul, Georges, review in *Les Lettres françaises* (3 November 1960).

Le Petit soldat:

Comolli, Jean-Louis, review in *Cahiers du cinéma,* no. 141 (March 1963).

Pétris, Michel, "Il 'mito vissato' di *Le Petit soldat,"* Filmcritica (November–December 1964).

Sadoul, Georges, "L'important est de se poser des questions," *Les Lettres françaises,* no. 848 (3 November 1969).

Une Femme est une femme:

Heifetz, Henry, review in *Film Quarterly* 18, no. 2 (Winter 1964).

Labarthe, André-Sylvain, "La Chance d'être femme," *Cahiers du cinéma,* no. 125 (November 1961). Essential reading.

Vivre sa vie:

Bory, Jean-Louis, "Un Documentaire pensant mais lucide qui cache un film d'amour," *Arts* (19 September 1962).

Chapier, Henry, *"Vivre sa vie* ou les difficultés de rester soi-même," *Combat* (24 September 1962).

Giroud, Françoise, "Un Message personnel," *L'Express* (20 September 1962).

Melville, Jean-Pierre, brief column in *Cinéma 63,* no. 75 (March 1963). A violent attack on Godard by one of France's most important filmmakers.

Sontag, Susan, "Godard's *Vivre sa vie,"* in *Against Interpretation.* New York: Dell, "Laurel" series, 1969. Also in Mussman anthology.

Les Carabiniers:

Gilliatt, Penelope, "The Folly of Soldiers," *The New Yorker* (11 May 1968).

Le Mépris:

Aprà, Adriano, *"Le Mépris e Il Disprezzo,"* Filmcritica, no. 151–52 (November–December 1964). Analysis of the differences between Italian and original versions.

Baroncelli, Jean de, review in *Le Monde* (23 December 1963).

Taylor, Stephen, "After the Nouvelle Vague," *Film Quarterly* 18, no. 3 (Spring 1965).

Bande à part:

Fruchter, Norm, review in *Film Quarterly* 18, no. 2 (Winter 1964).

Kael, Pauline, "Godard Among the Gangsters," *The New Republic* (10 September 1966). Also in Mussman anthology.

Kustow, Michael, review in *Sight and Sound* (Winter 1964).

Une Femme mariée:

Giroud, Françoise, "Jean-Luc et Bérénice," *L'Express* (7 December 1964).

Ropars-Wuilleumier, Marie-Claire, "De la mode," *Esprit* (February 1965).

Alphaville:

Jacob, Gilles, "Un Cauchemar non-climatisé," *Cinéma 65*, no. 97 (June 1965), pp. 115–18.

Ropars-Wuilleumier, "La Perte du langage," *Esprit* (September 1965).

Roud, Richard, "Alphaville: Anguish," introduction to Simon and Schuster film script (see above).

Pierrot le fou:

Cournot, Michel, two articles in *Le Nouvel observateur* (1 October and 3 November 1965).

Jacob, Gilles. "Sélection du 'Godard's Digest,'" *Cinéma 65*, no. 101 (October 1965).

Morgenstern, Joseph, review in *Film 69/70* (National Society of Film Critics Anthology), ed. Joseph Morgenstern and Stefan Kanfer. New York: Simon and Schuster, 1970.

Ropars-Wuilleumier, Marie-Claire, review in *Esprit* (February 1966).

Masculin-Féminin:

Albéra, François, review in *Travelling J* (Lausanne), no. 16 (April 1967).

Casty, Alan, review in *Film Quarterly 20*, no. 3 (Spring 1967).

Kael, Pauline, review in *Kiss Kiss Bang Bang*. Boston: Atlantic Monthly Press–Little, Brown, Inc., 1966.

Milne, Tom, review in *Sight and Sound* (Winter 1966–67).

Sadoul, Georges, "Godard ne passera pas," *Les Lettres françaises*, no. 1130 (5 May 1966).

(See also Grove Press film script, which contains eighteen reviews and review excerpts from French [translated], English, and American press. Includes the Kael, Milne, and Sadoul reviews mentioned above, in addition to reviews by Roud, Sarris, Crist, etc.)

Made in U.S.A.:

Daix, Pierre, review in *Les Lettres françaises*, no. 1162 (22 December 1966).

MacBean, James Roy, "Politics, Painting, and the Language of Signs in Godard's *Made in U.S.A.*," *Film Quarterly 22*, no. 3 (Spring 1969).

Ropars-Wuilleumier, "La Forme et le fond," *Esprit* (April 1967).

Sadoul, Georges, "Les Facettes d'un miroir brisé," *Les Lettres françaises*, no. 1163 (29 December 1966).

Deux ou trois choses que je sais d'elle:

Canby, Vincent, review in the *New York Times* (1 May 1970).

MacBean, James Roy, "Politics and Poetry in Two Recent Films by Godard" (*Deux ou trois choses . . .* and *La Chinoise*), *Film Quarterly 21*, no. 4 (Summer 1968).

Milner, Max, "Godard ambigu," *Esprit* (May 1965). An eloquent attack.

Zimmer, Christian, "Totalisation du vrac," *Les Temps modernes*, no. 252 (May 1967). One of the best articles ever written on a Godard film.

See also Seuil/Points film script of *Deux ou trois choses*; contains extracts of a number of reviews, plus four "commentaries," including ones by Marina Vlady and François Truffaut.

Loin du Viet-nam (entire film):

Ropars-Wuilleumier, Marie-Claire, review, in *Esprit* (April 1968). Reprinted in the author's *L'Écran de la mémoire*. Paris: Seuil, Collections Esprit "La Condition humaine," 1970.

Zimmer, Christian, "Cent-mille rizières," *Les Temps modernes*, no. 261 (February 1968).

La Chinoise:

Bontemps, Jacques, "Une Libre variation imaginative de certains faits," *Cahiers du cinéma*, no. 194 (October 1967). Written in the elitist, "chinois" style that makes most recent *Cahiers* articles all but unreadable.

Comolli, Jean-Louis, "Le Point sur l'image," *Cahiers du cinéma*, no. 194.

Duboeuf, Pierre, "Le Jaune en péril," *Cahiers du cinéma*, no. 195 (November 1967).

Greenspun, Roger, review in *New York Free Press* 1, no. 17 (18 April 1968).

Jouffroy, Alain, "Une affaire à régler avec le monde entier," *L'Avant-scène du cinéma*, no. 114 (May 1971).

Pouillon, Jean, "Il faut bien que jeunesse se passe," *Les Temps modernes*, no. 156 (September 1967). Negative article.

Ropars-Wuilleumier, Marie-Claire, review in *Esprit* (November 1967). Reprinted in *L'Écran de la mémoire*.

Sarris, Andrew, review in *The Village Voice* (4 April 1968).

Schickel, Richard, "The Trying Genius of M. Godard," *Life* (12 April 1968).

Weekend:

Adler, Renata, review in *A Year in the Dark*. California: Berkley Publishing Co., "Medallion" series, 1971.

Aumont, Jacques, review in *Cahiers du cinéma*, no. 199 (March 1968).

Cluny, Claude Michel, "Un Weekend loin du Viet-nam," *La Nouvelle revue française*, no. 183 (March 1968).

Collet, Jean, review in *Cahiers du cinéma*, no. 199.

Dawson, Jan, review in *Sight and Sound* (Summer 1968).

Kael, Pauline, review in *Film 68/69*, Hollis Alpert and Andrew Sarris, eds. New York: Simon and Schuster, 1969.

MacBean, James Roy, "Godard's *Weekend*, or the Self-Critical Cinema of Spectacle," *Film Quarterly* 22, no. 2 (Winter 1968–69).

Ropars-Wuilleumier, Marie-Claire, "Le Cru et le cuit," *Esprit* (March 1968). Reprinted in *L'Écran de la mémoire*.

Le Gai savoir:

Canby, Vincent, "Godard Treatise," the *New York Times* (28 September 1969, reprinted 5 June 1970).

One Plus One:

MacBean, James Roy, "*One Plus One,* or the *Praxis* of History," *The Partisan Review* (July 1971).

Oudert, Jean-Pierre, review in *Cahiers du cinéma,* no. 213 (June 1969).

One A.M.:

Dawson, Jan, review of the Pennebaker completion, *Monthly Film Bulletin* (British Film Institute), no. 451 (August 1971).

British Sounds (See You at Mao):

Greenspun, Roger, review (with *Pravda*), *New York Times* (22 May 1970).

MacBean, James Roy, "*See You At Mao:* Godard's Revolutionary *British Sounds,*" *Film Quarterly* 24, no. 2 (Winter 1970–71).

Pravda:

Mekas, Jonas, review in *The Village Voice* (May 1970).

Vent d'est:

MacBean, James Roy, "*Vent d'est,* or Godard and Rocha at the Crossroads," *Sight and Sound* (Summer 1971), pp. 144–50.

Mellon, Joan, review in *Film Comment* (Fall 1971). A strong and intelligent attack on the film and "anti-bourgeois" cinema in general.

Tout va bien:

Baroncelli, Jean de, review in *Le Monde,* 3 May 1972, p. 26.

Baby, Yvonne, "Pour mieux ecouter les autre" (interview with Godard), *Le Monde,* 27 April 1972, p. 17.

Curtis, Thomas Quinn, "Godard's Absorbing *Tout va bien,*" *International Herald Tribune,* 28 April 1972, p. 17.

Even, Martin, "Des travailleurs artistiques de l'information" (interview with Gorin), *Le Monde,* 27 April 1972, p. 17.

Nourissier, François, "Godard–Gorin: le souffle court," *l'Express,* 2–7 May 1972, pp. 88–89.

Vianey, Michel, "Deux petits soldats" (includes excerpt from script), *Le Nouvel Observateur,* 17 April 1972, pp. 49–52.

Vladimir and Rosa:

Canby, Vincent, "Godard's Social Mix, *Vladimir and Rosa,*" *New York Times* (30 April 1971).

Gilliatt, Penelope, "Godard Proceeding," *The New Yorker* (8 May 1971).

Index[1]

[1] Index covers pp. 5–173 only and excludes references to Jean-Luc Godard.

189